Programmer's Guide

to MS-DOS

Revised and Expanded

Dennis N. Jump

BRADY
New York

BRADY

Simon & Schuster, Inc.
Gulf+Western Building
One Gulf+Western Plaza
New York, NY 10023

DISTRIBUTED BY PRENTICE HALL TRADE

Manufactured in the United States of America

2 3 4 5 6 7 8 9 10

Library of Congress Cataloging-in-Publication Data

Jump, Dennis.
  Programmer's Guide to MS-DOS, Revised & Expanded

  "A Brady book."
   Includes index
   1. MS-DOS (Computer operating system)
   2. Microcomputers—Programming.   I. Title.
QA76.6.J85   1987   005.4'46   87-12803

ISBN 0-13-729096-9

Dedication

To all the people who still wonder what I do for a living

Contents

Limits of Liability and
Disclaimer of Warranty

Trademarks

Read.Me

Things certainly have changed from three years ago when *Programmer's Guide to MS-DOS* was first written. We've seen several new versions of MS-DOS come on the scene; computer languages have flourished and expanded, and the programming community has grown by leaps and bounds, not to mention in sophistication. With this new edition of *Programmer's Guide to MS-DOS*, I want to address these changes.

When the original version of this book was written, tree-structured directories, device drivers, and redirected I/O were foreign concepts to the users and programmers who cut their teeth in the microcomputer arena.

Certainly, the first software developers for the IBM PC were schooled in CP/M and the 8-bit world, and the move to MS-DOS (or PC-DOS, as the case may be) was very easy to make. MS-DOS was virtually a carbon copy of CP/M. This contributed to the awkwardness experienced by these early hackers (meant in the true sense of experimenter and hobbyist) when they were faced with the advanced features of MS-DOS 2.0.

Admittedly, the minicomputer and mainframe computer community had been working with these ideas for some years, and the transition was easier to make. One would suppose that when some of the concepts arrived on the micro stage, there was an influx of users from the other worlds into the microcomputer world.

In time, MS-DOS has moved away from its roots in CP/M and toward its more complex sibling, XENIX. We've seen the addition of tree-structured directories, networking, device drivers, hard disk drives, a multitude of load-and-stay-resident tools, and huge amounts of RAM memory. So it is part of the aim of this revision to talk about some of these topics as they relate to the programmers that have to work with them at a low level.

And languages! Where have they all come from? For the first edition of this work, there was BASIC, assembly language, and Pascal from Microsoft. These three covered (in my estimate) 85% of all the work being done. Today, C is moving ahead as the language of choice for serious software development on the microcomputer, and there is Turbo everything to run rings around the early Pascal compilers. The first edition of *Programmer's Guide to MS-DOS* made its programming references in Microsoft Pascal and 8088 assembly language.

Times have changed, and so do the references in this edition. A number of MS-DOS functions had to be summoned through assembly language interfaces if you were using Pascal. Naturally, in assembly language, the MS-DOS functions were the only way to get anything done. Now it turns out that for a C programmer, the library functions for C cover most of the MS-DOS functions. Since this is true, when functions are covered in this book, the corresponding C standard library function will be mentioned so that you can get an idea of what is happening in that function. Assembly language examples will spread throughout the book. This book has already been used extensively as a supplement to assembly language classes so that the I/O routines could be accessed.

HOW TO USE THIS BOOK

The main thrust of this text is to show programmers how to use the MS-DOS functions to complement their work. And to show how these functions can be used to cut down on the amount of work and creative energy these functions can save, examples will be liberally sprinkled through the text. Since a lot of time has gone by (things happen fast in this business, and one year can be half a lifetime for some projects), I have been able to expand some of my own horizons and have updated and expanded the examples. In addition to the examples for programming throughout the text, I have added a chapter on bringing the whole effort together. This chapter outlines a simple software problem, the steps to deciding upon an economical and sensible solution, and the programming involved to pull it off. This project will attempt to draw on several of the features of MS-DOS: programming functions in assembly language, redirection of I/O, and batch file execution.

In the older edition of this book, there was a communications device driver that was targeted for the NEC APC. To be honest, at the time of its writing, that was the current machine in the stable. There were certainly IBM PCs in and out the door for various software projects, but this was the current machine for software development at the time. So it is reasonable for proven software examples to be written on a machine close by. That computer is still in the lab, although it is somewhat underused at the moment, but the IBM and compatibles rule the roost at this time. With this superiority of numbers, the device driver for the communications program has been updated to the IBM standard. This communications software is an interrupt-driven RS-232 communications interface that can be accessed through the standard I/O functions of MS-DOS.

One of the newer innovations to hit the programming community is the expanded memory hardware cards and the Lotus-Intel-Microsoft interface. Strictly speaking, this is not an MS-DOS function or topic, but since it affects so many programmers, it is included with some primitive examples.

WHO THE BOOK IS FOR

Let me attempt to identify my audience for this book. Should you be reading this book? Will it meet your needs? I thought that there were an overwhelming number of computer books on the shelves of the bookstore when this book was first offered. Then there was a so-called "shake out" in the market. But, it seems as if there are more books now than ever before. Perhaps the quality has improved with the sophistication of the readership. But the question remains: Is this the right book for you?

MS-DOS is somewhat of an onion. I suppose for some people it is enough to make you cry, but that is not what I mean. What I really mean is that it is built in several layers. The end user sees the command level. This is where application programs are started, directories are displayed with DIR, and files are moved and copied with COPY. There are several books on this outer shell of MS-DOS. This is *not* one of them.

The next layer down is rather thin (if it rates as a layer at all). This would be the batch file processor. A batch file is a collection of regular MS-DOS commands to be executed as a predetermined sequence of commands. The batch file processor even has its own small programming language so that some decisions can be made to control the sequence of commands. This allows you to create your own commands or create shortcut commands for rather long and complicated command streams.

The next layer contains the MS-DOS programming functions. These are software functions that either perform certain I/O functions or perform hardware interactions that programmers would rather not know about. These functions are the center point of this text. We are interested in the use of these functions: how they are used, what they do, and when they should be considered in lieu of the library functions that are provided by the programming language.

So who is interested in this kind of information? For the programmer who is just venturing into the mysteries of MS-DOS, this can serve as a guide to understanding the abilities of the operating system and how to get to them. Beginning programmers are welcome. This book can also be used as a quick reference text for the experienced developer. I would never dream of remembering all the details that are required to implement some of the functions, and I would never expect it of anyone else. And I don't relish the idea of trying to decipher the technical document that IBM publishes when I need a quick answer. It's always easier to use an example in a real-life situation as a model to solve a problem or to understand the capabilities of the function. And for that other group that might be interested in the subject, those of you who are downright curious, I welcome you, too.

So let's get started at the beginning.

This book is intended for software developers who are looking for a way to get more out of their programs without expending the time and effort to develop the functions that may well already exist.

Chapter 1

A Quick Look at Operating Systems

INTRODUCTION

In the beginning, there was hardware.

Computer hardware being what it is, it is pretty useless without explicit instructions to follow. Therefore, with the development of the first computers came the first software programs. All of these programs were written in the machine's numerical language (no assembler language and no high-level languages).

These programs were developed by people (mathematicians, electronic engineers, and physicists) who worked very closely with the electronic engineers who built the first machines. Quite often, they were the people who built the hardware. This relationship between the programmers and the hardware builders was necessary since the complete control of the machine was in the hands of the programmer. If they wanted to type a message on the console typewriter, then they had to provide the correct instruction sequence to do this task. If they wanted to read data from a tape recorder, they had to issue the commands that started the tape recorder motors, enable the recorder's read and write heads, read the data into intermediate buffers and, finally, stop the motors. This took a great deal of knowledge about the peripheral devices.

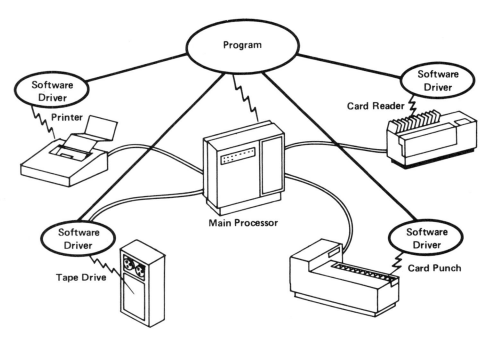

Figure 1-2. A Variety of Peripherals Driven by Software.

Like a novice programmer's first attempts at writing a BASIC program, the first programs were very rudimentary, aimed at finding out how the computer worked. Did it do what the engineers promised it would do? These programs were of no use to anybody, other than the scientists and engineers interested in the operation of the computers.

The sophistication of the first programmers grew. Soon, software application programs, containing complex groups of instructions for the operation of the hardware, were written: amortization tables, highly accurate mathematical calculations, population statistics. These programs had appeal to people other than the developers. The computer user did not have to understand anything about the computer because the application software assumed the responsibility of running the hardware. The application software became a *shell* around the hardware, protecting the user from the rigors of the computer.

It soon became apparent that the same groups of instructions were appearing in almost every program. These instruction groups usually were

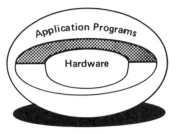

Figure 1-3. Adding an Application Program Shell to Hardware.

involved with the control of the input and output devices (printer, tape drives, and console typewriter). The next trend was to isolate these routines and place them in a memory location where every application could get to them. More and more programs relied on these routines to request hardware services from the peripheral I/O devices. Another shell was developing around the hardware. This particular shell was growing between the application software and the hardware.

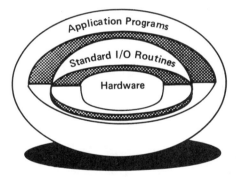

Figure 1-4. Separating the Application Program from the Hardware with an I/O Routine Shell.

This development had some real advantages. First, working and proven software was available for common tasks, and a programmer would not have to reinvent the wheel with every new program. Second, a person without an education in electronics could program since he did not have to understand the details of operating the peripheral I/O equipment. It was only necessary to group the proper information together and call one of the resident I/O routines.

Input and output routines were not the only software procedures to be added to this middle shell. There were other commonly used software *utilities* that joined the I/O routines. These routines included such common utilities as a random number generator, get the time, get the date, set the time, set the date, and load and execute a task. This entire group of software is the foundation of an operating system. They are collectively called the *kernel* of the operating system.

Applications Systems

At the same time, a duplicate action was taking place at the application program level. Instead of a group of well-used low-level routines being gathered, a group of often-used application programs were being collected. The applications included in this collection were utilities such as copy a file, delete a file, text editor, program debugger, and several other utilities. These utilities were useful tools that exploited the capabilities of the kernel routines. Since they were tightly associated with the kernel software, it only made sense that they be included with the operating system package.

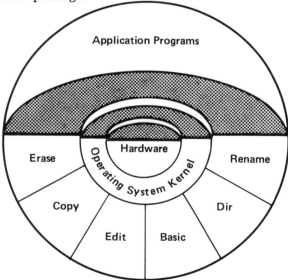

Figure 1-5. Operating System Utilities and Application Software.

All of the big computer companies had developed operating systems for their line of computers. This worked out fairly well. To sell software, an author only had to be sure that the host machine and operating system for the program was the same as the originating machine. This being true, the operating system kernel routines could be used to access the peripheral devices, regardless of small differences (logical addresses, operating speed, or capacity) in the hardware. Moving application programs to a machine of a different make (different machine language) or operating system (different kernel and interface) meant that the entire application program (at the machine-language level) had to be recreated. If the new operating system kernel was lacking in some of the required routines, the programmer would have to write those routines to add to the application program. (This is one of the places where programming languages come into the computing scenario, and tend to mask the operating system differences. But that's another story.) Wouldn't it be nice if all of the interfaces to all of the operating system kernels were the same?

EMERGENCE OF STANDARD OPERATING SYSTEMS

With the introduction of the microprocessor and the development of the personal computer, the operating system story takes another turn. We find the market loaded with many brands of home computers, all of them using one or more processors from a small group of microprocessors. It becomes easy to write software for a market of several computers, since they all use the *same* microprocessor (the same machine language).

However, if every brand of computer used a different operating system, then, although programs would not have to be recreated to get the proper machine language, they would have to be recreated to change the interfaces to the operating system kernel to perform I/O functions. And what was once a side task in a major job becomes the major job. Software companies would be forced to keep a version of a program for every operating system on the market.

The inconvenience (not to mention the dangers) of adapting software to several operating systems has caused the emergence of *standard operating systems* for the various microprocessors. With each microprocessor (and family of personal computers) on the market, there is an identifiable standard operating system.

Having an operating system shell around the hardware (which may have big differences in I/O devices), software authors can be confident that their works will be usable on any number of personal computers.

Well, now, you bought one of these personal computers and you received or bought an operating system with it. The manual talked about COPY, ERASE, FORMAT, RENAME, and DIR. There was nothing about an operating system kernel. What is all of this about?

Remember that the operating system is composed of two parts, the set of application utilities and the kernel. For the average user, knowledge about the application utilities (COPY, PRINT, DIR, FORMAT, and others) is sufficient to get the computer to do useful work for you. There are several books on the subject of using the utilities of the operating system. This is also the central theme of most user manuals.

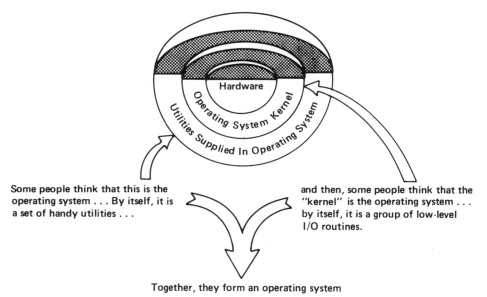

Some people think that this is the operating system . . . By itself, it is a set of handy utilities . . .

and then, some people think that the "kernel" is the operating system . . . by itself, it is a group of low-level I/O routines.

Together, they form an operating system

Figure 1-6. A Unified View of an Operating System.

SUMMARY

Knowledge about the kernel routines can be very useful to the application or system programmer. This knowledge allows the programmer to use the resources of the computer in a more efficient manner, write special purpose I/O packages, and add functions to a program that might not be included as a feature of a particular programming language.

This book explores the kernel of the *Microsoft Disk Operating System* (MS-DOS). The exploration will include a discussion of the data organizations required to use the operating system software, the interface conventions, and a detailed description of each routine.

MS-DOS has become the standard operating system for the IBM Personal Computer, the growing number of IBM-compatible computers (some by virtue of using MS-DOS), and other 8088/8086 microprocessor-based computers. Using this book as a guide for programming, you will be able to write programs that are usable on any computer using MS-DOS.

NOTE: Writing programs that use techniques that bypass MS-DOS (using the computer's BIOS routines or some unique hardware features) can lead to programs that will not run in other MS-DOS environments.

Chapter 2

A Look Inside MS-DOS

INTRODUCTION

Attempting to put a label on the various functions of MS-DOS must be like the group of blind wise men trying to describe an elephant. Each wise man, encountering a different part of the elephant, had a vastly different interpretation of what an elephant was. And so it is with MS-DOS or any other operating system.

In any given encounter with MS-DOS, you probably saw it as a file manager through the use of COPY, ERASE, and other utilities. While at another time, MS-DOS was a program supervisor where you named a program file and MS-DOS loaded the program's executable code and started the execution of the program. Or, following the directives of the batch file, it caused many functions and programs to be run.

In the following chapters, another view of MS-DOS will emerge. You will see how a program can use capabilities of MS-DOS to simplify the interface to some of the hardware functions and components. For these capabilities, the programmer uses the MS-DOS system calls.

WHAT ARE SYSTEM CALLS?

The MS-DOS *system calls* or *functions* are a part of the MS-DOS package. Their purpose is to allow you to write programs using the devices and processes of the computer, without needing to know the hardware characteristics and programming details of each one. The other aspect of this arrangement is that the system calls remain the same from one computer to the next (IBM, TI, NEC, Tandy, Sperry, AT&T, clone XYZ—

9

excuse me if I forgot yours), even though the actual hardware implementation is different. MS-DOS has covered the hardware differences with customized changes for each of the brands. This means that a program using the MS-DOS standard functions will run on any other MS-DOS compatible computer with no problems.

These routines can perform some primitive tasks, such as:

- Has a keyboard key been pressed?
- Get the ASCII character for the pressed key.
- Put a character on the screen.
- Write a line to the printer.
- What time is it?

And it can perform some tasks that are more sophisticated, such as:

- Open a disk file.
- Read a block of data from the disk.
- Delete a file.
- What is in the disk's directory?

These routines are an integral part of the basic MS-DOS and are loaded from the MS-DOS working diskette or fixed disk into the computer's memory when you turn on the machine or reinitialize the computer (by pressing the Ctrl-Alt-Del key combination on the IBM PC). Being required for the proper execution of the MS-DOS tools and utilities, these routines are in memory whether or not you use them. They do not cost you any memory by occupying space that you might use for your programs.

Why Are There System Calls in MS-DOS?

Part of this question was answered in the description of what the *system calls* are. The operating system calls perform functions that isolate the programmer from the rigors of hardware device control so that I/O operations can be executed in a simple and systematic manner.

But to answer the question better, let's go through a series of software development steps that would lead us to an operating system. These steps will let us see the reasons for the design and development of operating system calls.

To begin this scenario, assume that the programmer wants the program to control the operation of some device or function, and that there is no underlying operating system to assist. For example, getting a data record from a disk file without the benefit of an operating system, the user would have to know about turning on the drive motor; waiting for a certain length of time for it to get up to speed; positioning the read-write head at the proper track; waiting for the correct sector to rotate under the head; initiating the read sequence; and assembling the bytes of information as they are read. These actions would have to be repeated for all disk reads and writes, by all programs.

But disk operations aren't the only services that most programs use. The services required by most programs involve quite a few devices and hardware interfaces such as keyboard handlers, screen writers, and communications and clock functions.

Figure 2-1 shows the multitude of device interfaces that a program might have.

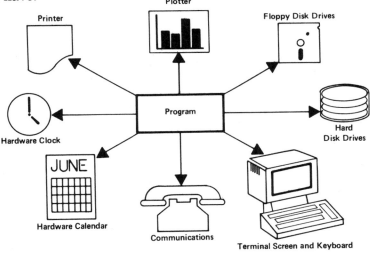

Figure 2-1. A Program Can Access a Multitude of Devices.

Pretty soon programmers have a collection of routines, appearing regularly in all of their programs. The natural thing to do is put the code for these routines in a common place so that all programs requiring these services would have them available. In this way, this collection of routines gets grouped together to form the nucleus of the operating system routines.

For these operating system routines to be useful to all of the application programs, the routines must require that data be arranged and presented in a certain way to be meaningful. This arrangement of data and its manipulation to meet the requirements of the operating system routine is called the *interface*.

Standardizing the Interface

Now, consistency is a virtue when it comes to using computers, and it is a two-way street. To get consistent and reliable results from the operating system routines, you must correctly prepare the data to be used or correctly interpret the results that you receive. To illustrate the point, you have probably found that it is not much fun to be surprised when you try something new on the computer using an approach that has worked in similar circumstances, only to find out that your results are not even close to what you expected.

The next step in the evolution toward an operating system is the standardization of the interface between the user program and the operating system. This standardization includes the following:

- A way to pass information to the operating system
- A method for getting the attention of the operating system to perform the task
- Getting information from the operating system
- Knowing if everything went okay

We now have a computer with a number of peripheral functions and devices, and a common set of software routines to operate these devices and functions. What happens when our Brand X disk drive fails and the only replacement for it is a Brand Y drive? If the individual programs provided their own disk routines, then all of the programs using the broken Brand X disk would need to be modified to properly use the new disk. However, relying on a single routine to get information from the disk, the programmer only has to change the disk interface software in one location and all of the application programs will run again.

But what if the computer has a Brand X and a Brand Y disk drive at the same time? This is a likely situation with a marketplace full of floppy disk drives, hard disk drives, and RAM pseudo-disks. One solution would be to have an operating system routine for each drive and the programmer would be responsible for calling the right one, depending upon which disk drive has the disk file.

A more realistic solution would be to allow the user to prepare the data for a disk in a standard method, regardless of model or type of disk drive, and the service routine would include routines for all of the drives. Instead of the programmer worrying about which was the proper routine to be used, the service routine, "seeing" which model of disk drive was being activated by the program's request, would call the proper disk-handling routine.

MS-DOS as the Operating System

To continue with the developmental phases of an operating system, suppose that your program was being sold to businesses, each having hardware configurations differing from installation to installation. One business may be using an IBM Personal Computer, while another is using a Zenith Z-100, and still another is using the NEC APC: same processor chip, different hardware layouts. But MS-DOS is available for all three.

Having assumed the role of the operating system, it becomes the responsibility of MS-DOS, through a uniform set of codes and data structures, to handle all of the hardware idiosyncrasies for a particular installation, thus leaving the application program with the responsibility of properly presenting the system calls and the data structures so that MS-DOS can provide consistent results from installation to installation.

Once again, why are there system calls in MS-DOS? There are system calls in MS-DOS so that programmers can:

- Write software for many different machines without having to know the exact details of each machine;

- Control devices and functions without knowing the details of that control; and,

- Use standard command and data structures to get consistent results regardless of the true nature of a peripheral device.

WHEN TO USE THE SYSTEM CALLS

We have seen that the operating system routines are collections of software that provide common interfaces to the computer peripherals and functions. The next avenue we are going to explore is the why and when of using the operating system routines.

At the end of this chapter, there is a list of all MS-DOS system calls. When you look over the list, you will see the multitude of functions that MS-DOS is capable of doing for you. These functions certainly imply *when* you would want to use the system calls to perform a service. The question that arises is: Why should I use these functions in my program when either the function is available through the language that I am using, or I could furnish those functions myself?

The following sections discuss some of the reasons for selecting an operating system function over the functions of a programming language or your own functions.

In the previous section, you learned that the operating system calls were an integral part of MS-DOS, and when the operating system is loaded, so are the system calls. By using the system calls to provide the basic I/O functions for your program, your program can be smaller and more efficient because you don't have to take up code space for functions that are already available.

When you are writing a program in a high-level language, the language's environment shields you from the fine details of the computer's mechanism. This is good, but if you are trying to make your program as compact and efficient as possible, the generalities of the programming environment can be counterproductive.

For instance, writing data to the printer is a simple matter in the high-level language. You give the command to perform the writing, followed by a list of variable names whose values are to be written to the printer. The variable name list may contain variables with *real numbers, integer numbers*, or *character strings*. The printer accepts only *characters*. This means that there must be some software that provides the *type conversion* so that only ASCII characters are sent to the printer.

Another example: When writing programs for real-time applications, you may want to use the system calls to speed up your program, minimizing the checking (e.g., value within range and type matching) that takes place in the high-level language run-time environment. If you are sure that certain conditions and values will always be within the proper operating limits, there is no need to employ the checking that accompanies the type conversions of the run-time support routines. All of this supporting software, value checking, and type conversions become a part of your program, being loaded from a library of run-time support routines. This is great if you take advantage of all of the built-in facilities, but if you only want to send ASCII characters to the printer as quickly as possible, you don't need the checking conversions to be present.

And that software is taking up space that could be used for other functions. Using the operating system function calls can eliminate those routines, making your program smaller. If there are conversions to be done, and you chose to use the system calls, you must provide the conversion software.

Sometimes the high-level programming languages allow you to do anything that you may want to do, and sometimes they don't provide all of the services you might need. For instance, FORTRAN, BASIC, COBOL, C, and Pascal (as defined by the various language standards committees) will not allow you to initiate a software interrupt. This isn't bad, just inconvenient. Software interrupts are dependent upon a particular machine and operating system environment, and one of the reasons for using a programming language is to express program ideas in a machine-independent manner. To get around this hurdle, you would have to write a compatible assembly language routine that would provide the software interrupt.

In the same way, there are functions of the operating system that would be useful to a program, but are not available (e.g., "read the disk directory"). In this case, you would have to write an assembly language routine that would invoke the proper system call and return the contents of the disk directory.

For assembly language programmers, the primary purpose of the system calls is to give you easy access to the computer peripherals without your having to reinvent the software functions to do so.

Sometimes there are oddities about the hardware/software interface that are not addressed in the documentation, but the operating system routines recognize these peculiarities and take them into consideration, sparing you from the fine details of getting a peripheral to work properly.

A case to consider: A hardware peripheral may have some hardware switches associated with it that turn it off and on or control its output. These switches may also be controlled through software. Although the principal peripheral is capable of doing its task without the switches, as the documentation will testify, these switches are designed into the system and require handling. The authors of the operating system probably consulted with the designers of the hardware and are aware of these switches. Their software works with the peripheral. On the other hand, if you are struggling with a software routine to run the peripheral, you may not have all of the information that you need. Use the operating system routines to access the peripherals; don't reinvent the process.

Since the operating system is supposed to understand the underlying hardware of your computer and provide a standard interface to the computer's functions, then it is reasonable to expect that if another computer with a different hardware configuration is using the same operating system, the interface should be the same as it is on your computer. In other words, creating your own machine-dependent functions could cause your program to be *nontransportable*.

These have been the *whys* of using the operating system calls. They are used to provide standard I/O services when the programming environment is too slow or bulky. They are also used when the programming language does not provide "almost-machine-dependent" features that are demanded by your application.

Certainly this list of reasons for considering the use of the MS-DOS system calls is incomplete. However, use the list as a starting guide for selecting an appropriate time and place for the specific functions of MS-DOS. You will probably find several more reasons that should be added to the list.

HOW ARE THE SYSTEM CALLS USED?

As previously mentioned, when dealing with MS-DOS, there are four things that are basic to the successful use of any of the system calls:

- Passing information to the operating system

- Getting the attention of the operating system to perform the task

- Getting information from the operating system

- Knowing if everything went okay.

Passing Information to MS-DOS

The system calls of MS-DOS can be thought of as very general routines that need specific guidance for their proper operation. The operation of the functions is given this direction through the data prepared for and passed to the functions. This section covers the four major methods of constructing and passing data to the operating system calls. These four methods are:

Direct register transfer

Disk transfer area

File control block

Pathnames and handles

Direct Register Transfer

We are going to see that all interaction with MS-DOS is initiated at the machine level through the interrupt system, and most of the information exchanges are done at the same primitive level, using the hardware registers.

For one thing, the action of MS-DOS is determined by the contents of certain hardware registers. The transfer of byte- and word-size pieces of data (character input and output to the console, printer, and communications adapter) to and from MS-DOS is through the registers.

Figure 2-2 illustrates the transfer of a character from an application program to the console screen through the hardware registers. This word and byte transfer is rather elementary and will be discussed for each of the individual MS-DOS calls.

For programmers using one of the higher-level languages (C or Pascal), the run-time library should contain a function that will set up the registers properly. In the Microsoft Pascal language, the routine is called *DOSXQQ*. In most C environments, the function is called *bdos*.

Although variations may exist, the following register assignments are typically found when providing information to MS-DOS:

Table 2-1. Input Register Uses.

Register	Uses
AH	MS-DOS function number
AL	Minor functional codes
BX	File Handle
DX	Time and Date
DL	Character to be output
DS:DX	Address of File Control Block
	Address of Data
	Disk Transfer Area Address
CX	Counts
	Time and Date

The Disk Transfer Area

You have seen that the normal medium of exchange, when transferring word- and byte-size information between your program and MS-DOS, is through the hardware registers. However, another method is available for the transfer of large chunks of information between external devices and your program such as a directory entry, an entire disk sector, or a single record from a file.

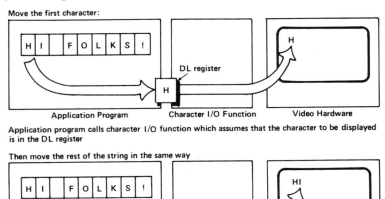

Figure 2-2. Direct Register Transfer

In these situations, your program must provide a location in memory that will serve as a common transfer point for these chunks of information. And MS-DOS must be notified through a system call of that location so that it can agree on the common exchange area. This exchange area is called the *Disk Transfer Area* (DTA).

For a disk write, your program deposits the data into the active DTA that is to be written, and MS-DOS will collect it and write it to the disk file. Figure 2-3 shows the exchange of data through a DTA.

The size of the DTA is determined by the application. For instance, the size of a DTA for reading a directory entry is 32 bytes (the size of a single directory entry). On the other hand, you might request the entire contents of a specific disk sector and need a DTA of 256, 512, or 1024 bytes long, so the size is determined by your requirements.

One word of caution, with the freedom to determine the actual size of the DTA comes the responsibility of calculating the proper size. There is no size checking when the transfer is taking place. MS-DOS assumes you know what you are doing. Murphy's Law implies that if you request 512 bytes of data and only provide a DTA of 256 bytes, you will surely overwrite 256 bytes of your most precious data.

When MS-DOS is loading and starting your program, it predefines a 256-byte area of memory at the base of your program as a *Program Seg-*

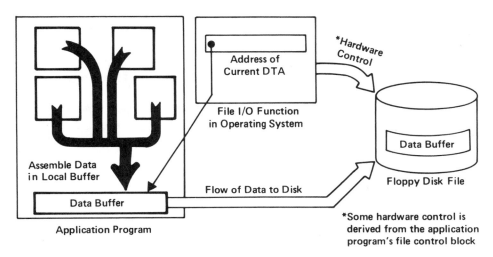

Figure 2-3. Data Flow through DTA.

ment Prefix area (PSP). Since most of the disk transfers in the system are through a DTA, MS-DOS insures that one is available by designating part of this area (the last 128 bytes) as the initial DTA. Unless you tell MS-DOS otherwise, this DTA could be the only one associated with your program.

If you are using assembly language, you are probably aware of the PSP (the PSP is the reason that your programs start at CS:100h) and are able to address this default area easily.

However, Pascal (and other language) programmers may have some difficulty in finding and addressing the area. They have two alternatives. One is to define your own DTAs for MS-DOS interfaces. Luckily, this is very easy to do and will be explained.

The second method is available with MS-DOS 2.0 and later versions. Using one of the MS-DOS system calls (Hex 2F), it is possible to get the address of the current DTA. The program segment prefix DTA, being the active DTA at the outset of the program, should be the address returned by MS-DOS.

If the program segment prefix DTA is already available, why tip the apple cart and create your own? Well, the default DTA is only 128 bytes long, which is sufficient for some transfers. However, if you are interested in full sector reads and doing your own data extractions and conversions from that point, you may need a 256- or 512-byte DTA and complete control of the use of that area. Why venture into this rat's nest of complexity if a programming language provides perfectly good I/O services? This is a tougher question to answer.

With high-level languages, I/O services have to be able to do everything for everybody. For instance, let's assume you are writing a Pascal program that deals only in character and byte data. When that program is linked (assembled for execution) with the Pascal run-time support routines, run-time object code may be included that handles real numbers. There is little you can do about this. When the program is growing large and memory space is precious, you don't want unnecessary code taking up memory in your program. Going directly to MS-DOS for I/O services allows you to have the basic I/O services required for characters and bytes, but you do not have to include the overhead of unwanted run-time routines.

When you choose this route, you need to play by the rules of MS-DOS, which includes the use of the DTA. I have had to do this and I had to pull the wool over the linker's eyes so that the Pascal I/O run-time routines would not be included, saving me approximately 12,000 bytes in the process.

Manipulating several DTAs with read/write operations on a number of files gives you power and flexibility to organize and control the flow of data through your program. In one of my programs, I had:

- A DTA for reading the directory from a disk;
- Another DTA for reading the contents of a text file to be edited;
- A third DTA as an intermediate buffer between a disk file and the system printer in a concurrent printing scheme;
- And, a final DTA for writing the contents of an edited file back onto a disk.

Juggling all of these file operations in one DTA would have been impossible, since the program could be busy printing a text file during the quiet moments between reading directories, manipulating files, and responding to user inputs.

Figure 2-4 is a diagram of DTAs and the corresponding files in this application. The trick to managing DTAs is to let MS-DOS know which one you are about to use, just before you use it. I will discuss the use of the DTA assignment function in more detail in Chapter 4, but it is necessary to know that this concept exists to fully exploit the block transfer capabilities of MS-DOS.

The File Control Block

When you are programming with MS-DOS 1.0 or 1.1, the primary method of designating a file or device as the target of an I/O process or other interrogation is through the *file control block* (FCB). In MS-DOS 2.0 and later versions, the FCB is valid in certain cases, but the preferred medium of designation is the *pathname* and the *file handle* (more details later).

The FCB is a 32-byte section of memory that serves as a common area for the application program and MS-DOS to exchange information about a file or peripheral device. It is not used for the exchange of information originating from the file or device, or information destined for the file or device (the job of the DTA), but should be regarded as a file status area. For instance, the filename is a component of a file. We can place the characters of the filename into the FCB, in prearranged format and at a specific location, thereby specifying a specific file, and with various requests of MS-DOS:

- Separate the physical device specifier, filename, and extension.
- Check for the existence of the file.
- Create the file if it does not exist.
- Perform a read or write to a specific location in a file (not necessarily the beginning or end of the file).
- Execute various functions based on the characteristics of the file.
- Give the file a new name.
- Remove the file from the disk directory.
- Find the length of the file.
- Alter the length of the file.

Another reason for throwing away the I/O routines of a higher-level language and using the MS-DOS routines directly is programming flexi-

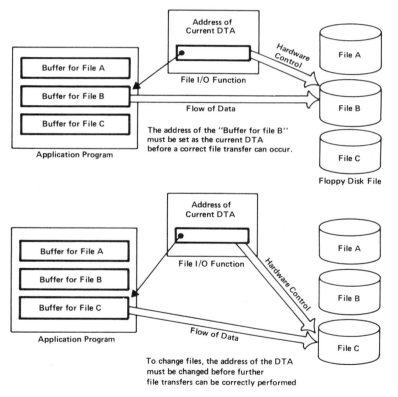

Figure 2-4. Using Several Data Buffers by Changing DTA Addresses.

bility. When you are programming with some Pascal language implementations, you will find that the Pascal file declarations must be located in very specific parts of the program. This is a language-dependent problem that is not a problem with the C language. It can limit your use of files and clutter up memory with file information that is used in some remote part of the program.

You can declare an FCB in any procedure in your program. The Pascal compiler can't tell what you are doing. With the FCB, you can open, manipulate, and close files without worrying about declaring them in the proper places in the program.

A caution: There are reasons that the Pascal file structure is built with these restrictions. The biggest reason is to protect the user from mishap. Circumventing this protection is not for novice programmers. For instance, creating and writing a file within a procedure, and then leaving the procedure without setting the file size and closing the file, can lead to all sorts of unpredictable problems. Be aware that exploring MS-DOS means assuming responsibilities.

In Pascal, the definition of the FCB is:

```
Type

    FCB_Type = Record
        Drive              [00] : Byte;
        Filename           [01] : String(8);
        Filetype           [09] : String(3);
        Block_Number       [12] : Integer;
        Record_Size        [14] : Integer;
        File_LSW_Size      [16] : Word;
        File_MSW_Size      [18] : Word;
        Date               [20] : Word;
        Reserved           [22] : String(10);
        Seq_Record_Num     [32] : Byte;
        Random_LSW_Num     [33] : Word;
        Random_MSW_Num     [35] : Word;
        End;
    Var
        Work_File                    : FCB_Type;
        Sort_File                    : FCB_Type;
```

In Assembler, the definition of the FCB is:

```
;
;declare the fields of the FCB
;these offsets can be used with
```

```
;any file control block
;
FCB        STRUC
Drive      DB     ?
Filename   DB     8 DUP (?)
Filetype   DB     3 DUP (?)
BlockNum   DW     ?
RecSize    DW     ?
FileSize   DD     ?
Date       DW     ?
Reserved   DB     10 DUP (?)
SeqRec     DB     ?
Random     DD     ?
FCB        ENDS
;
WorkFile   FCB    ; declare the memory for the file control blocks
MyFile     FCB


           mov    ax,workfile[drive]
           mov    myfile[seqrec],dx
```

If you do not have the ability to build structures, the file control block can be defined with EQUates like this:

```
Drive      EQU    00        ;Byte
Filename   EQU    01        ;String of 8 characters
Filetype   EQU    09        ;String of 3 characters
BlockNum   EQU    12        ;Word
RecSize    EQU    14        ;Word
FileSize   EQU    16        ;Double Word
Date       EQU    20        ;Word
Reserved   EQU    22        ;10 bytes
SeqRec     EQU    32        ;Byte
Random     EQU    33        ;Double Word


WorkFile   DB     32 DUP (?)
MyFile     DB     32 Dup (?)
```

Pathnames and Handles

Fooling with the addresses of the various DTAs and keeping the proper FCBs straight with their functions is virtually eliminated if you choose to manage your peripheral devices and file with Version 2.0 and later versions of MS-DOS. MS-DOS 2.0 introduced the concept of a tree-structured file system.

For the moment, recall that a disk contains a directory that will lead MS-DOS to the proper location on the disk so a file may be found. In the tree structure, the main directory serves as a root directory. The files found through the root directory may contain program object code, ASCII text, or various other forms of information.

One of the other file forms is the *subdirectory*. The purpose of the subdirectory is the same as the main or root directory; it provides a pathway to files within its scope. It is possible that the path to a particular file is found by passing through several directories and their subdirectories.

By chaining the names of the directories and the target file together, we produce a *pathname*, which describes the location of the file. The slashes, \ and /, are used as dividers or delimiters between the names of the various directories and filename. Normally, only the backslash, \, is used as a delimiter. However, when used through a system call, MS-DOS will recognize the normal forward slash as an acceptable delimiter. An example of a pathname would look like this:

```
C:\CLIENT1\PRODUCT.ABC\PASCAL\UTILITY\MAX.PAS
```

This pathname represents a Pascal program source file called *MAX*. (It finds the larger of two numbers.) MAX is a member of the group of utility routines written in the Pascal programming language on a project to produce product ABC for a certain client.

It should be obvious that this pathname is not going to fit into the filename and file type fields of an FCB. Obviously, not all pathnames are going to be the same length. To keep things orderly, MS-DOS has placed a length limit of 63 characters for a pathname.

You can't have every pathname being 63 characters long, so how do we tell when a pathname is 6 characters long and when one is 47 characters long? To tell MS-DOS exactly which characters are part of the pathname and which ones are garbage characters, MS-DOS will stop reading characters in your pathname when it finds a null (a byte with a binary zero) character in the path.

One of the nicest features of the innovations of MS-DOS 2.0 is the elimination of the FCB when using pathnames. With the later versions of MS-DOS, it is only necessary to reference a file through its pathname when the file is either being opened or created. Internally, MS-DOS maintains all of the data structures required to locate a file on a disk. To ease the burden of file identification, MS-DOS assigns a reference number to the file with the pathname that you constructed. All further references to that particular file are through this number, which has been called the *handle*. (Is there a CB radio ancestry to this term?)

The Microsoft Pascal language allows two data structures suitable for *string handling* (lists of characters for letter, word, and phrase manipulation).

The *LString* type is used for strings with variable lengths, storing the current length of the string in the first position (byte 0) of the list.

The *String* type is the other structure, similar to the LString, except that the length attribute is missing.

In the example below, the LString called A_NAME has been set to a maximum length of 64. This will allow the maximum pathname of 63 characters and still allow room for the trailing null character.

The *Open_File* procedure, however, requires a String as the parameter, which contains the pathname of the file to be opened. Pascal allows an LString to be used in place of a String as a parameter. Pascal conveniently ignores the length byte in this case, which is just the effect we want. MS-DOS will only "see" the characters in the pathname and not the length byte.

Notice the contortions required to get the null character on the end of the pathname:

1. Get the length of the valid portion of the string.

2. Add 1 to that length and place the null in that position. The null was not included in the valid portion of the string (the part within the length specified by the length byte), so the pathname is still valid for possible later operations, such as appending more characters to the pathname.

```
Var
A_Name   : LString(64);
A_Handle : Integer;
Status   : Integer;
Procedure Open_File (Vars FilePath : String;
     Var  Handle  : Integer;
     Var  Status  : Integer);
     Extern;
Begin
.
.
.
{form a pathname}
A_Name := 'A:/CLIENT1/PRODUCT.ABC/PASCAL/UTILITY/MAX.PAS';
{get the current length of valid characters }
```

```
{place a null (0) into the position after }
{the last character}
A_Name[A_NameLen + 1].:= Chr(0);
{let Pascal pass the string without the}
{length byte to the routine that will}
{eventually call MS-DOS}
Open_File (A_Name, A_Handle, Status);
  .
  .
  .
End.
```

We have looked at the data structures used by the application program in presenting data to the MS-DOS system calls. Now that we have the data prepared, it is time to get the attention of MS-DOS and have it do some work for us.

Getting the Attention of MS-DOS

Once the data is prepared, getting the attention of MS-DOS so that it will perform a requested function is one of the easiest parts of interfacing to the system calls. MS-DOS is alerted to your request through a software interrupt.

Hardware interrupts tell MS-DOS that something is happening in one of the peripheral devices and that it should stop whatever it is doing and pay attention to the hardware device. Typing on the keyboard causes a hardware interrupt that alerts MS-DOS that you have just pressed a key and it ought to respond to the interrupt so it doesn't miss any of the typed letters.

The same is true for software. One particular software interrupt notifies MS-DOS that there is a request for service pending. In the following chapters, you will get the information about setting up data structures and registers for each specific MS-DOS system call.

When that setup is complete, your request is forwarded to MS-DOS when an INT 21H machine instruction is executed. This software interrupt will temporarily halt the execution of your program while the system call performs the requested task. When the service is completed, MS-DOS allows your program to resume execution.

In Microsoft Pascal, the interface is a bit different. For one thing, there is not a software interrupt instruction in Pascal. However, the Pascal run-time support library provides a function called DOSXQQ. DOSXQQ will accept certain information (e.g., the identity of the requested function and a single parameter value) as parameters, set up the hardware registers, and perform the INT 21H.

Although DOSXQQ is very useful, it will not cover all of the system calls. You may be forced to write some assembler routines to provide these additional services.

In your Pascal program, declare DOSXQQ with the following line in the procedure declaration area:

```
Function DOSXQQ (Func : Byte; Parm : Word) : Byte;
EXTERN;
```

In the DOSXQQ function, the FUNC parameter is the number of the system call to be performed. The PARM parameter is a parameter to the system call, depending upon the system call requirements. Sometimes the parameter is a pointer to an FCB or DTA, and other times it is a character to be sent to the screen.

When a system call requires more than one parameter, DOSXQQ is unable to provide an interface to MS-DOS.

DOSXQQ is a function, so it returns with a value. The importance of that value, once again, depends upon the nature of the system call. Sometimes it is the completion status, and other times it may be the last character typed on the keyboard. The descriptions of the various system calls should make this value clear for each application.

When using Turbo Pascal, the interface to MS-DOS is through the predefined procedure called *MsDos*. This procedure is used only for functions that would be called with INT 21H in assembly language. There is a single parameter to this procedure, a record with a field for each register. The details for this record type can be found in the *Turbo Pascal Reference Manual*.

To make the listings for Microsoft Pascal and Turbo Pascal compatible, you might want to use the following Turbo Pascal function in your programs:

Listing 2-1. DOSXQQ Interface for Turbo Pascal.

```
Function DOSXQQ (Func : Byte; Param : Word) : Byte;
Type
   REGS = Record
      Case Integer of
      1: (AX,BX,CX,DX,BP,DI,SI,DS,ES,Flags : Integer);
```

```
        2: (AL,AH,BL,BH,CL,CH,DL,DH : Byte);
      End;
  Var
    R : REGS;
  Begin
    R.AH := Func;
    Case (Func) of {list here is incomplete}
      2, 4, 5, 6, $0E, $2E: R.DL = Param;
      9, $0A : R.DX = Param;
    End;
    MsDos(R);
    DOSXQQ := R.AL;
  End;
```

Getting Information from MS-DOS

The flow of data between a program and the operating system is a two-way street. Some functions of the operating system perform the output: They receive the characters in registers to be printed on the system printer, while other functions move data from a disk transfer area to a disk file. Still other functions do the input, reading disk files and putting the data into the disk transfer area, or getting a character from the keyboard.

In the case of the input functions, the applications program must have a way to receive the information generated through the operating system call. These transfers are just the reverse of the output functions. A call is placed to the function, and when the application program is started again, the data is available for use. This section briefly covers three methods of data transfer used by the MS-DOS. These three methods are:

- Direct Register Transfer
- Disk Transfer Area
- File Control Block

There are other methods of data transfer that will be covered with the specific system call in the later chapters.

Direct Register Transfer

We saw that the individual characters destined for the printer or the video monitor screen were passed through the hardware registers to the operating system. To complement this flow of characters, the operating system uses the hardware registers to pass the characters originated at the keyboard and other devices.

For high-level language programmers, the DOSXQQ (for Pascal users) function returns the value of the AX/AL register. This is the primary register for character transfers, so most of the character I/O system calls are available with DOSXQQ.

For the assembly language programmers, the following registers are used to get information from MS-DOS:

Table 2-2. Output Register Uses

Register	Uses
AX	File Handles
	Error Code
AL	Input Character Codes
	Completion Status Codes
DX	Time and Date
	Device Information
DS:DX	Disk Transfer Area Address
	Address of Data
CX	Counts
	Time and Date

The Disk Transfer Area

The Disk Transfer Area is also a two-way street. System functions that involve reading the disk place the results in the current DTA. These reads may be the contents of a regular file or entries in the disk directory. When the system function is complete, the data is ready for use by your program.

File Control Block

The File Control Block is mainly a collection point for information about a file. The program segments that show the detail of the FCB declaration list the names of these pieces of information. The placement of data into the FCB just prior to opening the file is the critical event for a program, and that is a data preparation step. However, the operating system also fills the FCB with information about the file; some of this information may be useful for your program. The exact details will be covered later, but the operating system can use the FCB to tell the program where the end of a file is; correctly load the FCB with a filename; and get the length of a file.

Making Sure That It Works

It is often out of the scope of a program to check all data for full validity. If a program asks a user for a filename, it is possible that a typing error could slip past your error-detection routine and end up in a file control block. Passing a bad filename to an operating system call shouldn't crash the program, but if you simply assume that the operating system successfully completed its task and your program continues using the bad filename, then you can expect an unhappy ending for your program.

The operating system tried to tell you that it was having problems, but how did you know?

Early MS-DOS system calls (Version 1.0 and 1.1) that involve files, and a couple of nonfile functions, use the AL register to return a *status code*. This status code should be checked by your program to make sure that everything was successfully performed.

If the AL register contains a value of zero, then the operation was properly completed. Any other value is a signal that some condition should be recognized. For instance, when reading a file and the end of the file is reached, the AL register will contain a 1 (no more data was read) or a 3 (a partial record was found before reaching the end of the file). These and other values are covered for each specific system call.

MS-DOS Version 2.0 system calls indicate the occurrence of an error by setting the processor's Carry flag. The program should check this flag after each call to MS-DOS. When the flag is set, a specific error code will be found in the AX register. Chapter 9, *Expanded Error Handling*, contains further details about this feature.

AVAILABLE INTERFACES

MS-DOS supplies a number of system calls to the programmer. In the following chapters, you will find specific information about each routine.

As we have seen, MS-DOS handles some simple tasks and some sophisticated tasks, so the system calls of MS-DOS have been classified into groups of related tasks. The following outline of chapters names each of the MS-DOS system calls with relation to its task group. You might mark this place in the book to use this list as a quick reference guide for the proper task group (chapter number) and function call number in hexadecimal (base-16) numbers of a system call.

Fundamental Character I/O Functions

Hex 01	Keyboard input
Hex 02	Display output
Hex 03	Auxiliary input
Hex 04	Auxiliary output
Hex 05	Printer output
Hex 06	Direct console I/O
Hex 07	Direct console input without echo
Hex 08	Console input without echo
Hex 09	Display string
Hex 0A	Buffered keyboard input
Hex 0B	Check standard input status
Hex 0C	Clear standard input buffer and invoke a standard input function

Fundamental Utility Functions

Hex 00	Program terminate
Hex 1A	Set disk transfer address
Hex 25	Set interrupt vector
Hex 26	Create a new program segment
Hex 2A	Get date
Hex 2B	Set date
Hex 2C	Get time
Hex 2D	Set time
Hex 2E	Set/reset verify switch
Hex 2F	Get DTA
Hex 30	Get DOS version number
Hex 31	Terminate process and remain resident
Hex 33	Ctrl-C and Ctrl-Break check
Hex 35	Get vector
Hex 36	Get disk free space
Hex 38	Return country dependent information
Hex 4C	Terminate a process

Hex 4D   Retrieve return code of a process
Hex 54   Get verify state
Hex 62   Get Program Segment Prefix address
Hex 65   Get Extended Country Information
Hex 66   Get/Set Global Code Page

Fundamental File Management

Hex 0D   Disk reset
Hex 0E   Select disk
Hex 0F   Open file
Hex 10   Close file
Hex 13   Delete file
Hex 14   Sequential read
Hex 15   Sequential write
Hex 16   Create file
Hex 19   Current disk
Hex 1B   Allocation table information
Hex 1C   Allocation table information for specific drive
Hex 21   Random read
Hex 22   Random write
Hex 23   File size
Hex 24   Set random record field
Hex 27   Random block read
Hex 28   Random block write
Hex 29   Parse filename

Directory Management

Hex 11   Search for the first directory entry
Hex 12   Search for the next directory entry
Hex 17   Rename file
Hex 39   Create a subdirectory
Hex 3A   Remove a directory entry
Hex 3B   Change the current directory
Hex 47   Get current directory
Hex 4E   Find first matching file
Hex 4F   Find next matching file
Hex 56   Rename a file
Hex 57   Get/set a file's date and time

Advanced File Management

Hex 3C	Create a file
Hex 3D	Open a file
Hex 3E	Close a file handle
Hex 3F	Read from a file or device
Hex 40	Write to a file or device
Hex 41	Delete a file from a specified directory
Hex 42	Move file read/write pointer
Hex 43	Change file attribute
Hex 44	I/O control of devices
Hex 45	Duplicate a file handle
Hex 46	Force a duplicate of a handle
Hex 5A	Create unique file
Hex 5B	Create new file
Hex 5C	Lock/unlock file access
Hex 67	Set handle count
Hex 68	Commit file

MS-DOS Memory Management

Hex 48	Allocate memory
Hex 49	Free allocated memory
Hex 4A	Modify allocated memory blocks
Hex 4B	Load or execute a program

Expanded Error Handling

Hex 59	Get extended error

Network Management

Hex 5E00	Get machine name
Hex 5E02	Set printer setup
Hex 5E03	Get printer setup
Hex 5F02	Get redirection list entry
Hex 5F03	Redirect device
Hex 5F04	Cancel redirection

Chapter 3

Fundamental Character I/O Functions

INTRODUCTION

This chapter is the first chapter covering the programming details of using MS-DOS. It describes the functions of the MS-DOS classified as the *fundamental character I/O functions*. These functions are responsible for the operation of peripheral devices that use single characters or bytes as their main component of manipulation. For example, the computer terminal's keyboard is a *character device*. It generates individual characters for the computer software to manipulate. The character I/O functions covered in this chapter are (in hexadecimal or base 16):

Hex 01	Keyboard input
Hex 02	Display output
Hex 03	Auxiliary input
Hex 04	Auxiliary output
Hex 05	Printer output
Hex 06	Direct console I/O
Hex 07	Direct console input without echo
Hex 08	Console input without echo
Hex 09	Display string
Hex 0A	Buffered keyboard input
Hex 0B	Check standard input status
Hex 0C	Clear standard input buffer and invoke a standard input function

DECIDING TO USE THESE FUNCTIONS

Of all of the function groups provided by the MS-DOS, this group probably offers the most diverse assortment of useful and worthless functions.

On the one hand, this group includes routines for getting characters and function key inputs from the computer's keyboard. This could be very handy in a real-time control program where you can't sit and wait for a language run time environment to gather and process a response from the user while some controlled process needs monitoring. The READLN command in Pascal and BASIC's INPUT command will both cause the program to wait until a character has been entered from the terminal keyboard. These routines have a design that goes something like this:

```
loop
   loop until key is struck
   get character from keyboard handler
   put character into input buffer
   until ENTER is found
```

The hang-up occurs in the "loop until key is struck" portion of the sequence. What is really wanted for more control is:

```
loop
   loop
   monitor processes
   until key is struck
   get character from keyboard
   put character into input buffer
   until ENTER is found
```

This is the kind of flexibility that is delivered by the better functions in this group.

On the other hand, this group also includes some very crude interfaces to the asynchronous communications and some old-fashioned functions to monitor.

Here is the problem: Once again, the purpose of MS-DOS is to provide a standard method of using the I/O devices and other functions of the computer. If you are going to write a program that can be used on any machine operating with MS-DOS, you have to allow for the use of the most primitive devices for each I/O function.

In the case of the interactive terminal, one of the most primitive devices is the teletypewriter terminal. This is stretching the point a bit, but when a computer uses the teletypewriter terminal as an I/O device, it becomes necessary to read and write in a line-oriented way (e.g., one line at a time). The teletypewriter can only operate on the current line at the current character position. Therefore, regardless of how sophisticated your personal computer might be, MS-DOS is going to treat that high-resolution color monitor as if it were a line-at-a-time TTY. That should explain why the MS-DOS monitor and most other MS-DOS-compatible software scroll lines of instructions at you from the bottom of the screen and the cursor keys don't work very well. There is no up and down on a TTY.

This sets you up for a dilemma: Should you stick with MS-DOS and make your program usable on other machines that use MS-DOS, or go with some of the goodies available on your brand of machine? The drawback is that to make a program machine dependent is to limit your market to that particular brand with your particular configuration. I'll try to get specific about some of these problems as each of the functions are discussed.

NON-ASCII KEYS ON THE IBM PC

Some of the following functions are used to get characters input through the computer's keyboard. The standard IBM PC keyboard and assorted spinoffs, however, allow more key stroke combinations than just the standard ASCII keys. Using functions 1, 6, 7, and 8, you will be able to read any combination allowed.

In normal operation, when the regular keys are used for entering information, MS-DOS functions will return the ASCII value of the key pressed. Moreover, pressing the Ctrl key at the same time as one of the letters or numbers will produce an ASCII character with a value relative to the letter's position in the alphabet (e.g., Ctrl-A = 1, Ctrl-B = 2, Ctrl-C = 3, etc.).

The function keys, the cursor keys and the Alt-combination keys are made available to your program by these MS-DOS functions through a somewhat different manner than just reading a simple value. When one of these non-ASCII keys or key combinations is pressed, MS-DOS returns a zero value to the calling program. This value will be in the AL register at the machine level. The zero value is a signal to your program that another call to the same MS-DOS function is required to get the value of the pressed key.

The following listing shows the use of the keyboard oriented functions. The program is written in Pascal. The DOSXQQ function is an MS-DOS interface function that allows a Pascal program to initiate MS-DOS functions and receive the results of the functions. In this particular example, the final value of the function (the AL register) is returned to the program as the result of the DOSXQQ function.

Listing 3-1. Detecting and Handling Function
Key Inputs.

```
Program Function_Key_Test;
Const
  Console_Input = 16 07;
Var
  C : Char;
  Quit_Command : Boolean;
Procedure Handle_Commands (Command : Byte); EXTERN;
Procedure Handle_Letters (Letter : Char); EXTERN;
Function DOSXQQ (Command : Byte; Parm : Word) : Byte;
  EXTERN;
Begin
  Quit_Command := False;
  Repeat
    {get a character from the keyboard}
    C := Chr(DOSXQQ (Console_Input, 0));
    {a value of zero means that a func/cursor/ALT key}
    {was pressed...need another call to get value}
    If C = Chr(0)
    Then
      {call the routine that handles commands with the}
      {value of the func/cursor/ALT key}
      Handle_Commands (DOSXQQ(Console_Input,0))
    Else
      {regular letter to be processed}
  Handle_Letters (C);
    {was the 'quit' command processed?}
    Until Quit_Command;
  End.
```

And for the C programmers in the crowd:

```
#define CONSOLE_INPUT    0x07
#define FALSE            0
#define TRUE             1

main()
char            c;
int             quit;
{
  quit = FALSE;
  while (!quit)
    if (c = _bdos(CONSOLE_INPUT,0)) /* get keyboard character */
      handle_letters(c); /* not NULL - must be good */
    else
        /* NULL means an ALT or FUNC key was pressed */
        /* get its value on the next access */
        /* set QUIT is command is QUIT */
    quit = handle_commands(_bdos(CONSOLE_INPUT,0));
}
```

A Word of Caution.   This almost always works. There seems to be a bug in this part of the early IBM PC software/hardware. The Alt-Q combination, which is a real natural as a command to quit a process, does not generate the proper code in some of the early IBM PCs. Instead, it causes each line of keyboard input to be sent to the printer. You may want to check this problem on your own machine since it was fixed on later versions of the IBM PC. If you are writing software to be used on IBM PCs in general, don't assume that if it works on your machine it will on every other one.

In the example, the routine called Handle—Commands receives the value of the pressed key when the main program calls the MS-DOS Console Input function again and passes the returned value as a parameter. The number that is returned from the function this time is the identity of the pressed key. The alphanumeric keys of the keyboard have been numbered. When an Alt key combination is entered and an alphanumeric key is pressed, the result is the key number.

Chapter 14 contains a section about the keyboard that gives the numeric value of each key. The function keys may have several values not shown on the chart because use of the Alt and Shift keys can influence the function key values. Also, using the Alt keys with the numbers at the top of the main keyboard will return valid values, but the values will not correspond to the numeric value of the key. These values are discussed in Chapter 14, *BIOS Programming*.

The body of the Handle—Commands routine would be a Pascal *CASE* statement to decode the key values and invoke whatever program sequence is required to accomplish the command, as shown here:

Listing 3-2. Details of Handling Alt Keys and Function Keys.

```
Procedure Handle_Commands (Command : Byte);
Begin
      CASE Command OF
      18 : {ALT-E} Quit_Command := True;
      30 : {ALT-A} Add;
      31 : {ALT-S} Subtract;
      Otherwise;
      End;
End;
```

And the same sequence in C:

```
int handle_commands (c)
char           c;
{
  int          q;
  q = FALSE;  /* assume that end is not near */
  switch (c)
    {
    case 18 : /* ALT-E */
               q = TRUE; /* time to end -- set quit flag */
               break;
    case 30 : /* ALT-A */
               add();
               break;
    case 31 : /* ALT-S */
               subtract();
               break;
    default : break;
    }
  return q;
}
```

If the Ctrl-Break or Ctrl-C keys are pressed when some of the keyboard functions are used, the MS-DOS function will initiate a software interrupt Hex 23 that handles this special situation. The normal outcome of a Ctrl-Break or Ctrl-C is a program abort. You can provide a customized handler (your own interrupt Hex 23 software) for these cases in your program. Then, pressing these key combinations will trigger the use of your handler. But if you should want to ignore their implied meanings (that is, stop the program), don't use that particular keyboard function.

As an example, a *Dumb Terminal* program has to be able to send a Ctrl-C to the host computer so that the terminal can control the operation of an application program. If the Dumb Terminal program allowed MS-DOS to detect the Ctrl-C and do its thing, two things would happen (or not happen): First, your Dumb Terminal program would crash (as a direct result of the Ctrl-C); and, if the application program on the host computer were in an endless loop (a good time for a Ctrl-C), you would never be able to stop it. Let's hope that the operating system on the host will cause your program to time out and stop.

The functions that are not sensitive to the Ctrl-C are noted as such so that you can pick the correct one for your application.

THE CHARACTER I/O FUNCTIONS

Keyboard Input

Function: Hex 01

Registers: AL = Character input

The purpose of the *Keyboard Input* function is to wait for a character to be entered by the user through the standard input device (console keyboard). When a character is entered, this function will display the character on the standard output device at the current cursor location. In the case of most microcomputers using MS-DOS, the standard output device is the video monitor, and the current cursor location is the position following the previous character (unless a new line was generated).

Since this function, as all of the other functions in this group, finds its origins in "one line at a time" output devices, such as printing terminals or remote terminals, compatibility with these types of terminals is maintained and the output is generated in "one line at a time" fashion, scrolling the finished lines up the screen. However, for a simple interface where a scrolling line is all that is necessary, this function will keep your programming task to a minimum.

The following program sequence shows the use of this function in a Pascal program.

Listing 3-3 Keyboard Input in Pascal.

```
Procedure Get_Char (Var C  : Char;
   Var Special_Key : Boolean);
Const
Console_Input_With_Echo = 16#01;
{ }
{the external function DOSXQQ is declared in the main}
{portion of the program as:  }
{FUNCTION DOSXQQ (Command : Byte; Parm : Word) : Byte;}
{EXTERN;}
{ }
Begin
  {get key presses from DOS}
  C := Chr(DOSXQQ (Console_Input_With_Echo, 0));
  Special_Key := False;
  {if func/cursor/ALT key. . .evidenced by zero}
  If C = Chr(0)
  Then
    Begin
    {set flag indicating a special key was pressed}
    Special_Key := True;
    {get value of the key}
    C := Chr(DOSXQQ (Console_Input_With_Echo, 0));
    End;
End;
```

This function is more or less already built into the C run-time librar-ies. But, the normal *getchar* doesn't deal with the extended key strokes. If it did, it might look something like this:

Listing 3-4. Keyboard Input in C.

```
int getkey (c)
char  *c;
#define CONSOLE_INPUT_WITH_ECHO 0x01
{
  /* get key presses from DOS */
  if (*c = _bdos (CONSOLE_INPUT_WITH_ECHO,0))   return
FALSE;
  /* if func/cursor/ALT key . . . evidenced by zero */
  *c = _bdos(CONSOLE_INPUT_WITH_ECHO,0);
  /* set return flag indicating a special key was pressed */
  return TRUE;
}
```

This function can be easily used in an assembly language program if the following macro were inserted at the front of the program:

Listing 3-5. Keyboard Input in Assembler.

```
getchar    macro    flag,key
           local    out
           mov      ax,1     ; get a character
           int      21h
           mov      flag,al  ; put char into flag variable
           Or       al,al    ; was that a 0 that was fetched?
           jnz      out      ; no - flag has ascii value
           mov      ax,1     ; get another char to find
           int      21h      ; which key is pressed
           mov      key,al   ; save in key variable
out:
           cmp      flag,0   ; generate flags
           endm
```

With this macro, you can place the next character entered into a variable (known as "flag" in the macro) that you name. If this value is zero, then the number of the pressed key will be placed into the second passed variable.

To use this macro, the assembly code would look like this:

```
    getchar  c,key       ; get character into c, key into key
    jnz      got_ascii   ; go and handle ascii char
;
;   code here to handle FUNC KEY, CTRL and ALT conditions
;
```

Display Output

Function: Hex 02

Registers: DL = Character to be displayed on console device

The purpose of the *Display Output* function is to display a character on the standard output device. On a video monitor, the character to be displayed will appear at the cursor's current position. The cursor is advanced after the character is written. When a character is placed at the end of a line, the cursor will move to the left edge of the screen and down one line, clearing that line to allow for further output. When the line is at the bottom of the screen, the contents of the screen are scrolled toward the top, and the bottom line is reused for the new output. The backspace character (ASCII value = 8) will cause the cursor to move one position to the left and place a space in that location, effectively erasing the previous character. If the Ctrl-Break or Ctrl-C keys are detected while this function is executing, a software interrupt Hex 23 will be initiated to handle that situation.

The following example illustrates the use of this function in an assembly language sequence. The program code assumes that there is a variable by the name of LINE which has some length corresponding to the number of characters to be displayed. Setting up a count in the CX register and a pointer to each of the characters with the SI register, the sequence will loop until all characters have been printed.

```
putchar     macro       char
            mov         ah,2
            mov         dl,char
            int         21h
            endp

            Mov         CX,LENGTH Line   ; get # of chars
            Mov         SI,0             ; start at first char
SHOWLINE:   Putchar     Line[SI]         ; show char on display
            Inc         SI               ; next char
            Loop        Showline         ; do it for all of them
```

Auxiliary Input

Function: Hex 03

Registers: AL = Character received from communications

The purpose of the *Auxiliary Input* function is to allow access to the asynchronous communications port (serial RS-232 adapter). This function will wait for a character to be received through the communications port and return it to the calling program. The use of this function is recommended only for compatibility with other MS-DOS programs that may use this function. If you are going to write a communications program, either use the ROM-based communications interface (software interrupt Hex 14 for the IBM PC and compatibles) or write your own.

This function is not interrupt-driven, which means that you will have to wait for each character and process it when the function returns with a value. This limits the amount of computing that could be done between characters.

This function will restrict you to half-duplex communications (two-way communications, but only one party talks at one time; CB radio is supposed to be half-duplex). During the receive portion of your program, you would have to call this function and wait for a character, and then when you've decided that it is your turn to talk, you use the next function (Hex 04) to send what you have to say.

In another way, you are almost forced to use the ROM-based communications interface because the communications port is initialized by MS-DOS to be:

- 2400 baud
- No parity
- 8 data bits
- One stop bit

Most popular communications (using a modem and the telephone system) use:

- 300, 1200, and 2400 baud
- Even parity
- 7 data bits
- one or two stop bits.

You can set this up using the MS-DOS MODE command through the command processor, or include some initialization in your program. The use of the software BIOS functions to use the ROM functions will be covered in Chapter 14.

Auxiliary Output

Function: Hex 04

Registers: DL = Character to be sent

The purpose of the *Auxiliary Output* function is to send a character to the asynchronous communications port for transmission. This function is the complement of the Auxiliary Input function and should/should not be used for most of the same reasons as function Hex 03.

This function is somewhat more useful than its receiving complement. The following sequence is a start at the transmitting side of a half-duplex Dumb Terminal program. The sequence fetches a character from the keyboard that also displays the character and then sends it out through the RS-232 port. Before you run off and use this code in a Dumb Terminal program, the MS-DOS functions used here will detect a Ctrl-C and crash your program:

```
XMIT    :   Mov     AH,01H      ; get character from keyboard
            Int     021H        ; have DOS do it
                                 ; char ==> AL
            Cmp     AL,0        ; func key pressed?
            Je      NoXMIT      ; let's quit if func key
            Mov     DL,AL       ; ready for sending
            Mov     AH,04H      ; async comm
            Int     021H        ; have DOS send it
                                 ; AL ==> RS-232 port
            Jmp     XMIT        ; back to keyboard read
NoXMIT:     Mov     AH,08H      ; flush other byte out
            Int     021H        ; ok, get other half of word
```

Printer Output

Function: Hex 05

Registers: DL = Character to be printed

The purpose of the *Printer Output* function is to send a single character to the printer. This function is almost an exact duplicate of Display Output, except that the character is printed on the system printer instead of being displayed on the screen.

This function makes the interface to the printer quite simple. There are normally a number of status checks to be made before a character can be sent to the printer (e.g., Is the printer ready? Is there room in the printer's buffer? Is there paper in the printer?). These status checks are handled by MS-DOS and appropriate warnings (e.g., "Out of Paper") are issued on the screen of the video monitor.

The code example given for Display Output can be used for Printer Output by changing the value in the AH register to "05H". A group of routines to set the modes of the printer could be quite useful. That is, routines to put the printer (Epson MX-80, in this case) into bold or condensed mode:

```
print     macro     char
          mov       ah,5
          mov       dl,char
          int       21h
          endm


BOLD      PROC      NEAR
          PUBLIC    BOLD
          ASSUME    CS:CODE
          print     27        ; escape character
          print     'E'       ; print in emphasize mode
          Ret                 ; and back to the caller
BOLD      ENDP
CONDENS   PROC      NEAR
          PUBLIC    CONDENS
          ASSUME    CS:CODE
          print     15        ; 'shift in' code
          Ret                 ; and back to the caller
CONDENS   ENDP
```

Direct Console I/O

Function: Hex 06

Registers: DL = I/O code and/or character to be displayed

AL = Character input from console

The purpose of the *Direct Console I/O* function is to provide a single routine for getting characters from the standard input device (keyboard) and sending characters to the standard output device (video monitor). The operations of this function are very similar to MS-DOS functions Hex 01 and Hex 02 with the major difference being that this function does not execute a software interrupt if Ctrl-Break or Ctrl-C is detected.

This function will conduct both the input and the output functions, so it is necessary to tell the function which to do. The value of the DL register determines the action of the function, shown in Table 3-1.

Table 3-1. DL Action Controls.

'DL' Register set to Hex FF

Action: Input from standard
input device
  If character is ready:
     Character in 'AL' register
     Zero flag in flag register
  is cleared
    If character is not ready:
     Zero flag in flag register
  is set

'DL' Register set to any other value :

Action: Character in 'DL' register is
displayed on standard output device

Here is an example:

```
GETCHAR :    Mov    AH,06H    ; direct i/o
             Mov    DL,0FFH   ; get a character
             Int    021H      ; DOS does it
             Jz     GOTONE    ; got a valid character
;
;    this code space could be used to do things while
;    you are waiting for a character to be typed
;
             Jmp    GETCHAR   ; processing done, try again
GOTONE:      . . .
```

Direct Console Input Without Echo

Function: Hex 07

Registers: AL = Character input from console

The purpose of the *Direct Console Input Without Echo* function is to fetch a character entered on the standard input device (the console keyboard). The character will not appear on the console output (the video screen).

This function is handy when you want the user to enter a response, but you want to control the way in which the typed characters are presented back to the user, if at all.

This function will retain program control until a key is pressed. If this is an undesirable condition, use the *Check Standard Input Status* function to find out whether a key has been pressed, prior to initiating this function.

Listing 3-6. Key Input without Screen Display (Pascal and C).

```
    Program Key_Press;
    Const
      Console_Input = 16#07;
      Console_Status = 16#0B;
    Var
      C  :   Char;
    Function DOSXQQ (Command : Byte; Parm : Word) : Byte;
      EXTERN;
    Begin
      While DOSXQQ (Console_Status, 0) = 0 Do
        Begin
        {things to be done while you are waiting}
        {such as:                                }
        {completing a backlog of requests        }
        {printing a file                         }
        {handling incoming communications        }
        {updating a digital clock on the screen  }
        End;
      C := Chr(DOSXQQ(Console_Input,0));
    End.


    #define CONSOLE_INPUT  0x07
    #define CONSOLE_STATUS 0x0B
    int kbhit() {return _bdos(CONSOLE_STATUS,0);}
    int getchar ()
    {
    while (!kbhit())
      {
     /* code here for printing or plotting */
     /* while you wait for a character to be entered */
      }
    return _bdos(CONSOLE_INPUT,0);
    }
```

The macro in the first function of this chapter can be easily modified for this and the next functions by changing the value of the AH register from 1 to either 7 or 8. Using either this function or the next with the display character, you have a chance to decide whether a keystroke should or should not appear on the screen. In the case of a function key, you would not want the "funny" character that may be produced by the key number to be displayed.

```
getchar      char,key      ; get a character
cmp          char,0        ; check for key number or ascii
jz           do_key        ; go someplace for key number
putchar      char          ; display ascii char just entered
```

The difference between this function and functions 1 and 8 (coming up next) is that these other functions will check for Ctrl-Break and Ctrl-C and this function will not. If you are writing a communications program in which you want to transmit the Ctrl-C character to a host computer, you will want to use this MS-DOS function because it will not terminate your program when it sees the Ctrl-C. The other functions will.

Console Input Without Echo

Function: Hex 08

Registers: AL = Character input from keyboard

The *Console Input Without Echo* function is identical to function 1 except that when the key is pressed, its value is returned to you without being displayed on the screen. This gives you the freedom to place the character (or not place it) wherever you wish.

If you are in a position to expect function key inputs or Alt key inputs, you will want to use this function (or function 7) so that the strange characters that could be echoed with function 1 don't appear on the screen.

Once again, this function checks for the Ctrl-C and Ctrl-Break key strokes. This can be handy to have when there is a chance that your program might get out of control and you want a way of stopping its execution without turning the whole computer off.

This function is capable of receiving inputs from the function keys, alternate key combinations, and the cursor keys on the key pad. These keys are signaled by getting a zero value on the first call to this function.

Display String

Function: Hex 09

Registers: DS:DX = Address of string to be printed

The purpose of the *Display (Print) String* function is to display a string of characters on the standard output device (console monitor). The previous console output functions dealt with the display of a single character. Repeating a call to these functions can be time-consuming (multiple calls) and resource-consuming (registers for counting characters and storing offsets into the array of characters). The Display String function requires only an address to the array of characters to be displayed. This address is placed into the DS and DX register pair.

There is a question of how to tell how long the string is. The answer is: MS-DOS will display all of the characters in the string, regardless of value, until a dollar sign ($) is found. This convention can put a real crimp in a business report where dollar signs are common. One solution is to leave a space where the dollar signs should be, and then display the dollar signs in the proper locations with the character-oriented display functions.

And don't accidentally forget to include the dollar sign. You can get screenfuls of strange characters, beeping, and squawking before a random dollar sign is encountered.

The following code segments show the sending of a line of text to the monitor with this function. Notice the carriage return (13) and the linefeed (10) characters in the text.

```
display     macro       stuff
            mov         dx,offset stuff
            mov         ah,9
            int         21h
            endm


TEXT        DB          'This is a string',13,10,'$'


            display     text       ; display string
```

Detection of Ctrl-Break or Ctrl-C is active during this function.

Buffered Keyboard Input

Function: Hex 0A

Registers: DS:DX = Address of input buffer

The purpose of the *Buffered Keyboard Input* function is to allow the entry of a complete line of text from the keyboard before allowing the application program to resume its execution. All of the previous keyboard input functions dealt with the entry of single characters. This function provides a means of gathering a large number of characters at one time. This eliminates multiple calls to the keyboard functions, moving single characters to a buffer, and maintaining the appropriate counters and indexes.

To use this function, a buffer for receiving the characters is prepared and its address is passed to MS-DOS. MS-DOS will place characters entered from the keyboard into this buffer until (1) a carriage return or Enter is encountered, or (2) the buffer is filled. Be aware that MS-DOS will not return the buffer until a carriage return or Enter is pressed, even though the buffer is full. If the buffer is filled before the carriage return occurs, MS-DOS will ring the console bell (beep the horn) for every overflow character.

Before this function is called, the receiving buffer must be prepared. To prevent character overflow or writing characters over sections of important data, it is necessary to tell MS-DOS how large the buffer is. In the first byte of the buffer, place the binary value of the number of characters the buffer can hold. This value must be between 1 and 255, since it must be contained in a single byte. Place the address of the buffer in the DS:DX register pair.

When MS-DOS returns the buffer, the second byte will contain the count of the number of characters that have been placed into the buffer (*excluding* the final carriage return, which is in the buffer, but not counted). The first character of the entered string is found in the third byte.

The following data declaration and code segment show one possible method of creating a buffer and passing its address to MS-DOS:

```
BUFFER     DB    80
COUNT      DB    0
CHARS      DB    80  DUP  (?)
```

```
            Mov DX,Offset BUFFER   ; where is buffer?
            Mov AH,0AH             ; get input in buffer
            Int 21H               ; call DOS
            Mov CX,COUNT          ; get count
   TOP:                           ; manipulate chars
            :
            :
            Loop TOP
```

The editing commands that are used by the MS-DOS command processor are useful in changing the letters entered through this function (before pressing Enter). These line editing commands are covered in the standard *MS-DOS User's Guide*.

Check Standard Input Status

Function: Hex 0B

Registers: AL = Status of keyboard

The purpose of the *Check Standard Input Status* function is to notify the calling program that a character has been entered from the keyboard. This interrogation ability allows an application program to operate in real time while the keyboard is idle. This function will check the keyboard to see if any keys have been pressed since the last time the program checked the status.

The example in function 7 shows the use of this function to check the status.

When there is a character available, the AL register will contain all ones (Hex FF). This is equivalent to the Boolean True, so you can check it using that method. The AL register will contain all zeroes (Boolean False) when a key has not been pressed.

The macro form of this function is:

Listing 3-7. Get Key Ready Status.

```
kbhit     macro
          mov     ah,0bh        ; check keyboard status
          int     21h
          or      al,al         ; generate comparison flags
          endm
   ;
   ;    implemented in code:
```

Listing 3-7. Continued

```
;
get_key:
        kbhit                       ; check for key stroke ready
        jnz         char_rdy        ; looks like a winner
;
;    do things while waiting for key input
;
        jmp         get_key
char_rdy:
        getchar     c,key
        jz          func_key
        putchar     c
;
;    do things to input
;
        jmp         get_key
func_key:
;
;    do things with func key, alt or ctrl input
;
        jmp         get_key
```

If the Ctrl-Break or Ctrl-C keys have been pressed when this function is called, this MS-DOS function will cause the appropriate action to be taken through the interrupt Hex 23 software. This means that if you want to detect the Ctrl-C yourself (so that you can send the Ctrl-C in a communications program, for instance), do not use this function. There is a BIOS routine for the IBM PC that will allow you to make this status check yourself. Using the BIOS will make your program unusable on some other machines using MS-DOS. For more information, refer to Chapter 14, *BIOS Programming*.

Clear Standard Input Buffer and Invoke a Standard Input Function

Function: Hex 0C

Registers: AL = type of input function character
input from standard input device

The purpose of *Clear Standard Input Buffer and Invoke a Standard Input Function* is to discard the collection of characters that may have accumulated in the standard input buffer, and initiate one of the input functions so that new and valid input may be gathered.

MS-DOS provides a type-ahead buffer so that typed characters can be accumulated and processed when the current program is ready to use them. This allows the user to type at a comfortable speed, and if the user should get ahead of the program, he will not have to reenter characters that the program may have lost while it was doing something else (writing to the disk, adjusting the margins in a word processor, etc.).

This feature can have some undesirable side effects. For instance, if the user should get ahead of the program in entering characters because the program was getting ready to crash, there would be quite a few characters in the buffer when the calling program or routine regained control. Whatever program gained control in the aftermath of the crash would start to read and use the letters remaining in the buffer. This could snowball into some other unwanted results. The recovering program does not want to wade through all of the garbage characters (possibly causing the execution of irrelevant or harmful routines) to get to the valid input from the user.

This function allows a program to clear all of the irrelevant characters from the type-ahead buffer so that valid inputs are readily available.

Besides the clearing feature, this function initiates a new keyboard input function. This function does not perform the input function, but transfers control to one of the regular input functions. It is the responsibility of the application program to identify which of the input functions should be used. The valid input functions are:

Hex 01 Keyboard input

Hex 06 Direct console I/O

Hex 07 Direct console input without echo

Hex 08 Console input without echo

Hex 0A Buffered keyboard input (DS:DX = Address of buffer)

To initiate a *Console Input Without Echo*, the following code could be used. The value of the function is placed in the AL register:

```
Mov AL,8       ; want input without echo
Mov AH,OCH     ; clear and start i/o
Int 21H        ; DOS call
               ; AL contains input character
```

The use of a function number other than those listed above will cause a return without a character (which can have its advantages).

Chapter 4

Fundamental Utility Functions

INTRODUCTION

This chapter provides programming details about the MS-DOS system calls classified as the *fundamental utility functions*. These functions are responsible for the operation of standard computer functions that are not related to input or output of information.

This function group allows machine-independent management of computer resources that are generally very machine-dependent. Interfacing with a computer's clock and calendar (Get/Set Time/Date) directly through a program can entail a great amount of understanding of the clock and calendar hardware and the data conversions required to satisfy the hardware data needs.

THE UTILITY FUNCTIONS

The list of system calls in this group does a good job of explaining the purpose of the group. The system calls covered in this chapter are:

Hex 00	Program terminate
Hex 1A	Set disk transfer address
Hex 25	Set interrupt vector
Hex 26	Create a new program segment
Hex 2A	Get date
Hex 2B	Set date
Hex 2C	Get time

Hex 2D	Set time
Hex 2E	Set/reset verify switch
Hex 2F	Get DTA
Hex 30	Get DOS version number
Hex 31	Terminate process and remain resident
Hex 33	Ctrl-C and Ctrl-break check
Hex 35	Get vector
Hex 36	Get disk free space
Hex 38	Return country dependent information
Hex 4C	Terminate a process
Hex 4D	Retrieve return code of a process
Hex 54	Get verify state
Hex 62	Get Program Segment Prefix address
Hex 65	Get extended county information
Hex 66	Get/set global page

Program Terminate

Function: Hex 00

Registers: CS = Code Segment

The purpose of the *Program Terminate* function is to terminate the execution of a program in an orderly fashion. When a program is ended, there are many things that have to be done. The main objective in getting all of these things done is to return the machine and the software to the conditions that existed prior to the starting of the program.

Before this function is called, the application program is responsible for two preparatory actions. First, all files should be closed. If a file was used for only reading, then the closing of the file is not critical. However, if data was written to the file, the size of the file probably changed and the newer size is not established until the file is closed.

Second, the action of terminating a program involves resetting some error addresses in the MS-DOS environment. These addresses are saved in the Program Segment Prefix. The application program *must* ensure that the Code Segment (CS) register is set to the same segment used in starting the program. Usually this is not a problem, since all of the program's code will be in the same code segment. If the program had wandered and the CS register had been changed, issuing a call to this function in a far-flung subroutine (in an attempt to abort the program) could lead to unpredictable results.

When MS-DOS receives control through this function, it performs several procedures. First, all of the disk file buffers are flushed. MS-DOS does not perform a physical disk write for every user request. The data from the user write requests is stored in a memory buffer (holding area). When the buffer is filled, MS-DOS writes the entire buffer to the disk. Therefore, it is possible to have a partially filled buffer when the program terminates. These partial buffers are written to the disk.

Second, the error addresses are restored. One of the prerogatives of a program is to change the error handling addresses which are usually maintained by MS-DOS. For instance, if a user should press the Ctrl-Break key combination, an MS-DOS-supplied routine would perform some halting or terminating process. However, a program can change the address that points to the error handler so that it addresses a special process. When a program terminates, the special handler is no longer valid. MS-DOS saves a copy of the old address so that it can be restored (overwriting the invalid address). During program initiation, the addresses are stored in the Program Segment Prefix. And, during program termination, they are restored from the same location.

Third, memory ownership is relinquished. The memory that was used for the program is returned to the MS-DOS memory management so that the same area can be used for further loading and executing of programs.

Last, machine control returns to the program that called the terminating program. More likely than not, control is passed to MS-DOS and the command processor, but another application could have spawned the program, and it is to this application that control would be returned.

Having said all of that, let's add the last part: Don't use this function. It is considered obsolete and included only for compatibility with older programs. Basically, it is tied to MS-DOS's roots with CP/M. Other terminating functions are preferred to this one. However, the actions of MS-DOS that are described above are still valid for other termination methods.

Set Disk Transfer Address

Function: Hex 1A

Registers: DS:DX = Address of DTA

There are usually two components used by MS-DOS when files are being read from or written to: the File Control Block, which contains information about the structure and location of the file; and the Disk Transfer

Areas, which are the exchange points of file data between the program and the operating system.

The purpose of this function is to notify MS-DOS of the address of the current Disk Transfer Area (DTA). This function must be used whenever the address of the transfer buffer is being changed.

Buffers are usually changed whenever different files are being used. One buffer may be used for an input file, and another buffer for the output stream. If operations on these files are being intertwined, then MS-DOS must be notified of which buffer to use for each input or output, switching between the two buffers.

The Pascal function, DOSXQQ, may be used for setting the DTA. The following sequence will establish the memory referenced by the pointer variable BUFFER as the DTA.

Here's an example in Pascal:

```
New(BUFFER);
Status := DOSXQQ (16#1A, BUFFER);
```

And, in C:

```
buffer = malloc(sizeof(required_input));
status = _bdos (SET_DTA,buffer);
```

Set Interrupt Vector

> **Function:** Hex 25
>
> **Registers:** DS:DX = address of interrupt routine (vector)
>
> AL = number of interrupt

In a normal processing environment, the program being executed is the focus of the computer resources. After all, the task of the computer is to process the instructions of the program. However, there may be external events occurring that demand the immediate attention of the computer's central processor. These events can get the attention of the processor through an electronic signal. This signal is called an *interrupt*. When the processor detects an interrupt, it stops executing the current program and saves what it is doing so that it may tend to the interrupt.

Interrupts are numbered. For the 8086/8088 processor, the numbers are from 0 to 255 (Hex FF).

There are hardware units that help the main processor with interrupts. When an interrupt occurs, these interrupt units determine the identity of the interrupt. Knowing the identity of the interrupt, the interrupt processor accesses a table of software routine addresses. It then forms and sends to the 8086/8088 processor a fake JUMP instruction to the selected software address. These addresses are called *interrupt vectors* because they point to the software routines that handle specific interrupts. The software routine for the interrupt now has control, so that whatever reason caused the interrupt can be fixed up or processed. When the interrupt's software routine has completed its task, the program that was stopped is resumed.

The purpose of the *Set Interrupt Vector* function is to name a software routine that is to receive control when a specific hardware or software interrupt occurs.

The interrupt vector table is stored in memory. Its location may not be the same from one brand of computer to the next. If you are writing software for the general MS-DOS market, you will want to use this function to set the interrupt vector to a software routine, instead of going directly to memory address as it might exist on your personal machine.

Here's an example of a communications program using the interrupt system: The interrupt and communications hardware can be set up so that when a character is received through asynchronous communications, an interrupt is generated. This received character must be read from the async board before the next character arrives—right now. By interrupting the main communications program, the received character can be retrieved by the software interrupt handler and saved somewhere until the main program is ready to use it. This must all be finished before the next character is received and wipes out the previous one.

The communications interrupt handler is not built into MS-DOS. The applications program must provide it. The applications program must also tell the operating system where the software handler is, so that it can be put into the interrupt vector table. This MS-DOS system call places the address of the handler into the vector table.

A word of caution: When the communications program is done, the vector should be reset to its previous value (probably no address at all). Otherwise, when the next program is started and an erroneous character (possibly caused by noise) shows up on the communications board, the appropriate vector may be pointing to an address within the new program that has nothing to do with communications or interrupts.

Here is a brief program segment that places the address of *COMM*, an interrupt handler, into the vector table:

```
; assign routine COMM as the interrupt vector Hex 0C
;
        Push DS                  ; save registers
        Push DX
        Mov  AX,Seg COMM         ; segment of COMM address
        Mov  DS,AX
        Mov  DX,Offset COMM      ; offset of COMM address
        Mov  AL,0CH              ; interrupt number
        Mov  AH,025H             ; function number
        Int  21H                ; call DOS
        Pop  DX                  ; restore original registers
        Pop  DS
```

Some interrupt processing hardware may have to be initialized or programmed for interrupts. For instance, the interrupt hardware has an internal masking register. This register controls which interrupts are to be processed and which interrupts are to be ignored by checking which bits, corresponding to specific interrupts, are set. The application program will have to *mask* (as in masking tape) these bits so that a specific interrupt is on or off. Also, in the case of the communications program, the communications hardware chip needs some simple programming to tell it to generate the interrupt signal when a character is received.

Create a New Program Segment

Function: Hex 26

Registers: DX = Memory segment number for program segment

At the beginning of every MS-DOS program is an area of 256 bytes (Hex 100) that is called either the Program Prefix Area (MS-DOS 1.0 and 1.1) or the Program Segment Prefix (MS-DOS 2.0 and later versions). The purpose of the *Create a New Program Segment* function is to transfer the contents of the program segment of the active program into a new program segment as a step in loading and executing a new program. The DX register must contain the number of the new segment. This can be accomplished through:

```
MOV DX,SEGMENT NEWPROG
```

This Program Segment Prefix area contains operating system environment information, file control blocks, and a disk transfer area. The operating system information is a set of critical addresses for error handling, program termination, and MS-DOS system call handling. The error handling addresses originate with the program that created the program segment prefix. This happens in the case of a new program changing an error handling address within MS-DOS; the old address can be restored when the new program terminates and the calling program resumes control.

The exact details of this area are generally not important to the programmer. To bear out this point, some MS-DOS references don't even list this system call. Other MS-DOS references will direct you to use the Load or Execute a Program (Hex 4B).

Get Date

Function: Hex 2A

Registers: CX = The year (1980–2099) in binary

DH = The month (Jan = 1, Feb = 2, etc.)

DL = The day of the month

AL = The day of the week

The purpose of the *Get Date* function is to allow the program to retrieve the current date, as stored within the computer. The current date is based on the date entered by the user or supplied by a clock/calendar unit at power-up initialization or reboot time.

This function would be useful for getting the current date for reports.

The timing problems, such as setting a new day at midnight and leap year checking, are done internally.

Notice that the date is returned in the CX:DX register pair. This combination makes the DOSXQQ function in Pascal and the __bdos function in C unusable. However, both Pascal and C languages make this function indirectly available through other built-in features.

The following sequence is a narrative design for placing the date on the video screen after using this system call:

Call MS-DOS for function Hex 2A

Decode the DL register into ASCII and save

Decode the CX register into ASCII and save

Use the DH register to look into a table for the spellings of the months

Move the month name to the video screen buffer

Move the saved day to the video screen buffer

Move a comma to the video screen buffer

Move the saved year to the video screen buffer

Set Date

Function: Hex 2B

Registers: CX = The year (1980–2099) in binary

DH = The month (Jan = 1, Feb = 2, etc.)

DL = The day of the month

AL = The status of set date

The purpose of the *Set Date* function is to reset the internal clock and calendar to a new date. This function is the complement to *Get Date*.

Its usefulness lies in the setting of the internal calendar using outside information. For instance, you may want to set the calendar from a clock and calendar board where the clock is always on with the correct time and date. When the computer is turned on, the auto start batch stream (AUTOEXEC.BAT) is started, and your date and time program is called. Using this function, the program could set the date from the information received from the clock/calendar board.

The status of the Set Date function is returned in the AL register. If the AL register is equal to zero, then the date was accepted as valid. When the register is filled with ones (Hex FF), then the date was not valid.

Get Time

Function: Hex 2C

Registers: CH = Hours (0–23)

CL = Minutes (0–59)

DH = Seconds (0–59)

DL = $\frac{1}{100}$ Seconds (0–99)

The purpose of the *Get Time* function is to allow a program to retrieve the current time from the internal clock/calendar. This routine is the companion of the *Get Date* function.

This function can provide the current time so that tests, reports, or other items can be given a time/date stamp. The Get Time function can also provide the current time so that a program could display a digital clock on the video monitor with the correct (if the internal clock is set to the correct time) or the elapsed time (if the internal clock is set to zeroes at the start of a process).

Notice that the time is returned in the CX:DX register pair. The Pascal DOSXQQ function is unusable with this register combination. However, the Pascal language makes this function indirectly available through other built-in features.

This function can be very useful as a countdown timer. I had an application where I needed to stop a process if it did not complete in a certain amount of time. At first, I used the C run-time routine called *time*. This seemed to be a reasonable thing to do since it returned the number of seconds since some past date. What I didn't realize is that the *time* routine corrected the passage of seconds for leap year, daylight savings time, and other parameters. When I analyzed the program, it turned out that 25 percent of program execution time was spent getting the time. I turned to this function as a countdown timer. Here is the code:

Listing 4-1. Countdown Timer.

```
int             time();
static int              current_second;
static int              timer_second;

int time(t)
int     *t;
```

Listing 4-1. Continued

```
{
union REGS      r_in;
union REGS      r_out;

  r_in.h.ah = 0 x2c;
  intdos(r_in,r _out);
  if (t) *t = r _out.h.dh;
  return r_out.h.dh;
}

int set_time()
{
 timer_second = 60 * time_limit;
 current_second = time(NULL);
}

int time_out()
{
int         tyme;
char        ch;

  if (timer_second)
    {
      if (time(tyme) != current_second)
        {
        current_second = tyme;
        timer_second--;
        }
    }
  return !timer_second;
}
```

To Display the Time as a Digital Clock

In Chapter 2, the Direct Console Input Without Echo function example showed an area of the routine that could be used for wasting time or doing things while waiting for a key to be pressed. The following steps could be performed in that area to get a digital clock display.

Call the DOS for function Hex 2C

(For regular am and pm times:

If value of CH > 12 Then Subtract 12

If value of CH = 0 Then set CH to 12)

Decode the CH register into ASCII and
move to video screen buffer

Move a colon to the video screen buffer

Decode the CL register into ASCII and
move to video screen buffer

Move a colon to the video screen buffer

Decode the DH register into ASCII and
move to video screen buffer

Set Time

Function: Hex 2D

Registers: CH = Hours (0–23)

CL = Minutes (0–59)

DH = Seconds (0–59)

DL = $\frac{1}{100}$ Seconds (0–99)

AL = status of set time

The purpose of the *Set Time* function is to reset the internal clock and
calendar to a new time. This function is the complement to *Set Date*.

Its usefulness lies in the setting and clearing of the internal calendar
using outside information. For instance, you may want to set the internal clock from a clock/calendar board where the clock is always on with
the correct time and date. When the computer is turned on, the auto
start batch stream (AUTOEXEC.BAT) is started, and your date and
time program is called. Using this function, it could set the time from the
information received from the clock/calendar board.

The Set Time function can also clear the clock to all zeroes so that the
clock can be used as an elapsed timer for timing events.

The status of the Set Time function is returned in the AL register. If
the AL register is equal to zero, then the time was accepted as valid.
When the register is filled with ones (Hex FF), then the time was not
valid.

The following program segment shows the clearing of the internal
clock so that an elapsed time clock can be started;

```
;
;   use the Get Time routine for elapsed timer
;   set the internal clock to zero to start the time
;
    Mov   CX,0        ; no hours, no minutes
    Mov   DX,0        ; no seconds, no 1/100ths
    Mov   AH,02DH     ; set time
    Int   21H         ; on your marks, get set, go!!
```

Set/Reset Verify Switch

Function: Hex 2E

Registers: DL = must contain 0

AL = toggle for setting and resetting verify

One of the services provided by the diskette drive controllers is to verify that information to be written to a disk file actually matches the data that is written. If the diskette controller is programmed properly, it will read data immediately after writing it to ensure that no errors had occurred in the writing.

The purpose of the *Set/Reset Verify Switch* is to turn the verifying program on and off.

The AL register contains the verify on and off command. If the AL register is set to zero, then the verifying program is turned off. Setting the AL register to one turns on the verify program. The DL register must be set to zero.

Diskette errors are not so common that the verify program must be used for most purposes. If the program is handling critical information, then verification may be warranted. Using the verify option will cause the diskette writing process to take twice as much time as the nonverified writing process.

Get DTA

Function: Hex 2F

Registers: ES:BX = Address of Active DTA

The purpose of the *Get DTA* function is to allow the program to get the address of the current DTA from MS-DOS. The DTA (Disk Transfer

Area) is a block of memory that MS-DOS will use for storing data from a disk read and accessing data for a disk write. For most programs, the DTA will be located in the program segment prefix. Once you have retrieved the DTA address, you can use the file and device I/O functions without having to reserve memory for the DTA or take the responsibility for declaring your own DTA. Knowing the address of the DTA, your program can access that memory before and after the I/O functions.

This function call does not tell you how much memory is reserved in the current DTA. When you are not sure of the size of the DTA, you do run the risk of overflowing information into adjacent program or data areas. When in doubt, use the Set DTA function to set the disk transfer address so that you are protected.

Since the AL register is not returning with a status word for this function, and since the ES and BX registers are going to contain the current address, the DOSXQQ function call from Pascal is not useful for this instance. You will have to call an assembler routing that does the function call and returns the value of the address to the calling program.

The following code sequence shows an example of the assembly language interface:

Listing 4-2. Get Address of DTA.

```
GETDTA      PROC      FAR
            PUBLIC    GETDTA
            ASSUME    CS:CODE
            Push      BP
            Mov       BP,SP
            Push      DS
            Push      ES
            Push      DI
            Push      BX
            Mov       AH,02Fh ; function number
            Int       21h
    ; return with ES:BX having address
            Lds       DI,DWORD PTR [BP+8]
            Mov       AX,ES
            Mov       DS:[DI],AX
            Mov       DS:[DI+2],BX
            Pop       BX
            Pop       DI
            Pop       ES
```

```
Listing 4-2. Continued
             Pop      DS
             Pop      BP
             Ret      4
   GETDTA    ENDP
```

Get DOS Version Number

Function: Hex 30

Registers: AL = Major version number

AH = Minor version number

Should you be in the position of writing software that will only operate with MS-DOS of a certain version, this function will inform your program of which version of MS-DOS is currently running on the system. For all versions of MS-DOS after version 2.0, this function will return the major version number in the AL register (a two, in the case of version 2.0) and the minor version number in the AH register (a zero, in this case). An earlier version of MS-DOS will return with a zero in both registers.

Checking the version with this function before getting too deeply into your program can let you decide whether the program is able to operate in the environment. If the version is wrong, you could issue a message telling the operator that the MS-DOS version is wrong and that you are aborting. For instance, if your program uses the version 2.0 pathnames and handle functions, then that program will work in the MS-DOS 1.1 environment. By using this function, you can find out if the program will work or not:

```
Program Version_Check (output);
Const
  Get_Version = 16#30;
Function DOSXQQ (Command:Byte; Parm:Word) : Byte;
  Extern;
Begin
  If DOSXQQ (Get_Version,0) < 2
  Then
    Writeln('This program will not work properly')
  Else
    Writeln('This works on MS-DOS 2.0 and later versions');
  End.
```

Terminate Process and Remain Resident

> **Function:** Hex 31
>
> **Registers:** AL = Exit code
>
> DX = Size (in paragraphs) of resident memory

The purpose of the *Terminate Process and Remain Resident* function is to stop the execution of a program and return control to the calling program (usually the command processor), but instead of letting MS-DOS reclaim the memory occupied by the process, the process remains in memory, untouched. This is not the normal method of leaving a program, for you would soon run out of available memory if you did. It is, however, a method of placing small software utilities into the computer's memory and leaving them there in a semipermanent way. If these utilities are activated through interrupts (hardware or software), then the utilities effectively become a part of MS-DOS. An interrupt handler for a communications-oriented machine could be installed this way. Most of the popular software print spoolers and keyboard utilities are put into memory and left resident.

The program is able to send a *return code* upon termination. The program that initiated this process can check this code and see if everything worked, or see if there were any problems. In a batch stream at the MS-DOS command level, checking this code can control the behavior of the remaining tasks in the stream. If this terminating task encountered a problem, running the remaining processes may not be valid. Or, perhaps, some other tasks should be invoked to clean up any messes left by the terminating task. This return code is available to the batch stream through the ERRORLEVEL selection in the batch stream IF command.

Part of the function's register setup is to determine how much of the process should be left in memory. This parameter is placed in the DX register and represents the number of 16-byte paragraphs to be given resident status. One of the ways that might be used to determine this value is to:

- Place a label at the front of the resident portion
- Place a label at the rear of the resident portion. This label would be in front of the portions of the program that are used as a one-time initialization process and can be returned to MS-DOS.
- Specify an EQU that is:

```
;
              Resident  EQU ((End - Front) / 16) + 11
;
;  The extra 11 is for the PSP in front of your
;  program (that's 11 paragraphs)
;
```

The code that uses this calculation would be:

```
Mov   DX,Resident  ; length of residency
Mov   AH,31h       ; quit, but stick around
Int   21h          ; bye
```

By specifying the length of only the resident portion of the routine, the loaded program may do some initializations, such as setting the interrupt vector table to the resident portion, and then letting that portion disappear when the program is terminated.

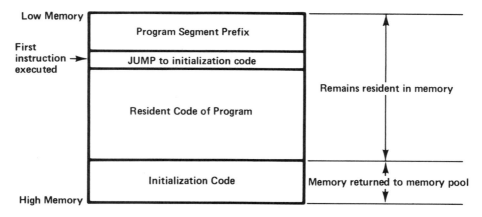

Figure 4-1. Program Layout for "Stay Resident" Program.

Ctrl-C and Ctrl-Break Check

Function: Hex 33

Registers: AL = Function command
DL = Toggle for set and reset

One of the properties of the *Traditional Character I/O* system calls (with a few exceptions) is that the Ctrl-C and Ctrl-Break codes were handled by MS-DOS, giving the user a chance to control or terminate an erroneous program. This capability is not normally extended to the other system calls. Thus, one of the actions of the *Ctrl-C and Ctrl-Break Check* function is to expand this capability to all other MS-DOS system calls. The other action of the function is to report whether the checking capability is active or inactive.

To control the Ctrl-C and Ctrl-Break checking, set the AL register to 1. The contents of the DL register controls whether the checking should be turned on or off. A zero in the DL register suspends checking, while a one in the DL register starts the checking.

To get the status of the checking operation, set the AL register to zero. When the system call is completed, the DL register will contain the current state of the Ctrl-C and Ctrl-Break checking. If the DL register is equal to zero, then the checking is not active. A one in the DL register shows that the Ctrl-C and Ctrl-Break keys will be sensed at every system call.

Get Vector

Function: Hex 35

Registers: AL = Interrupt number
ES:BX = Address of interrupt routine

The purpose of the *Get Vector* function is to report the interrupt vector address for a specific interrupt, as found in the interrupt vector table. The number of the interrupt to be checked is placed in the AL register. The address is returned in the ES:BX register pair.

This function can be of great service. Suppose that you wish to establish a routine as an interrupt handler. It is a wise move to save the vector address for the interrupt that you wish to change, so that you might restore that value when this particular process no longer needs the interrupt handler. Using the functions, the interrupt initialization routing can get the address and save it so that it is available for restoration when the process is closing.

If you just want to know if there really is an active interrupt handler available, checking the return registers for zeroes will tell you if there is or not. Making this check early in the development phase of a software project could save you from the task of developing a handler. A check at run time could keep you from reinstalling your own handler twice.

Get Disk Free Space

Function: Hex 36

Registers: DL = Disk drive

BX = Number of available allocation units

DX = Total number of clusters on the drive

CX = Number of bytes per sector

AX = Number of sectors per cluster (+ status)

The purpose of the *Get Disk Free Space* function is to allow a program to calculate the usage and/or free space on any disk drive. The function returns this information in a general form that can be confusing until you work through the definitions;

- Many contiguous bytes (usually 128, 256, or 512) form a sector.
- Depending upon the format of the disk, several sectors form a track.
- One or more sectors form a cluster.
- Clusters are the same thing as allocation units.

Thus,

Available bytes on the disk (in free sectors) = Available sectors * bytes per sector

Ratio if usable clusters - 1.0 - (Available clusters/total number of clusters)

These figures reflect only the unallocated clusters. A file may claim a number of allocation units, but if there is no information written into the file, or if it is only partially filled, then that unused space is not included in the space available byte count.

Return Country Dependent Information

Function: Hex 38

Registers: AL = Country code

DS:DX = 32 byte memory block

For international computing, MS-DOS has provided a means of determining the proper formatting required in various countries. The purpose of the *Return Country Dependent Information* function is to retrieve the formatting information.

For MS-DOS 2.0, only a subset of the function is available. The *current country* (AL=0) is the only country available with only the first four fields being valid.

To retrieve the country dependent information, place the country code into the AL register. The country code for the current country is zero. The country codes are the international telephone *area codes*. You can find these in your telephone directory.

MS-DOS 3.0 supports more features of the Return Country Dependent Information function.

There are some changes in designating country codes with MS-DOS 3.0. The country code is loaded into the AL register if the country code will fit into a byte (0 through 255). If the country code is greater that 255, it will take a 16-bit register to contain the code. The AH register half of the AX register is in use, so this register is not available. However, the BX register is available. Whenever the country code is too large for the AL register, set the AL register to Hex FF and use the BX register for the country code.

With MS-DOS 3.0, error conditions are supported by the Get Extended Error function.

The system call will deposit the information into a 32-byte buffer. The calling program is responsible for reserving the memory area. When the function is finished, the information will be in the 32-byte memory area, according to the following layout.

To set the current country, place the country code in the AL register and set the DX register to −1 (Hex FFFF) prior to the system call.

The 32 bytes of the country dependent information are organized as:

Bytes 0–1 Date and Time Format.   This field is coded to specify the format for presenting the time and date by different standards. The values of this field are shown in Table 4-1.

Table 4-1. Month/Year/Day Formats.

0	USA	h:m:s	m/d/y
1	Europe	h:m:s	d/m/y
2	Japan	h:m:s	y/m/d

Bytes 2–6 Currency Symbol.   This field is a 5-byte ASCIIZ string (up to 4 characters, allowing for the binary zero at the end of the string) with the country's currency symbol.

Bytes 7–8 Thousands Separator.   This field is a 2-byte ASCIIZ string with the punctuation used to denote the thousands place (e.g., 23,000) in a number.

Bytes 9–10 Decimal Separator.   This field is a 2-byte ASCIIZ string with the punctuation used to denote the separation of whole numbers from the fractional parts (e.g., 45.9).

Bytes 11–12 Date Separator.   This field is a 2-byte ASCIIZ string with the punctuation used to separate the month, day, and year fields in a date (e.g., 1/1/88 and 2-5-89).

Bytes 13–14 Time Separator.   This field is a 2-byte ASCIIZ string with the symbol used to separate the fields in the time (e.g., 11:45:34).

Byte 15 Bit Field.   This field is a set of flags that control the presentation of information found in other fields. The meanings of the bits are:

Bit 0	**Bit 1**
0 = Currency symbol is in front of currency amount	0 = No space between currency symbol and the amount
1 = Currency symbol is behind the currency amount	1 = There is a space between the currency symbol and the amount.

Byte 16 Currency Places.   This field specifies the number of decimal places (to the right of the decimal point) that the country's currency has.

Byte 17 Time Format. This field specifies whether the country uses a 12- or 24-hour clock (e.g., 1:23 or 13:23). The values of this field are:

0 = 12-hour time
1 = 24-hour time

Bytes 18–21 Case Mapping Call. This field contains a FAR (32-bit) address (segment:offset) of a country specific procedure that converts lowercase characters to the proper uppercase. The procedure only converts characters with Hex values in the Hex 80 to Hex FF range. ASCII characters sent to the routing will not be converted. The character to be converted is placed into the AL register. Upon return from the routine, the AL register will contain the proper upper case code. If a conversion cannot be done, the AL register is unchanged.

Bytes 22–23 Data List Separator.

Bytes 24–32 Reserved for future expansion.

Terminate a Process

Function: Hex 4C

Register: AL = Return code

The purpose of the *Terminate a Process* function is to provide a method for a program to correctly stop execution, and return program control to the calling program.

Using this function, the program is able to send a *return code* to the calling program. The return code is placed in the AL register prior to calling the termination function. The program that initiated this terminating process can check this code and see if everything worked, or see if there were any problems.

In a batch stream at the MS-DOS command level, checking this code can control the behavior of the remaining task in the stream. If this terminating task encountered a problem, running the remaining processes may not be valid. Or, perhaps, some other tasks should be invoked to clean up any messes left by the terminating task. This return code is available to the batch stream through the ERRORLEVEL selection of the batch stream IF command.

Retrieve Return Code of a Process

Function: Hex 4D

Registers: AX = Return code and status

The purpose of the *Retrieve Return Code of a Process* function is to get the return code that was sent from a terminating process using the Terminate a Process and Terminate a Process and Remain Resident functions. The value is returned in the AH register. This function could be called directly from a program in Pascal or C with the operating system interface procedure. Using the value of the return code, a receiving process can determine its course of action.

Get Verify State

Function: Hex 54

Registers: AL = Status of verify state

The purpose of *Get Verify State* is to find the current status of the Disk Write with Verify option in MS-DOS. If disks are being written with verification (read data immediately after writing it to check for errors occurring in the writing process), then the AL register will return with a value of one. A zero value in the register indicates that the disks are not being verified during the disk write process. This is the normal setting. The Set and Reset Verify Switch function (Hex 2E) can be used to turn the verification process on and off.

Get Program Segment Prefix Address

Function: Hex 62

Registers: BX = Segment address of PSP for current task

This function was added in MS-DOS 3.0. The Program Segment Prefix is a 256-byte area at the front of a loaded program where MS-DOS saves an initial DTA, FCB, terminating address, and a copy of the initiating command line. Execution of the program starts (usually) at Hex 100.

With a complex program, the value of the segment register pointing to the PSP can get lost before your program even gains full control of the process. In the case of programs written in Pascal or C, program execution passes through several run-time support routines before the first line of your program gets used.

The purpose of the *Get Program Segment Prefix Address* function is to give the application program a chance to retrieve the segment number of the PSP so that it can access that area of the program.

This function will return the segment number of the PSP in the BX register. This PSP is for the currently running task.

Get Extended Country Information

Function: Hex 65

Registers: AL = Minor function code

BX = Code Page

CX = Count of bytes to return

DX = Country code

DS:DI = Address of buffer for returned information

This function was added in MS-DOS 3.3. It allows a program to get a country-dependent information block for countries other than the default country. The default country information is held in MS-DOS memory and is always available. This function allows the program to get information about other countries from the system file, COUNTRY.SYS.

The type of extended operation is specified by the AL register. The operations allowed are:

1 Return standard information (see funtion Hex 38).

2 Return pointer to uppercase table. For extended ASCII codes (greater than 127), this table will provide lowercase to uppercase conversions.

4 Return pointer to filename. Country dependent information does not necessarily have to reside in COUNTRY.SYS. The "COUNTRY =" command in CONFIG.SYS can specify another file from which country information is to be taken.

6 Return pointer to ASCII collating sequence. The collating table is 258 bytes. The first two bytes contain the number of entries in the table. The remainder of the table is ASCII characters in ascending sort order as appropriate for the current country.

The value in the BX register specifies the "code page" to be used in preparing the country information. MS-DOS has five code pages that are used in converting numeric codes to display and print characters. These code pages may be activated to suit the needs of a particular country. The idea is to provide a universal translation table for device drivers using the console screen or the printer. The five code pages are:

850 Multilingual
437 USA
860 Portugal
863 Canada-France
865 Norway

A single country can use up to two code pages.

Setting the BX register to −1 will cause the current code page for the console device to be used. Set the CX register to the number of bytes you expect to have returned.

The information returned by this function follows the structure of the country dependent information block in function Hex 38, Get or Set Country Dependent Information. The address of this buffer is placed into the DS:DI register pair.

Since this function was added after MS-DOS 3.0, error codes are handled through the Get Extended Error function.

Get/Set Global Code Page

Function: Hex 66

Registers: AL = Minor function code

BX = Active code page

DX = Default code page

This function was added in MS-DOS 3.3. A single country can use up to two code pages. This function can change the code page being used by the current MS-DOS country. It can also get the values of the code pages associated with the current country.

The value of the AL register directs the action of the function. The function codes for the AL register are:

1 Get Code Page. This returns the current code pages assigned to the current country. The active code page number is returned in the BX register. The alternative code page is returned in the DX register.

2 Set Code Page. This toggles the code pages assigned to the current country. All device drivers that support the new code page are switched.

Since this function was added after MS-DOS 3.0, error codes are handled through the Get Extended Error function.

Chapter 5

Fundamental File Management

INTRODUCTION

This chapter covers the functions that handle the disk file operations for MS-DOS versions 1.0 and 1.1. Since disk I/O operations usually involve the transfer of large blocks of data, these functions are often referred to as the block-oriented I/O functions. This is in contrast to the character- (single byte) oriented I/O operations encountered in Chapter 3. The functions discussed in this chapter are:

Hex 0D	Disk reset
Hex 0E	Select disk
Hex 0F	Open file
Hex 10	Close file
Hex 13	Delete file
Hex 14	Sequential read
Hex 15	Sequential write
Hex 16	Create file
Hex 19	Current disk
Hex 1B	Allocation table information
Hex 1C	Allocation table information for specific drive
Hex 21	Random read
Hex 22	Random write
Hex 23	File size
Hex 24	Set random record field
Hex 27	Random block read
Hex 28	Random block write
Hex 29	Parse filename

FILE CONTROL BLOCK

The MS-DOS functions that directly interface with disk files use the *File Control Block (FCB)* to hold and pass information used in the operation. The FCB is a 37-byte block of memory, where the bytes are numbered 0 through 36. MS-DOS expects certain information in specific locations in the FCB. The fields of the File Control Block are defined as follows (by byte offsets).

Byte 0 Drive Designator

0 = use default drive (before *Open File* function only)

1 = use drive A

2 = use drive B

etc.

Bytes 1–8 Filename   Start in byte 1 and use spaces to fill to byte 8 when using special peripheral names (e.g., LPT1 or COM1), use only the letters of the name, discarding the colon (:).

Bytes 9–11 Filename Extension (filetype)   Start in byte 9 and use spaces (as required) to file to byte 11 (use of all the spaces is acceptable).

Bytes 12–13 Current Block Number   The block number is relative to beginning of file, where the block number is zero. A block is 128 records of the size specified in the logical record size field. This field is set to zero by the *Open File* function.

Bytes 14–15 Logical Record Size in Bytes   This field designates the number of bytes contained in the fundamental record of the file. For example, if the file contains text characters, then the record size would be 1. This field is set to Hex 80 (decimal 128) by the Open File function. The programmer must correctly set this field, if the record size is not 128 bytes, prior to disk operations.

Bytes 16–19 File Size in Bytes   This is a two-word field with the exact count of bytes recorded in the file. The first of the two words is the least significant.

Bytes 20–21 File Date   This field contains the date, showing the creation date or the latest date of update. The date is in m/d/y (month-day-year) form as follows:

```
    < byte 21 >      < byte 20 >
7 6 5 4 3 2 1 0  7 6 5 4 3 2 1 0
y y y y y y y m  m m m d d d d d

Months (mmmm)   = 1-12
Days (ddddd)    = 1-31
Year (yyyyyyy)  = 0-119
(added to 1980, gives proper year)
```

The diagram of the bytes is reversed to show the continuity of the year-month-day structure. There would be no problem if this entire structure were handled as an integer, the reversed bytes being normal 8088 format.

Bytes 22–31   Reserved for system use (the time is in here, too).

Byte 32 Current Relative Record Number   This field contains the number of the current record within the current block of records. The field at bytes 12–13 designates the current block with 128 records (regardless of size) in a block. This field may have a value of 0 through 127, designating which of the 128 records is the current record. This field must be set before performing any sequential read or write operations. The Open File function does not initialize this field.

Bytes 33–36 Relative Record Number   The block number is relative to beginning of file, where the block number is zero. This field must be set before performing and random read or write operations. The *Open File* function does not initialize this field. In this two-word field, the first word is the least significant. When the logical record length is greater than 64 bytes, then only the first byte (least significant byte) of the second word (most significant) is accessed by the MS-DOS functions.

```
      33         34                  35         36
< least significant word > < most significant word >
< LS Byte  > <   MS byte > < LS byte  > <   MS byte >
```

The declaration of the FCB can be constructed with a high-level language. The declarations in Microsoft Pascal and C are as follows:

Listing 5-1. The File Control Block in MS-DOS 1.1.

```
Type
  FCB_Type      =      Record
    Drive            [00]:    Byte;
    Filename         [01]:    String(8);
    Filetype         [09]:    String(3);
    Block_Number     [12]:    Integer;
    Record_Size      [14]:    Integer;
    File_LSW_Size    [16]:    Word;
    File_MSW_Size    [18]:    Word;
    Date             [20]:    Word;
    Reserved         [22]:    String(10);
    Seq_Record_Num   [32]:    Byte;
    Random_LSW_Num   [33]:    Word;
    Random_MSW_Num   [35]:    Word;
    End;
Var
  Work_File                        : FCB_Type;
  Sort_File                        : FCB_Type;


typedef
  struct
    {
    char        drive;
    char        filename[8];
    char        filetype[3];
    int         block_number;
    int         record_size;
    long        file_size;
    int         date;
    int         reserved[5];
    char        seq_record_num;
    long        random_num;
    }           fcb_type;

  fcb_type      work_file;
  fcb_type      sort_file;
```

There probably isn't much use in using a high-level language with a file control block. The later versions of MS-DOS have improved file handling capabilities. However, these examples are given in case you find yourself needing to talk to an older version of MS-DOS.

An unopened File Control Block is an FCB with the drive designator, filename, and (if necessary) the file extension fields filled in. An opened

File Control Block is the result of an Open File or Create File function filling the remaining fields of an unopened File Control Block.

FILE MANAGEMENT FUNCTIONS

Disk Reset

Function: Hex 0D

Registers: None

The purpose of the *Disk Reset* function is to flush all of the file buffers. Not all commands to MS-DOS that call for writing to a file actually cause data to be physically written to the disk. An internal buffer is used to gather enough data (for sequential operations) to fill a disk sector before it is actually transferred to the disk. When the buffer is full, the physical write occurs.

The Disk Reset function will write the residual bytes in a partially filled buffer to the file. The function will also reset any indexes into buffers being used for reading operations.

The Disk Reset function will not modify the file size entry in the disk directory. Therefore, enlarged files with open FCBs will not have the correct file size. A properly closed file, using the Close File function, is the only way to insure that the file size entry in the disk directory has been properly set.

Select Disk

Function: Hex 0E

Registers: DL = Specify selected disk

AL = Returns the number of logical drives

The purposes of the *Select Disk* function are to specify a default disk and to get the total number of drives attached to the computer system.

The DL register is used to select a default drive. The drives are selected by using a numeric code for the drive (e.g., 0 = drive A, 1 = drive B, etc.).

The value returned in the AL register indicates the number of disk drives in the system. However, the value returned is not reliable when a single- or double-drive system is encountered. MS-DOS assumes that all systems have logical drives A and B, even if these two logical drives occupy the same physical space. To protect this assumption, this function will return a value of 2 (for A: and B:) when the system only has 1 (A:) diskette drive. Since you can't really understand what this value is telling you—Is it a single? or a double?—the results of the function are unreliable. For the user of the IBM PC, the *Equipment Check* BIOS function will return a reliable value for a disk drive count.

Open File

Function: Hex 0F

Registers: DS:DX = Address of unopened FCB

AL = Status of open function

The purpose of the *Open File* function is to properly prepare a File Control Block (FCB) for I/O operations and to associate the FCB with a disk file. This function must be called before any reading or writing operations may be performed on the file.

The FCB must be an unopened FCB prior to the function call. The address of the FCB is placed into the DS:DX register pair. The address to the opened FCB will be returned in the same registers.

The filename and its extension are placed into their respective fields. If the names are less than the field sizes, pad the extra room with trailing blanks.

Set the value of the disk drive into the disk drive field. This value will designate which disk will be searched in an attempt to find and open the file. The value is a number that corresponds to the drives, where drive A = 1 and drive B = 2. If you should choose to search the default disk, set the disk drive value to 0. MS-DOS will substitute the zero with the value of the current default drive.

The *Parse Filename* function can be used to fill in the disk drive, filename, and extension information. This function accepts an MS-DOS filename, such as A:THEFILE.X, and places the components of the name into the proper fields. The details of the Parse Filename function will be covered later in this chapter.

When the Open File function is called, it searches the specified disk's directory for the named file. When the search is completed, MS-DOS returns a completion code in the AL register.

If the file is not found during the search, the status returned in the AL register is Hex FF. It may seem disappointing to get the *Not found* flag from MS-DOS, but this information can be useful.

Suppose you wanted to create a file, but didn't want to accidentally name an already existing file. To use an existing file's name in the Create File function will cause the file to be opened with zero length (as if it were a newly created file). That destroys the contents of the file! To prevent this problem, attempt a file opening before creating the file. Getting the Hex FF status code is a signal to go ahead with the file creation.

If the file to be opened does exist, the AL register returns with a zero value and the returned FCB is filled with the following information:

If the disk drive field was set to request the default drive (set to zero), the actual drive number is placed into the field. With this field now set to the proper drive, the system default drive value can be changed without affecting the file operations for this file.

The current block field is set to zero. The record size is set to the system default size of Hex 80 (128 in decimal) bytes. If your program is using records of a different size, such as single-byte records for text, it is the responsibility of the program to set the proper record size after the Open File function is finished and before the first I/O operation.

The file's time and date are retrieved from the directory entry for the file and placed into the FCB.

The Open File function does not set or modify the random record field or the current record fields. These fields are within the domain of the random and sequential I/O operations. And although the read and write functions will update the contents of these fields after these operations are complete, initial values are not set by any MS-DOS function (except the *File Size* function), making this activity the responsibility of the application program.

The following assembly language routine is a Pascal-callable procedure that accepts a filename and attempts to open the corresponding file. Notice how the procedure uses the Parse Filename function to ensure that the filename is correctly located in the FCB.

```
Listing 5-2. Open File With FCB.
;
; Open a file
; Parameters : Address of FCB
;               Address of Filename
;               Reference to Status word
OPENFILE        PROC            FAR
                ASSUME          CS:CODE
                PUBLIC          OPENFILE
                Push            BP
                Mov             BP,SP
                Push            DS
                Push            ES
                Lds             SI,DWORD PTR [BP+8]    ; get addr of FCB
                Les             DI,DWORD PTR [BP+12]   ; get addr of name
                Mov             AH,29H                 ; parse filename
                Mov             AL,0FH                 ; control the parse
                Int             21H
                Cmp             AL,0FFH                ; OK?
                Je              OPENEND                ; No, return bad status
                Mov             DX,SI                  ; correct FCB addressing
                Mov             AH,0FH                 ; OPEN command
                Int             21H
OPENEND:        Pop             ES
                Pop             DS
                Mov             BP,SP
                Mov             BP,[BP+6]              ; get address of status word
                Mov             [BP],AL                ; return status to caller
                Pop             BP
                Ret             10
OPENFILE        ENDP
```

Close File

Function: Hex 10

Registers: DS:DX = Address of open FCB

AL = Status of close function

The purpose of the *Close File* function is to properly terminate the use of a file. Closing a file involves the updating of the disk's directory to reflect changes made to the file. The directory fields that are affected are the time, date, and file size fields.

Files that were used exclusively for reading do not need to be closed. However, if a large number of files are being used by the application, it may be advisable to close any unused files, regardless of type of access. This will prevent the situation of needing to open a file, but already having open the maximum number of files allowed by MS-DOS. This maximum number is controlled by the FILES = n command in the CONFIG.SYS file (n is the maximum number of files allowed open at one time).

To close a file, the address of the open FCB of the file is placed into the DS:DX register pair and the MS-DOS function is requested.

The Close File function searches the disk directory of the disk named in the FCB. If the entry is found, the directory is updated and the AL register is set to zero to indicate the successful closure. If the entry is not found, the AL register is set to hex FF. In this case, it can be assumed that the disk has been changed, and the application program should take appropriate steps, with the possibility of the issuing of a message that prompts the user to return the disk for another try.

The following segment of code shows the use of the Close File function. This procedure is callable from Pascal and is expecting an FCB as its parameter. The application that used this procedure was performed and does not include a status check.

```
; Close a file
; parameters : Address of FCB
;
CLOSEFIL  PROC    FAR
          ASSUME  CS:CODE
          PUBLIC  CLOSEFIL
          Push    BP
          Mov     BP,SP
          Push    DS
          Lds     DX,DWORD PTR [BP+6] ; get addr of FCB
          Mov     AH,10H              ; close file
          Int     21H
          Pop     DS
          Pop     BP
          Ret     4
CLOSEFIL  ENDP
```

Delete File

Function: Hex 13

Registers: DS:DX = Address of unopened FCB
AL = Status of delete function

The purpose of the *Delete File* function is to remove a file from a directory, effectively erasing it from the disk.

The file to be deleted is named in an unopened FCB. The filename can be placed into the FCB with the Parse Filename function.

Deletion occurs when MS-DOS finds a directory entry that matches the filename in the FCB. Multiple deletions are possible if the "?" is used in the filename to denote positions where any letter in the directory entry's name will match. Deleting the filename "????????.???" will clear the disk because all filenames will match the pattern.

The Delete File function returns a completion code to the calling program in the AL register. If the AL register returns with a 0, then at least one file was deleted. An AL register with the value of Hex FF indicates that no files were found that matched the filename, and none were deleted.

The following code sequence shows the call to the Delete File function. This routine is callable from Pascal. The Delete File function could also be called through the DOSXQQ function. That code would look like this:

```
        Status := DOSXQQ (Delete_File, File_FCB);

; delete a file
; parameter : Address of FCB
;
DELETE    PROC    FAR
          ASSUME  CS:CODE
          PUBLIC  DELETE
          Push    BP
          Mov     BP,SP
          Push    DS
          Lds     DX,DWORD PTR [BP+6] ; get addr of FCB
          Mov     AH,13H              ; delete command
          Int     21H
          Pop     DS
          Pop     BP
          Ret     4
DELETE    ENDP
```

Sequential Read

Function: Hex 14

Registers: DS:DX = Address of opened FCB

AL = Status of sequential read

The purpose of the *Sequential Read* function is to transfer a single record from a disk file to the Disk Transfer Area. The sequential nature of the read is that the file address in the file's FCB points to the record immediately following the one that was read.

The read operation is performed on the file whose FCB is passed to the function in the DS:DX register pair. The FCB must be opened before any I/O operations can be correctly performed.

This function will read a record from the indicated file. The size of the record is determined by the record-size field in the FCB. When a file is opened, the record size is set to 128 bytes. It is the responsibility of the program to set the proper record size. The record size field is used to determine the location of the next record in the file.

The location of the file record is determined through the current-block and current-record fields of the FCB. The current-block field is set to zero by the Open File function. However, the current-record field is not initialized for this function's use by any MS-DOS function. Setting an initial value in this field is the responsibility of the program. To begin reading the file from the start of the file, this field should be set to zero.

The record will be read into the current DTA. Make sure that the declared DTA is large enough to hold the record. MS-DOS declares a DTA before the program starts, but it is only 128 bytes in length. If the records are larger than that, overflowing bytes may damage program data or instructions. The Set Disk Transfer Address function describes the steps needed to declare the DTA.

When the Sequential Read function is finished, it returns a completion code in the AL register. The value in the AL register indicates the status of the read operation. The status may have any of the following values:

0 The file transfer was completed successfully.

1 The end of the file was reached during the read operation. No bytes were available to read, and none were placed into the DTA.

2 The end of the disk transfer segment was reached before the end of the transfer. A partial record was read. This is not an overflow of the DTA. In this case, the end of the segment's (either the Data or Extra segment register's) address space was reached when the offset in the segment reached Hex FFFF (DS:FFFF) during the transfer of bytes.

3 The end of the file was reached during the read operation. There were bytes available to read before the end-of-file was encountered. A partial record was read into the DTA.

The Sequential Read function may be called directly from a Pascal language program by using the DOSXQQ function. Before the Sequential Read function can be called, the target file must be opened, the record size set, the current record field cleared, and a suitable DTA declared. The following Pascal and C code sequences could be used to read a file record until the end of file (or other error condition) is encountered.

And, quickly shown in Pascal:

```
While DOSXQQ (Read_Seq, File_FCB) <> 1 do Perform_Work (DTA);
```

and in C:

```
while (_bdos(READ_SEQ,file_fcb) != 1) perform_work(dta);
```

Sequential Write

Function: Hex 15

Registers: DS:DX = Address of opened FCB

AL = Status of sequential write

The purpose of the *Sequential Write* function is to transfer a single record from the Disk Transfer Area to a disk file. The sequential nature of the write is identical to the Sequential Read function by the fact that the file address in the file's FCB points to the record space immediately following the one that was written.

The write operation is performed on the file whose FCB is passed to the function in the DS:DX register pair. The FCB must be opened before any I/O operations can be correctly performed.

This function will write a record to the indicated file. The size of the record is determined by the record-size field in the FCB. When a file is opened, the record size is set to 128 bytes. It is the responsibility of the program to set the proper record size. The record size field is used to determine the location of the next record in the file.

When the record size of a file is less than the sector size of the disk, MS-DOS will hold the record in an intermediate buffer until an entire record can be written. When a file is closed, MS-DOS will physically write any partially filled buffers to the disk so all data will be placed onto the disk. This is why it is important to properly close files that have been written.

The location of the file record is determined through the current-block and current-record fields of the FCB. The current-block field is set to zero by the Open File function. However, the current-record field is not initialized for this function's use by any MS-DOS function. Setting an initial value in this field is the responsibility of the program. To begin writing the file from the start of the file, this field should be set to zero.

The record will be written from the current DTA. Make sure that the declared DTA is large enough to hold the record. If the records are larger than the DTA, extra bytes from program data or instructions may be transferred to the disk file.

When the Sequential Write function is finished, it returns a completion code in the AL register. The value in the AL register indicates the status of the write operation. The status may have any of the following values:

0 The file transfer was completed successfully.

1 The disk media is full. A partial record may have been written, but its value would probably be worthless.

2 The end of the segment's (either the Data or Extra segment register's) address space was reached when the offset in the segment reached Hex FFFF (DS:FFFF) during the transfer of bytes. A partial record was written.

The Sequential Write function may be called directly from a Pascal language program by using the DOSXQQ function. Before the Sequential Write function can be called, the target file must be opened, the record size set, the current-record field cleared, and data moved into the DTA. The following code could be used to write a file of records:

```
Repeat
  Perform_Work (DTA, More_to_Write);
  If More_To_Write
  Then
     Status := DOSXQQ (Write_Seq, File_FCB);
Until (Status <> 0) or Not (More_to_Write);
CloseFil (File_FCB);
```

We can turn the loop around to get another look to the program. This
time in C, we'll add some messages to tell us why we encountered
problems (if there were any) with the writing process.

```
while (perform_work(dta)) /* returns TRUE for more to do */
  if (status = _bdos(WRITE_SEQ,file_fcb))
    {
    switch(status)
      {
      case 1 : printf("Disk is full\n");
               break;
      case 2 : printf("Segment addressing error\n");
               break;
      }
    break;
    }
```

Create File

Function: Hex 16

Registers: DS:DX = Address of unopened FCB

AL = Status of create file

The purpose of the *Create File* function is to insert a new directory
entry into the disk directory. This creates a new file, but does not allocate any data area to the file.

The information for the new directory entry is supplied in an unopened
FCB. The only necessary information is the name of the file. The filename can be placed in the FCB with the Parse Filename function. All
other information in the directory is either set to zero (file size and starting sector) or retrieved from MS-DOS (time and date).

The Create File function will search the directory of the indicated disk
for a matching filename.

If a matching file is found, the directory entry is reset to a file length of zero bytes. The FCB is opened.

If a matching file is not found, MS-DOS will search for an available directory entry. When one is found, the entry is initialized, the file size is set to zero, and the FCB opened.

The Create File returns a completion code in the AL register. If the file was successfully created and opened, the AL register will return with a zero value. If an available position in the directory was not found and the file was not created, then the AL register is set to Hex FF.

The following code is an example of using the Create File function. The name of the file to be created and an unopened FCB are passed to the routine. The Parse Filename function is called to put the filename into the FCB. Following the favorable completion of the parser, the file is created.

```
Listing 5-3. Create a File With FCB.
; Create a file
; Parameters : Address of FCB
;               Address of Filename
;               Reference to Status word
CREATE          PROC        FAR
                ASSUME      CS:CODE
                PUBLIC      CREATE
                Push        BP
                Mov         BP,SP
                Push        DS
                Push        ES
                Lds         SI,DWORD PTR [BP+8]   ; get addr of FCB
                Les         DI,DWORD PTR [BP+12]  ; get addr of name
                Mov         AH,29H                ; parse filename
                Mov         AL,0FH                ; control the parse
                Int         21H
                Cmp         AL,0FFH               ; OK?
                Je          CREATED               ; No, return bad status
                Mov         DX,SI                 ; correct FCB addressing
                Mov         AH,16H                ; CREATE command
                Int         21H
CREATED:        Pop         ES
                Pop         DS
                Mov         BP,SP
                Mov         BP,[BP+6]
                Mov         [BP],AL
                Pop         BP
                Ret         10
CREATE          ENDP
```

Current Disk

Function: Hex 19

Register: AL = Value of current disk drive

The purpose of the *Current Disk* function is to fetch the drive specifier of the current default drive. The value is returned in the AL register. The drives are identified with numeric code for the drive (e.g., 0 = drive A, 1 = drive B, etc.).

Allocation Table Information

Function: Hex 1B

Registers: DS:BX = Address of default drive FAT ID

DX = Number of allocation units

AL = Number of sectors per allocation unit

CX = Number of bytes in a physical disk sector

The purpose of the *Allocation Table Information* function is to get the address of the File Allocation Table (FAT) for the current default drive and to get other disk organization information.

This function is MS-DOS-version-dependent. Prior to MS-DOS 2.0, the FAT was resident in memory, and this function performed as described in this section. Starting with MS-DOS 2.0, the FAT is left on the disk and the DS:DX registers will return the address of the *media descriptor* found in the first byte of the FAT. Further information about the media descriptor can be found in Chapter 12, Device Drivers. The other pieces of information are returned in all versions.

Besides the address to the File Allocation Table, which will be covered in detail, this function provides some basic information on the organization of files on the disk.

The DX register is set to the number of allocation units (or clusters) that the disk contains. An allocation unit is one or more consecutive sectors. The use of the allocation unit standardizes block transfer sizes for a particular installation. For instance, a computer may be using a floppy diskette with 1,024 byte sectors and a hard disk with 512 byte sectors. To make the source of information transparent to the application program, all data accesses are made in blocks of 1,024 bytes (one allocation unit). This means that a cluster on the diskette is a single sector, while the cluster on the hard disk is two 512-byte sectors.

The AL register is set to the number of sectors in each allocation unit.

The CX register is set to the number of bytes in a sector.

The contents of these registers can be used to calculate the total capacity of the disk. This information is also useful in calculating the disk address of a sector when the File Allocation Table is being used to locate sectors.

The File Allocation Table is used by MS-DOS to link the clusters on the disk to form a contiguous file. The cluster number of the first cluster of a file is located in the disk directory entry for the file. Each entry in the table represents a cluster on the disk. The FAT entry may be either 12 or 16 bits long. An entry with 12 bits means that each entry shares one half a byte with an adjacent entry.

The 16-bit FAT entries were introduced in MS-DOS version 3.0. These were created to handle the larger hard disk drives being supported by the newer MS-DOS. The 12-bit FAT entry was enough to handle a 10M disk with 20,740 sectors of 512 bytes each. Larger disk drives would require larger entries to handle the number of sectors. You can tell which size of FAT entry that you will be encountering by inspecting the value of the DX and AL register values. The DX register reports the number of allocation units on the disk. The AL indicates the number of sectors in an allocation unit. Multiplying these values together will give the number of sectors on the drive. If the number is greater than 20,740, use 16 bits as the size of the FAT entry.

The entry's value indicates one of the following items:

- The cluster is not currently in a file (entry = Hex [0]000).
- The cluster number of the next cluster in an active file.
- The cluster is the last cluster in an active file (entry = Hex [F]FF8 through Hex [F]FFF).
- The cluster is reserved (entry = Hex [F]FF0 through Hex [F]FF6).
- The cluster is bad (entry = Hex [F]FF7).

In the case where the entries in the FAT are one and a half bytes each with adjacent entries sharing bytes, some calculations will have to be performed to find the FAT entry for a particular cluster. The algorithm for finding the address and contents of an entry is:

Multiply the cluster number by 1.5;
Convert the product to an integer (drop any fraction);
Use this value as the offset into the FAT;
Read an entire 16-bit word;
If the cluster is an even-numbered cluster, keep the 12 least significant bits. Perform an "AND" with a Hex 0FFF mask.
If the cluster is an odd-numbered cluster, keep the 12 most significant bits. Shift the register by 4 bits to the right.

If all of these words were a bit confusing, try the C code for doing the same thing:

```
char    *get_fat();

int get_12_cluster(cluster,drive)
int     cluster;
int     drive;
{
   char    *fat;
   int     c_index;

   fat = get_fat(drive);
   c_index = (cluster * 3) >> 1;   /* multiply by 1.5 */
   return (cluster  1) ? ((int)*(fat + c_index) >> 4) :
                         ((int)*(fat + c_index) 0x0fff);
}
```

The 16-bit entry is simply the value of the FAT address plus the offset for the cluster (twice the cluster number).

```
int get_16_cluster(cluster,drive)
int     cluster;
int     drive;
{
   return (int) *(get_fat(drive) + (cluster + cluster));
}
```

The result is the cluster number of the next cluster or other cluster code. Finding a particular sector in a cluster (for clusters with more than one sector) will require multiplying the cluster number by the number of sectors within the cluster.

To modify the entry, the new value must be prepared and placed into the register without disturbing the 4 bits of the adjacent entry. If the entry is modified, the disk version of the FAT will have to be updated. The DS:BX register pair contains the address of the FAT. The byte in front of the FAT is the flag byte to indicate a changed FAT. Set this byte to 1 to indicate to MS-DOS that the FAT has been changed.

It is not an easy task, but access to the FAT and a disk's directory (by reading it directly from the disk) can be used by a programmer to retrieve lost files. A crashed-disk fix-up program would:

- Find the actual sectors that had belonged to a file through inspection of the sectors.

- Link the sectors in the FAT.

- Anchor the chain of sectors in a directory entry. The deleted directory entry is fairly easy (if you've gotten this far) to find and reset to being an active entry.

Allocation Table Information for Specific Drive

Function: Hex 1C

Registers: DL = Identification of specific drive

DS:BX = Address of default drive FAT ID

DX = Number of allocation units

AL = Number of sectors per allocation unit

CX = Number of bytes in a physical disk sector

The *Allocation Table Information for Specific Drive* function is identical to the Allocation Table Information function, except that the identification of the drive is placed in the DL register before the function is called. The disk drive is a numerical value with the default drive = 0, drive A = 1, and so on.

Random Read

Function: Hex 21

Registers: DS:DX = Address of open FCB

AL = Status of random read

The purpose of the *Random Read* function is to transfer a single record from a disk file to the Disk Transfer Area. The random nature of the read is that the file address in the file's FCB is set to agree with the random-record field before the read is performed. In other words, if the random-record field is set to 83 so that the eighty-third record will be read, MS-DOS will calculate the position of the eighty-third record and set that disk address into the current-block and record fields before the disk transfer is made.

The read operation is performed on the file whose FCB is passed to the function in the DS:DX register pair. The FCB must be opened before any I/O operations can be correctly performed.

This function will read a record from the indicated file. The size and location of the record is determined by the record-size field in the FCB. When a file is opened, the record size is set to 128 bytes. It is the responsibility of the program to set the proper record size.

The random-record field of the FCB is used to indicate the numerical position of the record in the file. This number is combined with the record size, disk sector size, and number of sectors per cluster to calculate the address of the record on the disk.

A file of random records does not necessarily have to be filled with valid records. It is quite appropriate to have a sparsely populated file of randomly numbered records. A magic number might be calculated to determine the record number of a record, and this function could be used to fetch the record without regard to the presence or absence of records around it.

The record will be read into the current DTA. Make sure that the declared DTA is large enough to hold the record. MS-DOS declares a DTA before the program starts, but it is only 128 bytes in length. If the records are larger than that, overflowing bytes may damage program data or instructions. The Set Disk Transfer Address function describes the steps needed to declare the DTA.

When the Random Read function is finished, it returns a completion code in the AL register. The value in the AL register indicates the status of the read operation. The status may have any of the following values:

0 The file transfer was completed successfully.

1 The end of the file was reached during the read operation. No bytes were available to read and none were placed into the DTA.

2 The end of the disk transfer segment was reached before the end of the transfer. A partial record was read. This is not an overflow of the DTA. In this case, the end of the segment's (either the Data or Extra segment register's) address space was reached when the offset in the segment reached Hex FFFF (DS:FFFF) during the transfer of bytes.

3 The end of the file was reached during the read operation. There were bytes available to read before the end-of-file was encountered. A partial record was read into the DTA. The remainder of the record's area is filled with zeroes.

The Random Read function may be called directly from a Pascal language program by using the DOSXQQ function. Before the Random Read function can be called, the target file must be opened, the record size set, and a suitable DTA declared. The following code could be used to read random records until a command is received to stop reading records:

```
Repeat
   {ask the user for a random record number}
   {or have the program generate a number  }
   {if the user enters a 0, then quit       }
   Record_Num := Get_Command;
   If Record_Num <> 0
   Then
     Begin
     File_FCB.RANDOM_REC := Record_Num;
     Status := DOSXQQ (Read_Ran, File_FCB);
     If Status = 0 Then Perform_Work (DTA);
     End;
Until Record_Num = 0;
```

Random Write

Function: Hex 22

Registers: DS:DX = Address of open FCB

AL = Status of random write

The purpose of the *Random Write* function is to transfer a single record from the Disk Transfer Area to a disk file. The random nature of the write operation is that the file address (current block and record) in the file's FCB is set to agree with the random-record field before the write is performed. In other words, if the random-record field is set to 83 so that the eighty-third record will be written, MS-DOS will calculate the position of the eighty-third record and set that disk address into the current-block and record fields before the disk transfer is made.

This write operation is performed on the file whose FCB is passed to the function in the DS:DX register pair. The FCB must be opened before any I/O operations can be correctly performed.

This function will write a record to the indicated file. The size and location of the record is determined by the record-size field in the FCB. When a file is opened, the record size is set to 128 bytes. It is the responsibility of the program to set the proper record size.

The random-record field of the FCB is used to indicate the numerical position of the record in the file. This number is combined with the record size, disk sector size, and number of sectors per cluster to calculate the address of the record on the disk.

Writing to a randomly accessed file can mean that not all record positions in the file actually contain valid data. It is quite permissible to write records to the file in a shotgun manner. There is one thing to watch when you are creating a random file. A wild random-record number may expand the file to a very large size. If the record number is large enough, the file may have to include all of the available sectors on the disk so that the record number can be included in the file. This fills a disk quicker than a runaway word processor.

The record will be written from the current DTA. Make sure that the declared DTA is large enough to hold the record.

When the Random Write function is finished, it returns a completion code in the AL register. The value in the AL register indicates the status of the write operation. The status may have any of the following values:

0 The file transfer was completed successfully.

1 The disk has been filled. Check the program for the use of a very large random-record number. Trying to write a record outside the bounds of the file (having assimilated all available sectors) will generate this error.

2 The end of the disk transfer segment was reached before the end of the transfer. A partial record was write. This is not an overflow of the DTA. In this case, the end of the segment's (either the Data or Extra segment register's) address space was reached when the offset in the segment reached Hex FFFF (DS:FFFF) during the transfer of bytes.

The Random Write function may be called directly from a Pascal language program by using the DOSXQQ function. Before the Random Write function can be called, the target file must be opened, the record size set, and the DTA filled with record data. The following code could be used to write random records until a command is received to stop writing records:

```
Repeat
   {ask the user for a random record number}
   {or have the program generate a number  }
   {if the user enters a 0, then quit       }
   Record_Num := Get_Command;
   If Record_Num <> 0
   Then
      Begin
      File_FCB.RANDOM_REC := Record_Num;
      If Status = 0 Then Perform_Work (DTA);
      Status := DOSXQQ (Write_Ran, File_FCB);
      End;
Until Record_Num = 0;
```

File Size

Function: Hex 23

Registers: DS:DX = Address of unopened FCB

AL = Status of file size

The purpose of the *File Size* function is to get the number of records that a file contains.

The file size count is based on a record count, not a byte count. The number of bytes in the file divided by record size in the FCB (the logical record-size field) determines the file size figure.

To use this function:

- Fill an unopened FCB with the filename of the file for which the count is being requested (use the *Parse Filename* function).

- Set the logical record size field to the size of one record. Use a size of one to get the true file size.

- Call the function passing the address of the FCB in the DS:DX register pair.

The function searches the directory for the filename and fills in the random-record field of the FCB.

The FCB is now pointing at the last record in the file. You may open the FCB at this time.

The Open File function will not disturb the random-record field, but it will destroy the record-size field. Reset the record-size field when the Open File function is finished.

Performing a random write, after this process is through, will allow you to append data to a file. If the file contains text material of any other ASCII characters (set the record size to 1 before calling the File Size function and after returning from the Open File function), an end-of-file character should be the last character in the file. Appending characters after the EOF may be a waste of time and energy. If you are going to append an ASCII file, subtract 1 from the random-record field and proceed. Remember to involve both words in the random-record field in your calculations.

The following code sequence is for a Pascal-callable procedure that prepares a file to be extended:

Listing 5-4. Prepare File for Append with FCB.

```
; use file size to append another file
; FCB already contains name of file
; logical record size in set in FCB
; Rec Size = 1 for file of characters or bytes
; Procedure Append (Vars FCB
;                    Var  Status)

APPEND    Proc Far
```

```
        PUBLIC      APPEND
        ASSUME      CS:CODE
        Push        BP
        Mov         BP,SP
        Push        DS
        Lds         DX,DWORD PTR [BP+8]
        Mov         AH,10H
        Int         21H
; Get filesize in random record number -- points to eof
        Mov         AH,23H
        Int         21H
; FCB now references last byte (record) in file
        Mov         AH,0FH
        Int         21H
        Pop         DS
        Mov         BP,SP
        Mov         BP,[BP+6]
        Mov         [BP],AL
        Pop         BP
        Ret         6
APPEND  ENDP
```

Set Random Record Field

Function: Hex 24

Registers: DS:DX = Address of open FCB

The purpose of the *Set Random Record Field* function is to convert the current disk file address in an FCB's current-block and current-record fields to the equivalent random record value.

The random-record field is converted to a disk address whenever one of the random I/O operations is used. This function is the inverse of that operation.

The address of the open FCB is passed to the Set Random Record Field function in the DS:DX register pair.

There are no completion codes for this function.

Random Block Read

Function: Hex 27

Registers: DS:DX = Address of open FCB

CX = Count of bytes read

AL = Status of random block read

The purpose of the *Random Block Read* function is to transfer several records from a file to a program buffer. This function is similar to the Random Read function because the file may be accessed randomly by setting the random-record field of the FCB. This function is different because it will transfer more than one record (block-oriented transfer) from the disk at one time.

This function is terrific for reading several small records in one operation. If a file contains ASCII text, it may be convenient, not knowing how long a text line might be, to set the record size to 1 byte. However, reading byte by byte sequentially with the Sequential Read function can take a long time. This function makes large block reads a practical alternative.

The file records are transferred to the current Disk Transfer Area. There must be enough memory reserved by the DTA to hold all of the records being read. Overflowing the DTA with data can damage program data or instructions.

The file to be read is selected with the open FCB passed to the function by putting its address in the DS:DX register pair.

Make sure that the record-size field is properly set in the FCB. When a file is opened, the record-size field is set to 128 bytes (Hex 80). It is the responsibility of the application program to set the correct record size value in the FCB.

The number of the record to be read is placed into the FCB's random-record field. MS-DOS will use the value of the record-size field and the random-record field to calculate the disk address of the requested record number. This address is placed into the current-block and current-record fields of the FCB.

The location of the first record to be read is set up in the FCB. However, the purpose of this function is to read several records. There is no field in the FCB for counting records. The number of records to be read is placed into the CX register. This count must not be zero. For an ASCII text file and a record size of 1, using a count of 512, will cause a whole sector to be read into the DTA. Keeping the total number of bytes as close to 512 as possible can help to increase the efficiency of the I/O process.

The Random Block Read function returns a completion code after it has performed its data transfer. The AL register holds the completion code. The values for this code are:

0 The file transfer was completed successfully.

1 The end of the file was reached during the read operation. No bytes were available to read, and none were placed into the DTA.

2 The end-of-disk transfer segment was reached before the end of the transfer. A partial record was read. This is not an overflow of the DTA. In this case, the end of the segment's (either the Data or Extra segment register's) address space was reached when the offset in the segment reached Hex FFFF (DS:FFFF) during the transfer of bytes.

3 The end of the file was reached during the read operation. There were bytes available to read before the end-of-file was encountered. A partial record was read into the DTA. The remainder of the record's area is filled with zeroes.

The CX register returns with the actual number of records transferred to the DTA. This number may be less than the requested number if the end of the file was reached.

The current-block, current-record, and random-record fields of the FCB are set to address the next record in the file. This allows several more reads, using either the Sequential Read, Random Read, or Random Block Read functions.

The following code shows the Random Block Read being used to read blocks of single-byte records (ASCII characters) from a file. The requested count is passed as a parameter and ends up in the CX register. The Random Block Read is doing duty as a sequential file reader in this case.

Listing 5-5. Random Block Read with FCB.

```
; read a random block from a file
; note : the DTA must have been specified already
; parameters  :  address of FCB
;                reference to number of records to read
;                reference to status word
BLOCREAD        PROC    FAR
                ASSUME  CS:CODE
                PUBLIC  BLOCREAD
                Push    BP
                Mov     BP,SP
                Push    DS                          ; save
                Lds     DX,DWORD PTR [BP+10] ; addr of FCB
                Mov     BP,[BP+8]
                Mov     CX,[BP]                     ; get count
                Mov     AH,27H                      ; random block read
                Int     21H
                Pop     DS                          ; restore
                Mov     BP,SP                       ; reset base pointer
                Mov     BP,[BP+6]                   ; get reference
                Mov     [BP],AL                     ; return status
                Mov     BP,SP                       ; reset again
                Mov     BP,[BP+8]                   ; get reference
                Mov     CX,[BP]                     ; return actual read count
                Pop     BP
                Ret     8
BLOCREAD        ENDP
```

Random Block Write

Function: Hex 28

Registers: DS:DX = Address of open FCB

CX = Count of bytes to write

AL = Status of random block write

The purpose of the *Random Block Write* function is to transfer several records from a program buffer to a file. This function is similar to the Random Write function because the file may be accessed randomly by setting the random-record field of the FCB. This function is different because it will transfer more than one record (block-oriented transfer) to the disk at one time.

This function is tailor-made for writing several small records in one operation. For example, you may need to write some text strings to a file. Not knowing how long a string might be, it may be convenient to set the record size to one byte and vary the number of records (single characters) to be written according to the lengths of the individual strings. Writing single characters to a file using the Sequential Write function could take a long time.

The file records are transferred from the current Disk Transfer Area. There must be enough memory reserved by the DTA to hold all of the records being written. Writing more data than the program expected to write can cause the transfer of irrelevant (soon to become erroneous) data to the disk file.

The file is selected with an open FCB passed to the function by putting its address in the DS:DX register pair.

Make sure that the record-size field is properly set in the FCB. When a file is opened, the record size field is set to 128 bytes (Hex 80). It is the responsibility of the application program to correctly set the record-size field in the FCB.

The number of the record to be written is placed into the FCB's random-record field. MS-DOS will use the value of the record size field and the random record number to calculate the disk address of the requested record number. This address is placed into the current-block and current-record fields of the FCB.

The disk address of the first record is set up in the FCB. However, the purpose of this function is to write several records. There is no field in the FCB for counting records. The number of records is placed into the CX register.

If the CX register is set to zero, the Random Block Write will not write to the file, but will set the FILE SIZE entry in the FCB and the disk directory to the current position of the random record number (expressed in number of bytes from the beginning of the file). This file size may be larger or smaller than the current directory value. Allocation units are added or dropped from the file's chain of sectors to set the file to this size.

The Random Block Write function returns a completion code after it has performed its data transfer. The AL register holds the completion code. The values for this code are:

0 The file transfer was completed successfully.

1 The disk has been filled. Check the program for the use of a very large random-record number. Trying to write a record outside the bounds of the file (having assimilated all available sectors) will generate this error.

2 The end of the disk transfer segment was reached before the end of the transfer. A partial record was Write. This is not an overflow of the DTA. In this case, the end of the segment's (either the Data or Extra segment register's) address space was reached when the offset in the segment reached hex FFFF (DS:FFFF) during the transfer of bytes.

The current-block, current-record, and random-record fields of the FCB are set to address the next record in the file. This allows several more writes, using either the *Sequential Write, Random Write* or Random Block Write functions.

The following code shows the Random Block Write being used to write blocks of single-byte records (ASCII characters) to a file. The count value is actually the length of a string variable that is being transferred to a disk file. The requested count is passed as a parameter and ends up in the CX register. The Random Block Write is doing duty as a sequential file writer in this case.

Listing 5-6. Random Block Write With FCB.

```
; write a random block from a file
; note : the DTA must have been specified already
; parameters : address of FCB
;              reference to number of records to read
;              reference to status word
BLOCWRIT   PROC     FAR
           ASSUME   CS:CODE
           PUBLIC   BLOCWRIT
           Push     BP
           Mov      BP,SP
           Push     DS                   ; save
           Lds      DX,DWORD PTR [BP+10] ; addr of FCB
           Mov      BP,[BP+8]
           Mov      CX,[BP]              ; get count
           Mov      AH,28H               ; random block write
           Int      21H
           Pop      DS                   ; restore
           Mov      BP,SP                ; reset base pointer
           Mov      BP,[BP+6]            ; get reference
```

```
          Mov      [BP],AL          ; return status
          Mov      BP,SP            ; reset again
          Mov      BP,[BP+8]        ; get reference
          Mov      CX,[BP]          ; return actual write count
          Pop      BP
          Ret      8
BLOCWRIT  ENDP
```

Parse Filename

Function: Hex 29

Registers: DS:SI = Address of string with filename

ES:DI = Address of FCB (no initialization required)

AL = Command to parse filename function

The purpose of the *Parse Filename* function is to transform a filename from the normal user form

```
Drive:Filename.Extension
```

as in:

```
B:MYFILE.TXT
```

into the form required by the File Control Block. This function is a real time-saver when it comes to stuffing filenames into FCBs. When this function is used in conjunction with the Open File or Create File functions, you can write a routine that will accept a user's filename and return with a properly opened FCB. This function requires three things: the filename, the FCB in which to place it, and some command bits set in the AL register to control the parsing.

The Parse Filename commands are:

Bit 0 = 1 Ignore the following characters if they are encountered before finding the filename: . ; , = + TAB SPACE.

Bit 1 = 1 Set or change the drive byte in the FCB only if the filename explicitly names a drive.

Bit 2 = 1   Set or change the filename in the FCB only if the passed string of characters contains a filename.

Bit 3 = 1   Set or change the filename extension in the FCB only if the passed string of characters contains an extension.

The original purpose of this function was to search a command line, entered by the user, for a filename and extension. By setting the bits in the AL register, the program can control what is actually placed in the FCB. To use this function as a tool to parse a filename and place it in the FCB, clear the AL register prior to calling it.

Since this function is concerned with parsing command lines, the function expands the wildcard "*" symbol to fill all trailing spaces in the filename with the "?" wildcard.

The major items (Filename and FCB) are passed to the routine as addresses. The FCB does not have to be initialized in any way. The result of this function is a properly set up unopened File Control Block. When the function is finished, your program will have to move the contents of the ES:DI register pair into the DS:DX register pair as required for the Open File and Create File functions.

The AL register will return to the calling procedure with a status of the parsing process. If the AL register is equal to zero, then the parse was satisfactory. When the AL register returns a value of Hex FF (decimal 255), then the drive specifier was in error. Returning with a value of one, the AL register signifies that a wildcard character was found in the filename.

The programming examples in the Create File and Open File functions contain passages that use the Parse Filename function to put a filename received from a user into an FCB.

Chapter 6

Directory Management

INTRODUCTION

The previous chapters covered fundamental functions that have been a part of MS-DOS since its introduction. There were also a couple of utility functions that were introduced in version 2.0. This chapter deals with the functions that are required to manage disk directory structures.

One of the big innovations of MS-DOS 2.0 is the concept of tree-structured disk directories. The use of tree structures allows the user greater control in organizing and maintaining files.

Briefly, a disk contains a directory which is used to find the file's physical location on the disk. This file usually contains text, program code, or portions of a program to be assembled later. All of these types of files would be listed in a directory. In MS-DOS 2.0, another type of file is available, the subdirectory. This file is another directory (a subdirectory) through which files can be classified and found.

The functions covered in this chapter are:

Hex 11	Search for the first directory entry
Hex 12	Search for the next directory entry
Hex 17	Rename file
Hex 39	Create a subdirectory
Hex 3A	Remove a directory entry
Hex 3B	Change the current directory
Hex 47	Get current directory
Hex 4E	Find first matching file
Hex 4F	Find next matching file
Hex 56	Rename a file
Hex 57	Get/set a file's date and time

DIRECTORY FUNCTIONS

Since this is the first chapter to deal with functions that were introduced in version 2.0, it is also the first to show the extended error codes that MS-DOS will return upon completion of a function. Chapter 9, Expanded Error Handling, covers the details of the error codes.

Search for the First Directory Entry

> **Function:** Hex 11
>
> **Registers:** DS:DX = Address of FCB
>
> AL = Status of search function

The purpose of the *Search for the First Directory Entry* function is to retrieve the first disk directory entry that matches a filename or filename pattern. This function also initializes an FCB for further directory searches.

The subject of the directory search is a filename or filename pattern. The MS-DOS function will search through the disk directory, attempting to match the given filename with the filenames in the directory entries. When a match is found, the search is terminated and the contents of the matched entry are placed into the current Disk Transfer Area.

The filename may contain "?" characters, indicating that any letter in the directory name will match for that position. This allows a great deal of flexibility in searching the directory. By setting the filename to "????????" and the filename extension to "???", all directory entries will match the filename. This function will find and return the first entry in the directory for this pattern. Using a specific filename extension, such as BAS, will cause the function to find the first BASIC program in the directory.

Directory entries are not necessarily in alphabetical order, so don't count on getting ACCOUNT.BAS before PAYROLL.BAS in a directory search.

The filename pattern is placed in an unopened FCB, which will be passed to the function by setting the DS:DX register pair to the address of the FCB.

When the Search for the First Directory Entry has finished its search, it returns a completion code in the AL register. The value of this code indicates whether or not the search was successful. If the AL register is set to Hex FF, the search was not successful because no directory entries matched the filename in the FCB. If the AL register is set to Hex 00, the search was successful and a copy of the directory entry was put into the DTA.

A successful search results in a copy of the directory entry being transferred to the DTA. Actually, the first byte of the DTA will contain numerical value of the disk drive where the searched disk is mounted. Following that byte is the directory entry.

With the inclusion of the drive identification byte, the DTA appears to be an unopened FCB. The DTA could be used as an FCB to open the matched file. However, with the exception of the filename and extension fields, the directory entry and an FCB are different. Don't get trapped into thinking of an FCB and a directory entry as being the same structure. The directory entry is a 32-byte block with the following definitions of its fields:

Bytes 0–7 Filename

Bytes 8–10 Filename Extension

Byte 11 Attributes The setting of the bits in the attribute byte describes the properties of the file. The setting of some bits will cause this function to exclude the entry from the search, and you should never see some of the following attributes. Reading the directory directly from the disk without this function will provide the identities of files with restrictive attributes. The attribute bits are defined as:

Bit 0 File is read-only.

Bit 1 File is a hidden file. This function will exclude this file from its searches.

Bit 2 File is a system file. This function will exclude this file from its searches.

Bit 3 This entry is the disk volume name. The only information in this entry is an 11-byte name. This is an MS-DOS 2.0 introduction.

Bit 4 This entry is for a subdirectory. This function will exclude this entry from its search. This is an MS-DOS 2.0 introduction.

Bit 5 This file is a backed-up archive file for a hard disk file. This is an MS-DOS 2.0 introduction.

Bit 6   Unused

Bit 7   Unused

Bytes 12–21   Reserved

Bytes 22–23 File Time   This field contains the creation time or the latest time of update. The time is in hour/minute/second form as follows:

```
<           byte 23      >  <         byte 22         >
7  6  5  4  3  2  1  0  7  6  5  4  3  2  1  0
h  h  h  h  h  m  m  m  m  m  m  d  d  d  d  d

Hours    (hhhhh)   = 0 - 23
Minutes  (mmmmm)   = 0 - 59
Seconds  (sssss)   = 0 - 30
(To compensate for the lack of enough bits,
seconds are recorded in 2 second increments)
```

Bytes 24–25 File Date   This field contains the date, showing the creation date or the latest date of update. The date is in month/day/year form as follows:

```
<           byte 25      >  <         byte 24         >
7  6  5  4  3  2  1  0  7  6  5  4  3  2  1  0
y  y  y  y  y  y  y  m  m  m  m  d  d  d  d  d

Months (mmmm)     = 1 - 12
Days   (ddddd)    = 1 - 31
Year   (yyyyyyy)  = 0 - 119
(added to 1980, gives proper year)
```

Bytes 26–27 Cluster Number   This number represents the disk address of the first cluster of the file. Other clusters of the file are found in the chain of clusters in the File Allocation Table. The chain begins with this cluster. To find the first disk sector (for multiple sectors per cluster), the cluster number is multiplied by the number of sectors in the cluster. This value is the relative sector number, based on the first data cluster (cluster #2).

Bytes 28–31 File Size   This field represents the total byte count of the file. This is a true byte count. It is not calculated from the number of sectors in the file multiplied by the number of bytes in a sector. Other methods count unused bytes in the last sector of the file. This count is based upon the number of bytes actually used in the last sector of the file. This field contains two words worth of byte count. The least significant of the two words is stored in bytes 28 and 29, while the most significant word is stored in bytes 30 and 31. If that sounds confusing, remember that the least significant byte of a word is stored in the first byte, and the most significant byte in the second.

This function can be called from a Pascal program through the DOSXQQ function. The results of the search function are returned as the result of the DOSXQQ. Before using this function call, establish the DTA and set up the filename pattern in the FCB. The following code sequence shows the steps to find the first entry in the disk directory:

```
{DTA has been established}
Dir_FCB.Filename := '????????';
Dir_FCB.Filetype := '???';
Dir_FCB.Drive    := 1; {search on drive A:}
Status  := DOSXQQ (First_Directory, Dir_FCB);
```

This function may also be called from C. In this case, the FCB for the directory entry (dir_fcb) is a local variable structure. It would also be possible to use *malloc()* to acquire the memory for the FCB and then reference the area with pointers. The address of the FCB would be passed directly to *_bdos* as a parameter.

```
/* DTA has been established */
strcpy(dir_fcb.filename,"????????");
strcpy(dir_fcb.filetype,"???");
dir_fcb.drive = 1;
```

Search for the Next Directory Entry

Function: Hex 12

Registers: DS:DX = Address of FCB

AL = Status of search function

The Search for the Next Directory Entry function is an extension of the Search for the First Directory Entry function. If the FCB used in finding the first matching entry in a directory contained the "?" character, there is a possibility that several matching entries may be found in the directory. The purpose of this function is to continue the search for the remaining entries.

The Search for the First Directory Entry function must be called at least once before this function will operate correctly. The first search initializes data for a continuing search. The Search for the First Directory Entry function saves some of its search information in the reserved fields of the FCB. Therefore, to continue the search, the same FCB must be passed to this function. The FCB must not be modified in any manner, including not opening the original FCB. Opening the FCB created in the DTA is permitted.

Put the address of the FCB into the DS:DX register pair as you did with the Search for the First Directory Entry function.

The Search for the Next Directory Entry function executes in the same manner as the first search function. The AL register returns the same completion codes.

A good programming strategy would be to call this function and some procedure to use the directory information until all available entries are scanned. The following code sequence illustrates that strategy:

Listing 6-1. Read and Process Directory (in Pascal and C).

```
{DTA has been established}
Dir_FCB.Filename := '????????';
Dir_FCB.Filetype := '???';
Dir_FCB.Drive    := 1; {search on drive} A:
Status := DOSXQQ (First_Directory, Dir_FCB);
{check that the last search was successful}
While Status = 0 Do
  Begin
  Process_Directory;
  {search for the next directory and try again}
  Status := DOSXQQ (Next_Directory, Dir_FCB);
  End;


/* DTA has been established */
strcpy(dir_fcb.filename,"????????");
strcpy(dir_fcb.filetype,"???");
dir_fcb.drive = 1; /* search on drive A: */
status = _bdos(FIRST_DIRECTORY,dir_fcb);
/* check that the last search was successful */
while (!status)
  {
  process_directory(dta);
  /* search for the next directory and try again */
  status = _bdos (NEXT_DIRECTORY, dir_fcb);
  }
```

Rename File

Function: Hex 17

Registers: DS:DX = Address of special FCB
AL = Status of rename

The purpose of the *Rename File* function is to change the filename in a directory to another filename. The filename in the directory entry of the original file is changed to a second name.

Both filenames for the function are passed in the same unopened FCB. The original filename is placed into the normal filename fields of the FCB. The old filename may include "?"s in place of letters to allow multiple renames by matching with several directory entries. The Parse Filename function could be used to set the first filename.

The new filename is placed into the reserved portion of the FCB. The format of the filename is identical to the normal FCB filename. If the "?" character is used in the new filename, the filename that is eventually placed into the directory will assume the letters of the directory's original filename in the corresponding positions. Eight bytes are used for the filename, and three bytes are used for the filename extension. The start of the new filename is at location 17 (Hex 11) from the front of the FCB.

Creating a new FCB type for this function may be a simple way to handle the two names. A Pascal FCB might be declared as follows:

```
Listing 6-2. FCB to Rename File in Pascal and
C.
```

```
Rename_FCB   = Record
  Drive      [00]: Byte;
  Old_Name   [01]: String[8];
  Old_Ext    [09]: String[3];
  Unused     [12]: String[5];
  New_Name   [17]: String[8];
  New_Ext    [25]: String[3];
  Vacant     [28]: String[10];
  End;
```

and in C:

```
typedef
  struct
    {
    char   drive;
    char   old_name[8];
    char   old_ext[3];
    char   unused[5];
    char   new_name[8];
    char   new_ext[3];
    int    vacant[5];
    }    rename_fcb;
```

If you use *strcpy()* to move the filenames and filetypes into position in this example, be mindful of the order in which you copy the strings. C strings terminate in a binary zero and are actually one character longer than you might think, to allow for that zero. If you were to move the filetype into position first, the first character would be changed to a binary zero when the filename is entered. Instead, move the filename first and let the filetype overwrite the trailing zero with a proper character. The binary zero from the filetype will not cause any problems in the unused portion of the FCB.

With the filenames securely in the FCB, the Rename File function can be called. The function searches the directory for filename or pattern matches. When a match is found, the new filename, with "?" editing applied, is installed in the directory entry.

When the function is finished, the AL register is set to indicate the completion status of the function. If the value of the AL register is zero, the rename process was successful. If the value of the AL register is Hex FF, then no files were renamed.

The following bit of code uses the Rename_FCB to rename all files with the filename starting with the letter "P" and the extension of SRC to a filename with the first letter of "X" and a filename extension of BAK. It doesn't make much sense, but it illustrates the use of the "?" feature.

```
With REN_FCB Do
  Begin
  Drive      := 1;
  Old_Name  := 'P???????';
  Old_Ext   := 'SRC';
  New_Name  := 'X???????';
  New_Ext   := 'BAK';
  Status    :=   DOSXQQ (Rename_File, REN_FCB);
  End;
```

More of the same:

```
ren_fcb = (rename_fcb *) malloc(sizeof(rename_fcb),1);
ren_fcb->drive = 1;
strcpy(ren_fcb->old_name,"P???????");
strcpy(ren_fcb->old_ext,"SRC");
strcpy(ren_fcb->new_name,"X???????");
strcpy(ren_fcb->new_ext,"BAK");
status = _bdos (RENAME_FILE,ren_fcb);
```

Create a Subdirectory

Function: Hex 39

Registers: DS:DX = Address of pathname

Errors: 3, 5

The purpose of the *Create a Subdirectory* function is to create a new file on the disk which will act as a subdirectory, pointing to other files instead of a file holding textual information, program code, or raw data. The new subdirectory is seen as a file by the directory in which it is listed. However, certain bits are set in the parent directory entry to designate this new subdirectory as being a directory and not a data file. Being a subdirectory, the new file will have the ability to point to its own files and subdirectories.

Using this and other MS-DOS functions and the command processor, your programs are able to create new entries within this subdirectory. This function will not create a new data file.

The following errors can be generated by this function:

```
3 Path Not Found
5 Access denied
```

If these errors occur (the Carry Flag is set upon returning from the function), check to see that the pathname is valid by checking that all of the elements of the pathname really exist and are spelled correctly. Your request may be denied if a file with that name has already been created or you are choosing to create a subdirectory with a special name (e.g., PRN:).

The following code can be used to create a new directory from inside a program. The main parameter to this routine is the pathname of the new directory. This pathname is an ASCIIZ string, that is, the last character in the pathname is followed by a byte with a binary zero value.

Listing 6-3. Make a Directory.

```
;  Make a Directory (MKDIR)
;  Procedure MKDIR  (Vars F_Name  : String;
;                         Var  Status  : Integer); EXTERN;
MKDIR      PROC    FAR
           ASSUME  CS:CODE
           PUBLIC  MKDIR
           Push    BP
           Mov     BP,SP
           Push    DS
           Push    DX
           Lds     DX,DWORD PTR [BP+8]  ; addr of pathname
           Mov     AH,39H               ; make a directory
           Int     21H                  ; and call DOS
           Pop     DX
           Pop     DS
           Jc      MKDIRST              ; everything work?
           Sub     AL,AL                ; yes, return 0
MKDIRST:   Mov     BP,[BP+6]
           Mov     [BP],AL              ; return status
           Pop     BP
           Ret     6
MKDIR      ENDP
```

Remove a Directory Entry

Function: Hex 3A

Registers: DS:DX = Address of pathname

Errors: 3, 5

Just as in the case of files, the existence of the subdirectory depends upon the whims of the user and current needs of the system. The purpose of the *Remove a Directory Entry* function is to delete the file which represents the subdirectory. The removal of a subdirectory may be warranted during cleanup times, when files from old projects are removed to make room for the next project or, perhaps, next year's accounts are backed up to make room for the new year's accounts. When all of the files of a subdirectory are removed, the next logical thing to do is to remove the subdirectory for those old files (unless leaving it there serves a purpose).

Notice that you must remove the files within the subdirectory before removing the subdirectory itself. This function will not remove a directory if it contains files. Now, writing a program that will do a clean-sweep of the files and then remove the subdirectory is quite possible. But the power of such a program is so great, in terms of destroying more than you really want to, that it is neither worth having nor safe to use. When you delete single files in preparation for deleting the directory, you get a chance to see what is being deleted and can save certain files if you wish. Mass destruction of files will not allow you to be so selective or lucky.

The following errors can be generated by this function:

3 Path Not Found

5 Access denied

If these errors occur, check to see that the pathname is valid by checking that all of the elements of the pathname exist and are spelled correctly. Your request may be denied if the subdirectory you are deleting is actually a file, a special device, or the current directory (see the next function).

The following code will cause a subdirectory to be removed from its directory:

Listing 6-4. Remove a Directory.

```
; Discard a Directory
; Procedure DISCARDD (Vars PathName : String;
;                     Var  Status   : Integer); EXTERN;
DISCARDD  PROC    FAR
          ASSUME  CS:CODE
          PUBLIC  DISCARDD
          Push    BP
          Mov     BP,SP
          Push    DS
          Lds     DX,DWORD PTR [BP+8]   ; get addr of path
          Mov     AH,3AH                ; remove directory
          Int     21H                   ; DOS does it
          Jc      DIRSTAT               ; everything ok?
          Sub     AL,AL                 ; ok! status = 0
DIRSTAT:  Mov     BP,[BP+6]
          Mov     [BP],AL               ; return status
```

Listing 6-4. Continued

```
            Pop     DS
            Pop     BP
            Ret     6
DISCARDD    ENDP
```

Change the Current Directory

Function: Hex 3B

Registers: DS:DX = Address of pathname

Errors: 3

Using pathnames to locate each file, especially with long pathnames, can be a bulky operation. The longer the pathname, the better the chances are that a typing mistake will occur. Couple this to the fact that most of the work done by a program will occur within a single subdirectory in the file system. It makes sense to designate a subdirectory as the default (current) directory so that the pathname of a file is assumed to contain the pathname of the current subdirectory, and all files within the subdirectory can be called by their simple names. This is the purpose of the *Change the Current Directory* function.

The pathname passed to the system call is checked to see if the path really exists (error code 3 is returned if there is a problem) and, being a valid path, becomes the pathname that will prefix all pathnames being subsequently used.

The following program segment shows how to set the current directory by passing its pathname to MS-DOS.

Listing 6-5. Change a Current Directory.

```
;  Set the current directory
;  Procedure SETDIR (Vars Pathname : String;
;                    Var Status    : Integer); EXTERN;
SETDIR    PROC   FAR
          ASSUME CS:CODE
          PUBLIC SETDIR
          Push   BP
          Mov    BP,SP
          Push   DS
          Push   DX
```

Listing 6-5. Continued

```
            Lds     DX,DWORD PTR [BP+8]   ; get addr of path
            Mov     AH,3BH                ; set directory
            Int     21H                   ; system call
            Jc      SETSTAT               ; everything ok?
            Sub     AL,AL                 ; yes status = 0
SETSTAT:    Mov     BP,[BP+6]
            Mov     [BP],AL               ; return status
            Pop     DX
            Pop     DS
            Pop     BP
            Ret     6
SETDIR      ENDP
```

Get Current Directory

Function: Hex 47

Registers: DL = Drive number

DS:DI = Address of area to receive pathname

Errors: 15

The purpose of the *Get Current Directory* is to report the pathname of the current directory on a specific disk drive. The DL register is loaded with the designator for a specific drive (0 = default drive, 1 = drive A, 2 = drive B, etc.) The program must reserve a 64 byte area (addressed by the DS:DI register pair) to receive the pathname. When the function is called, the disk drive is specified in the DL register, so the letter designator should be understood and is not returned as part of the string. The string will not start with a backslash, but will terminate with a byte of binary zeroes.

Listing 6-6. Get Current Directory.

```
; Get the current directory
; Procedure GETDIR (     Drive : Integer;
;                   Vars Pathname : String;
;                   Var Status    : Integer); EXTERN;
; Note: Pathname is assumed to be 64 bytes long (minimum)
;
```

Listing 6-6. Continued

```
GETDIR    PROC    FAR
          ASSUME  CS:CODE
          PUBLIC  GETDIR
          Push    BP
          Mov     BP,SP
          Push    DS
          Push    DI
          Push    DX
          Mov     DL,[BP+12]              ; get id of drive
          Lds     DI,DWORD PTR [BP+8]     ; get addr of path
          Mov     AH,47H                  ; get directory
          Int     21H                     ; system call
          Jc      GETSTAT                 ; everything ok?
          Sub     AL,AL                   ; yes status = 0
GETSTAT   Mov     BP,[BP+6]
          Mov     [BP],AL                 ; return status
          Pop     DX
          Pop     DI
          Pop     DS
          Pop     BP
          Ret     8
GETDIR    ENDP
```

Find First Matching File

Function: Hex 4E

Registers: DS:DX = Address of pathname
                CX = Search attribute

Errors: 2, 18

The purpose of the *Find First Matching File* function is to search a named subdirectory for the first filename that matches a given pattern. For instance, in the pathname:

ROOT.DIR\MYSTUFF\LETTERS.DIR\????????.TXT

the first three segments of the pathname designate the subdirectory name, and the pattern for the filename match is the last section. With a general pattern of all question marks, the first file in the directory will be found. The use of wildcard characters was covered in an earlier chapter.

This system call is the MS-DOS 2.0 version of function Hex 11 (Search for the First Entry). This earlier version operated through the FCB to designate the pattern for searching (the directory had to be the disk directory) and the results were returned in a 32-byte DTA in the form of another FCB. This newer version uses a pathname to designate the subdirectory and the pattern. Again the DTA handles the returning directory entry. The format of the DTA is different from the earlier version's FCB.

The DTA has this layout:

Table 6-1. Directory Organization in DTA.

Bytes	Meanings
0–20	Reserved for DOS use in searching
21	Attribute found
22–23	File's time
24–25	File's date
26–27	Least significant word (filesize)
28–29	Most significant word (filesize)
30–42	Filename and extension (filetype)

The filename and extension will have all spaces removed, and the string will be terminated with a byte of binary zeroes. If the extension/filetype is present, it will be prefixed with a period.

The next code sequence is a subroutine that calls MS-DOS to get the first entry in a subdirectory. The pathname of the subdirectory and filename pattern are passed to this routine as address parameters. The DTA that is to receive the directory entry must have been previously declared to the operating system.

Listing 6-7. Get First Entry in Subdirectory.

```
; Get first entry in a subdirectory
; Procedure GETFIRST (Vars Pathname : String;
;                         Var Status    : Integer); EXTERN;
; Note: DTA must be declared prior to this call
;
GETFIRST   PROC    FAR
           ASSUME  CS:CODE
           PUBLIC  GETFIRST
           Push    BP
```

Listing 6-7. Continued

```
              Mov      BP,SP
              Push     DS
              Push     DX
              Lds      DI,DWORD PTR [BP+8]  ; get addr of path
              Mov      AH,4EH              ; search directory
              Int      21H                 ; system call
              Jc       FIRSTST             ; everything ok?
              Sub      AL,AL               ; yes status = 0
    FIRSTST:  Mov      BP,[BP+6]
              Mov      [BP],AL             ; return status
              Pop      DX
              Pop      DS
              Pop      BP
              Ret      6
    GETFIRST  ENDP
```

Find Next Matching File

Function: Hex 4F

Registers: None

Errors: 18

The purpose of the *Find Next Matching File* function is to continue the directory search started in the Find First Matching File function. Repeated calls to this function will cause additional directory entries to be returned to the calling program until all entries matching the pattern are found. The error code 18 (no more files) is returned when all directory entries have been searched. The DTA used in the Find First Matching File will contain the data on the entries. There is no need to submit a pattern with every call, since the pattern searching parameters are contained in the reserved bytes of the DTA.

The following sequence of code illustrates how simple the request for another directory entry can be with MS-DOS 2.0:

```
;
; Get next entry in directory
; Procedure GETNEXT (Var Status : Integer); EXTERN;
; Note: Same DTA as GETFIRST
;
GETNEXT   PROC    FAR
```

```
        ASSUME   CS:CODE
        PUBLIC   GETNEXT
        Push     BP
        Mov      BP,SP
        Mov      AH,47H            ; get directory
        Int      21H               ; system call
        Jc       NEXTSTAT          ; everything ok?
        Sub      AL,AL             ; yes status = 0
NEXTSTAT: Mov     BP,[BP+6]
        Mov      [BP],AL           ; return status
        Pop      BP
        Ret      2
GETNEXT ENDP
```

Rename a File

Function: Hex 56

Registers: DS:DX = Address of pathname of current file

ES:DI = Address of new pathname of the file

Errors: 3, 5, 17

The purpose of the *Rename a File* function is to allow the user to change the name of a file. This is the MS-DOS 2.0 version of the Hex 17 function (Rename File) with an interesting feature. Since the structure of DOS 2.0 allows subdirectories, it is possible to rename a file from one subdirectory to another. This is comparable to copying the file to another directory and erasing the original, but this function merely moves the entry from one directory to another. It also allows simple name changes within a single directory.

The ability to change a file's pathname is not available through the REN*ame* command in the command processor.

Listing 6-8. Rename or Move a File.

```
;
; Rename a file
; Procedure RENAME (Vars Oldname : String;
;                   Vars Newname : String;
;                   Var Status   : Integer); EXTERN;
```

Listing 6-8. Continued

```
;
RENAME      PROC    FAR
            ASSUME  CS:CODE,DS:NOTHING,ES:NOTHING
            PUBLIC  RENAME
            Push    BP
            Mov     BP,SP
            Push    DS
            Push    DI
            Push    DX
            Lds     DX,DWORD PTR [BP+14]  ; get addr of old
            Les     DI,DWORD PTR [BP+8]   ; get addr of new
            Mov     AH,56H                ; rename a file
            Int     21H                   ; system call
            Jc      RENSTAT               ; everything ok?
            Sub     AL,AL                 ; yes status = 0
RENSTAT:    Mov     BP,[BP+6]
            Mov     [BP],AL               ; return status
            Pop     DX
            Pop     DI
            Pop     DS
            Pop     BP
            Ret     12
RENAME      ENDP
```

Get/Set a File's Date and Time

Function: Hex 57

Registers: AL = Command to function
BX = Handle of file
DX = Date
CX = Time

Errors: 1, 6

The purpose of the *Get/Set a File's Date and Time* system call is to allow a program to interrogate and change the time and date fields of a file's directory entry. The BX register is used to specify the file's handle for getting and setting the time and date.

To get the time and date of a file, the AL register is set to zero. Upon return from the operating system, the CX register contains the time and the DX register contains the date.

To set the time and date for a file, the AL register is set to one; the CX register is set to the time parameter; and the DX register is set to the date.

The CX register's time value is formatted in the following manner:

```
   FCB Time Field
15   14   13 12   11 10 9    8  7  6   5 4 3 2   1 0
< hour  (0-23)  > < minute (0-59) > <   2 sec >
   CX Register Setup (Bytes Swapped)
15 14   13 12 11 10 9 8 7 6 5 4 3 2 1 0
m   >  <   xx > <    hh   > <    m
```

The DX register's date value is formatted as follows:

```
   FCB Date Field
15 14    13 12 11 10  9  8  7  6 5   4  3   2   1   0
<          year       > < month > <   day   >
      0-119 for 1980-2099  1-12 1-31

   DX Register Setup (Bytes Swapped)
   15 14   13 12 11 10 9 8 7 6 5 4 3 2 1 0
month >  <  day  > <     year    > <
```

Chapter 7

Advanced File Management

INTRODUCTION

This chapter describes the advanced file and device management capabilities of MS-DOS introduced in version 2.0.

In earlier versions of MS-DOS, the separation of character-oriented I/O devices and related functions from the block-oriented I/O devices and functions was highly visible. There were read and write routines for moving characters from the console keyboard to the console monitor, and other routines for reading records to and from a disk file.

MS-DOS 2.0 (and later) does not draw the same distinction between the device types at the system function call level. An application program can make I/O requests to MS-DOS with little regard for the type of device being accessed. This is because the interface to the operating system is the same for character and block I/O. There are still some differences, though. For instance, it can be difficult to correctly read random characters from the keyboard. However, there are auxiliary functions for maintaining control of the specific peripheral devices.

The distinction between the device types occurs at the device driver level. The creation and use of device drivers is covered in Chapter 12.

FILE AND DIRECTORY MANAGEMENT FUNCTIONS

One of the magic features that MS-DOS 2.0 (and later versions) allows is I/O redirection. I/O redirection is the substitution of another device or file for one of the standard input or output devices during program execution. This is possible since the I/O interface to all devices is exactly the same. It becomes a matter of tying the file and device identifications (file handle numbers) together.

This is what redirection allows you to do: Some programs are written that expect to receive their input from the standard input device; the keyboard, and send their output to the standard output device, the console monitor. The standard input handle can be forced, using this function, to track with another handle, perhaps a file handle. Whenever input is expected from the standard device, the file is actually used as a source of input data. The input has been redirected to the file.

The extended file and device management functions are:

Hex 3C	Create a file
Hex 3D	Open a file
Hex 3E	Close a file handle
Hex 3F	Read from a file or device
Hex 40	Write to a file or device
Hex 41	Delete a file from a specified directory
Hex 42	Move file read/write pointer
Hex 43	Change file attribute
Hex 44	I/O control of devices
Hex 45	Duplicate a file handle
Hex 46	Force a duplicate of a handle
Hex 5A	Create unique file
Hex 5B	Create new file
Hex 5C	Lock/unlock file access
Hex 67	Set handle count
Hex 68	Commit file

Create a File

Function: Hex 3C

Registers: DS:DX = Address of ASCIIZ pathname
CX = Attribute of new file
AX = Returned file handle

Errors: 3, 4, 5

The purpose of the *Create a File* function is to create a new file in a directory or subdirectory. The creation of the file only takes place when the file does not already exist. If the file exists, it is opened and its length is set to zero, making it appear to be a new file. The file is opened with read and write access capabilities.

The new file is identified by its pathname. The pathname includes the subdirectory name to which the file is to be assigned. MS-DOS returns the file handle identification number for use with other I/O activities.

Load the CX register with the appropriate attributes for the new file. Setting an attribute bit to one will activate the attribute. A good policy for most file creations is not to set any attributes (normal file) and use the Change File Attributes function (Hex 43) to set the desired attributes after the file has been correctly established. The attribute bits are defined as:

Bit 0 File is read-only. Attempting to open this file with a write access request will generate an error. Creating a file with this attribute is not suggested. After data has been written to the file, the attribute can be changed with the Change Attribute function.

Bit 1 Hidden file. When normal searches are made in the directory that contains this file, this file is excluded.

Bit 2 System file. This file is also excluded from directory searches.

Bit 3 Volume Label Entry. This is a special file in the root directory and contains the name of the diskette volume. This should not be of importance to most programmers.

Bit 4 Subdirectory. This file is a subdirectory of the current directory. It is excluded from normal directory searches.

Bit 5 Archive file. This file is created during a hard disk backup or restore operation. The bit is used to test the integrity of the file.

The system-assigned handle will be returned in the AX register. However, if there is an error condition detected during the file creation, the Carry bit in the Flag register will be set. In this case, the AX register will contain an error code. The errors that can be detected by the Create a File function are:

3 Path Not Found. Check the spelling of the components of the pathname, and check for a binary zero byte at the end of the name.

4 Too Many Open Files. MS-DOS is handling its maximum number of open files and there are no more available file handles.

5 Access Denied. Check the attribute byte in CX for a combination of attributes that might restrict the creation of a data file (such as setting the subdirectory or volume name attribute). Check for another subdirectory with the same name.

The following code sequence illustrates the use of the Create a File function. This function is callable from Pascal. It returns the file handle through a different parameter than the status byte. It allows the calling program to check the status parameter as being zero before using the handle, since the value of the Carry bit may have been destroyed by the time the calling program regains control.

Listing 7-1. Create a File.

```
;
; Create a File
; Procedure CREATE (Pathname, Handle, Status);
; Offsets :    Ref Pathname   : C (Segment), A (Offset)
;              Ref Handle     : 8
;              Ref Status     : 6
;              Ret            : 0
;
CREATE     PROC    FAR
           ASSUME  CS:CODE;
           PUBLIC  CREATE
           Push    BP                      ; save frame ptr
           Mov     BP,SP
           Push    DS                      ; save data segment
           Push    DX                      ; going to use DX also
           Lds     DX,DWORD PTR [BP+10]     ; get pathname
           Mov     CX,0                    ; file attribute (regular)
           Mov     AH,3CH                  ; 'create' command
           Int     21H                     ; call DOS
           Pop     DX                      ; get set to return
           Pop     DS
           Push    AX                      ; may have error or handle
           Jc      CREATST                 ; error if carry is set
           Sub     AL,AL                   ; no error--clear status
CREATST:   Mov     BP,[BP+6]               ; set status word
           Mov     [BP],AL
           Pop     AX                      ; get possible handle
           Mov     BP,SP                   ; get back to stack area
           Mov     BP,[BP+8]               ; get handle address
           Mov     [BP],AX                 ; return the handle
           Pop     BP                      ; ready to return
           Ret     8
CREATE     ENDP
```

Open a File

Function: Hex 3D

Registers: DS:DX = Address of ASCIIZ pathname

AL = File access code

AX = Returned file handle

Errors: 2, 4, 5, 12

The purpose of the *Open a File* function is to associate an existing file, identified by a pathname, with a numerical handle, and prepare that file for read and/or write operations. The address of the pathname (in ASCIIZ format) is placed into the DS:DX register pair.

A file access code is passed to MS-DOS in the AL register. This access code controls the types of operations that may be used with the file. The access codes are:

0 Open file for reading

1 Open file for writing

2 Open file for reading and writing

The system-assigned handle will be returned in the AX register. However, if there is an error condition detected during the file opening, the Carry bit in the Flag register will be set. In this case, the AX register will contain an error code. The errors that can be detected by the Open a File function are:

2 File Not Found. Check the spelling of the components of the pathname and check for a binary zero byte at the end of the name.

4 Too Many Open Files. MS-DOS is handling its maximum number of open files and there are no more available file handles.

5 Access Denied. Check the access byte in AL for opening a read-only file for a writing access. Check that the file to be opened is not a subdirectory or volume label file.

12 Invalid Access. Check that the access value placed in the AL register was in the range of 0 to 2.

The following code sequence illustrates the use of the Open a File function. This function is callable from Pascal. It returns the file handle through a different parameter than the status byte.

Listing 7-2. Open a File.

```
;
; Open a File
; Procedure OpenFile (Pathname, Handle, Status);
; Offsets :   Ref   Pathname : C (Segment), A (Offset)
;             Ref   Handle   : 8
;             Ref   Status   : 6
;                   Ret      : 0
;
OPENFILE   PROC     FAR
           ASSUME   CS:CODE
           PUBLIC   OPENFILE
           Push     BP                        ; save frame ptr
           Mov      BP,SP
           Push     DS                        ; save data segment
           Push     DX                        ; going to use DX also
           Lds      DX,DWORD PTR [BP+10]       ; get pathname
           Mov      BP,[BP+6]
           Mov      AL,[BP]                    ; get file access value
           Mov      AH,3DH                     ; 'open' command
           Int      21H                        ; call DOS
           Pop      DX                         ; get set to return
           Pop      DS
           Mov      BP,SP                      ; get back to stack
           Push     AX                         ; may have error or handle
           Jc       OPENST                     ; error if carry is set
           Sub      AL,AL                      ; no error--clear status
OPENST:    Mov      BP,[BP+6]                  ; set status word
           Mov      [BP],AL
           Pop      AX                         ; get possible handle
           Mov      BP;SP                      ; get back to stack area
           Mov      BP,[BP+8]                  ; get handle address
           Mov      [BP],AX                    ; return the handle
           Pop      BP                         ; ready to return
           Ret      8
OPENFILE   ENDP
```

In MS-DOS 3.0, the File Access Code set into the AL register to control the action of the opened file has been expanded. The earlier settings of the register as designated in MS-DOS 2.0 are still valid.

The AL register is now split into four fields:

Bit 7 Inheritance Flag (I)   This flag specifies whether a spawned process (child task) can inherit the opened file.

- If the I is set to zero, then child processes may inherit the file.
- If the I is set to one, then the current process has exclusive rights to the file.

Bits 4–6 Sharing Mode Field (S)   This field specifies what operations can be performed on this opened file by other tasks (networking or multitasking). Restrictions listed here apply to other tasks attempting to perform operations on the file. The following values may be used:

- S is set to 000—Deny any attempt to read or write to the file (this value is compatible with versions of MS-DOS before 3.0).
- S is set to 001—Deny any attempt to read or write to this file.
- S is set to 010—Deny any attempt to write to this file.
- S is set to 011—Deny any attempt to read from this file.
- S is set to 100—Allow all operations to the file.

Bit 3 Reserved (R)

Bits 0–2 Access Field (A)   This field defines the access restrictions to the opened file (read only, write only, or read/write).

- A is set to 00—Read only access
- A is set to 01—Write only access
- A is set to 10—Read/write access

Close a File Handle

> **Function:** Hex 3E
>
> **Register:** BX = File handle
>
> **Errors:** 6

The purpose of the *Close a File Handle* function is to mark the end of current operations on a file. The only parameter to this function is the numerical handle identifier of the file. For a file that was open for reading, the close function returns the file handle to MS-DOS so that it can be used with another file. For a file that has been opened for writing, the close function flushes any partially filled buffers to the file and sets the file size.

If there is an error condition detected during the file opening, the Carry bit in the Flag register will be set. In this case, the AX register will contain an error code. The errors that can be detected by the Close a File Handle function are:

6 Invalid Handle. The handle passed to MS-DOS was not the handle of an open file.

The following code sequence illustrates the use of the Close a File Handle function. This function is callable from Pascal.

```
;
; Close a File
; Procedure CLOSEFIL (Handle);
; Offsets :   Ref   Handle   : 6
;                   Ret      : 0
;
CLOSEFIL      PROC    FAR
              ASSUME  CS:CODE
              PUBLIC  CLOSEFIL
              Push    BP            ; save frame ptr
              Mov     BP,SP
              Mov     BX,[BP+6]     ; get handle
              Mov     AH,3EH        ; 'close' command
              Int     21H           ; call DOS
              Pop     BP            ; ready to return
              Ret     2
CLOSEFIL      ENDP
```

Read from a File or Device

Function: Hex 3F

Registers: BX = File handle

CX = Number of bytes to read (record size)

DS:DX = Address of buffer

AX = Number of bytes actually read

Errors: 5, 6

The purpose of the *Read from a File or Device* function is to move bytes from an external file or peripheral device into a buffer. This single function replaces the several different reading functions (sequential, random,

block, and character string) of MS-DOS 1.1. The file or device is identified through the handle identifier. For reading from devices, MS-DOS
has permanently assigned the following handles to these devices:

0 Standard Input Device. This device is normally the console keyboard, but
it may be redirected to read characters from other devices and files.

3 Standard Auxiliary Device. This device is usually the communications
processor.

The opened file or device is identified by its file handle, which is
passed to MS-DOS in the BX register.

The Disk Transfer Area of MS-DOS 1.1 is not used for this function.
The application program must provide its own buffer. The address of this
buffer is passed to the function in the DS:DX register pair. This method
of managing buffers proves to be easier than switching the DTA address
every time an I/O operation is made to a different file.

The number of bytes to be read is placed into the CX register. This
byte count can represent:

- the expected number of bytes to be read from a character device;
- the number of bytes in the file's record size; or
- the number of bytes in the application program's buffer.

The actual number of bytes transferred will not exceed the count in
the CX register, but could possibly be less than the CX register count.
For instance, if this function were being used to read characters from a
character-oriented device such as the keyboard, the number of characters actually transferred would depend upon the length of the line that
was entered, since the input function would terminate with a carriage
return. Also, if an attempt is made to read from the end of the file, no
characters are read. The actual number of characters transferred is returned in the AX register (unless an error occurs).

If there is an error condition detected during the file or device read
operation, the Carry bit in the Flag register will be set. In this case, the
AX register will not contain the number of transferred bytes, but the
error code instead. The errors that can be detected by the Read From a
File or Device function are:

5 Access Denied. Check the file handle for a file or device that did not support reading (trying to read from the printer).

6 Invalid Handle. The handle passed to MS-DOS was not the handle of an open file.

The following code shows the Read from a File or Device function being used to implement a block read routine. The target file is an ASCII text file, so it is very effective to read a sector at a time and reconstruct the lines of text in another routine. The parameter that is used to designate the number of characters to be read (CX register value) is also used as an output parameter to return the number of characters actually read (AX register value). The status parameter is an output parameter that returns the error code in the AX register if the Carry flag is set.

Listing 7-3. Read a Block of Records from a File.

```
;
; Read a block from a file
; Procedure BLOCREAD (Handle, Buffer_Addr, Count, Status)
; FRAME:    Val  Handle  : E
;           Ref  Buffer  : C (Segment), A (Offset)
;           Ref  Count   : 8
;           Ref  Status  : 6
;                Ret  : 0
;
BLOCREAD    PROC    FAR
            ASSUME  CS:CODE
            PUBLIC  BLOCREAD
            Push    BP
            Mov     BP,SP
            Push    DS
            Push    DX
            Push    BX
            Mov     BX,[BP+14]              ; get file handle
            Lds     DX,DWORD PTR [BP+10]    ; get buffer addr
            Mov     BP,[BP+8]              ; get addr of count
            Mov     CX,[BP]                ; get char count
            Mov     AH,3FH                 ; read from a file
            Int     21H                    ; DOS function call
            Pop     BX
            Pop     DX
            Pop     DS
            Mov     BP,SP                  ; reestablish addr of stack
```

Listing 7-3. Continued

```
            Push    AX              ; save count/error code
            Jc      STAT            ; if CARRY set, then error
            Sub     AL,AL           ; no error set status to 0
    STAT:   Mov     BP,[BP+6]       ; get addr of status word
            Mov     [BP],AL         ; save status
            Pop     AX              ; bring back count
            Mov     BP,SP           ; find stack again
            Mov     BP,[BP+8]       ; get addr of count var
            Mov     [BP],AX         ; return actual count
            Pop     BP
            Ret     10
    BLOCREAD ENDP
```

Write to a File or Device

Function: Hex 40

Registers: BX = File handle

CX = Number of bytes to write

DS:DX = Address of buffer with data to write

AX = Number of bytes actually written

Errors: 5, 6

The purpose of the *Write to a File or Device* function is to move bytes from a buffer to an external file or peripheral device. This single function replaces the several different writing functions (sequential, random, block, and character string) of MS-DOS 1.1.

The file or device is identified through the handle identifier. For writing to peripheral devices, MS-DOS has permanently assigned the following handles to these devices:

1 Standard Output Device. This device is normally the console monitor, but it may be redirected to write characters to other devices and files.

2 Standard Error Output Device. This device is normally the console monitor. It may not be redirected to other devices and files.

3 Standard Auxiliary Device. This device is usually the communications processor.

4 Standard Printer Device. This device is usually the first printer.

The opened file or device is identified by its file handle, which is passed to MS-DOS in the BX register.

As in the Read from a File or Device function, the application program must provide its own buffer. The contents of this buffer are written to the file or device starting at the address in the DS:DX register pair.

The number of bytes to be written is placed into the CX register. This byte count can represent:

- the number of valid bytes in the buffer to be written to a device;
- the number of bytes in the file's record size; or
- the number of bytes in the application program's buffer.

The actual number of bytes transferred will not exceed the count in the CX register, but could possibly be less than the CX register count. This should be considered as an error condition. For example, if the disk is physically filled during a writing operation, not all of the bytes will be transferred to the disk, making the actual transfer count less than the requested transfer count. All correct write operations should successfully move all of the bytes to the output media.

If there is an error condition detected during the file or device write operation, the Carry bit in the Flag register will be set. In this case, the AX register will not contain the number of transferred bytes, but the error code instead. The errors that can be detected by the Write to a File or Device function are:

5 Access Denied. Check the file handle for a file or device that did not support writing (read-only file or trying to write to the keyboard).

6 Invalid Handle. The handle passed to MS-DOS was not the handle of an open file.

The following code shows the Write to a File or Device function being used to implement a block write routine. The target file is an ASCII text file, so it is very effective to write a sector or block at a time, rather than a character at a time. The parameter that is used to designate the number of characters to be written (CX register value) is also used as an output parameter to return the number of characters actually moved (AX register value). The status parameter is an output parameter that returns the error code in the AX register if the Carry flag is set.

Listing 7-4. Write a Block of Records to a File.

```
;
; Write a block to a file
; Procedure BLOCWRIT (Handle, Buffer_Addr, Count, Status)
; FRAME:       Val  Handle  : E
;              Ref  Buffer  : C (Segment), A (Offset)
;              Ref  Count   : 8
;              Ref  Status  : 6
;                   Ret     : 0
;
BLOCWRIT     PROC     FAR
             ASSUME   CS:CODE
             PUBLIC   BLOCWRIT
             Push     BP
             Mov      BP,SP
             Push     DS
             Push     DX
             Push     BX
             Mov      BX,[BP+14]          ; get file handle
             Lds      DX,DWORD PTR [BP+10] ; get buffer addr
             Mov      BP,[BP+8]           ; get addr of count
             Mov      CX,[BP]             ; get char count
             Mov      AH,40H              ; write to a file
             Int      21H                 ; DOS function call
             Pop      BX
             Pop      DX
             Pop      DS
             Mov      BP,SP               ; reestablish addr of stack
             Push     AX                  ; save count/error code
             Jc       ST                  ; if CARRY set, then error
             Sub      AL,AL               ; no error set status to 0
ST:          Mov      BP,[BP+6]           ; get addr of status word
             Mov      [BP],AL             ; save status
             Pop      AX                  ; bring back count
             Mov      BP,SP               ; find stack again
             Mov      BP,[BP+8]           ; get addr of count var
             Mov      [BP],AX             ; return actual count
             Pop      BP
             Ret      10
BLOCWRIT     ENDP
```

Delete a File from a Specified Directory

Function: Hex 41

Registers: DS:DX = Address of ASCIIZ pathname

Errors: 2, 5

The purpose of the *Delete a File from a Specified Directory* function is to remove a file entry from a directory or subdirectory. The identity of the file is the ASCIIZ pathname addressed by the DS:DX register pair. The file must not be open (have an associated file handle).

If there is an error condition detected while the file is being deleted, the Carry bit in the Flag register will be set. In this case, the AX register will contain an error code. The errors that can be detected by the Delete a File from a Specified Directory function are:

2 File Not Found. Check the spelling of the components of the pathname and check for a binary zero byte at the end of the name.

5 Access Denied. Check the pathname for a file that is read-only or a subdirectory.

The following assembly language subroutine illustrates the deletion of a file using this function when the pathname is passed from a Pascal program:

```
;
; Remove a file from a directory
; Procedure DISCARD (pathname)
; FRAME    Ref Pathname : 8 (segment), 6 (offset)
;                Ret        : 0
;
DISCARD   PROC    FAR
          ASSUME  CS:CODE
          PUBLIC  DISCARD
          Push    BP
          Mov     BP,SP
          Push    DS
          Lds     DX,DWORD PTR [BP+6]   ; addr of pathname
          Mov     AH,41H                ; delete this file
```

```
            Int     21H
            Pop     DS
            Pop     BP
            Ret     4
DISCARD     ENDP
```

Move File Read/Write Pointer

> **Function:** Hex 42

> **Registers:** BX = File handle
>
> CX:DX = Offset (in bytes)
>
> AL = Pointer move method
>
> DX:AX = New location after move

> **Errors:** 1, 6

In MS-DOS 2.0, the requirement for an FCB has been eliminated. However, with that elimination, the ability to set the random-record field of the FCB, giving a random I/O capability to a file, was also eliminated. Random movement through a file is a basic computing requirement, so the capability had to be offered in another form. The purpose of the *Move File Read/Write Pointer* is to give random file capabilities to the read and write functions. The file to be randomly accessed is identified through its file handle which is placed into the BX register. The file must be open.

There are three methods of moving through a file with this function. The method of movement is set into the AL register. The movement types are:

AL = 0   The file pointer is moved to a position CX:DX bytes from the beginning of the file.

AL = 1   The file pointer is moved to a position CX:DX bytes beyond the current position of the file pointer.

AL = 2   The file pointer is moved to a position CX:DX bytes beyond the end of the file. This move is ideal for appending data to the end of the file.

The number of bytes to move is set into the CX:DX register pair. The byte count is a 32-bit number where the CX register contains the most significant word, and the DX register has the least significant word.

When the function returns, the current position of the file pointer (relative to the beginning of the file) is in the DX:AX register pair (DX has the most significant word).

If there is an error condition detected when the file pointer is being moved, the Carry bit in the Flag register will be set. In this case, the AX register will contain an error code. The errors that can be detected by the Move File Read/Write Pointer function are:

1 Invalid Function. Check that the movement method value placed in the AL register was either 0, 1, or 2.

6 Invalid Handle. The handle passed to MS-DOS was not the handle of an open file.

The following code sequence shows the steps for using this function to position the file pointer in preparation for appending data to the file. The assumption is made that the file is an ASCII text file and the end-of-file character is at the end of the file. The offset position is set to −1 so that the end-of-file character is deleted from the file.

Listing 7-5. Prepare File to Append Records.

```
;
; Procedure APPEND (Handle)
; Set up File Pointer to Append at End of File
; FRAME:   Handle  : 6
;          Ret     : 0
;
APPEND  PROC    FAR
        ASSUME  CS:CODE
        PUBLIC  APPEND
        Push    BP
        Mov     BP,SP
        Push    BX
        Push    DX
;
; method 1
;
        Mov     BX,[BP+6]  ; get handle
        Mov     CX,-1      ; set relative position of
        Mov     DX,-1      ; a minus one
        Mov     AL,2       ; relative to end of file
        Mov     AH,42H     ; move file pointer
        Mov     21H        ; DOS Does it
;
; end of method 1
```

Listing 7-5. Continued

```
        ;
                Pop     DX
                Pop     BX
                Pop     BP
                Ret     2
        APPEND  ENDP
        ;
        ; method 2
        ;
                Mov     BX,[BP+6]   ; get handle
                Mov     CX,0        ; set pointer to end of file
                Mov     DX,0        ; with no offset
                Mov     AL,2        ; relative to end of file
                Mov     AH,42H      ; move file pointer
                Mov     21H         ; DOS Does it
                                    ; returns length of file
                Mov     CX,DX       ; register shuffle
                Mov     DX,AX       ;
                Dec     DX          ; calculate a length of one less
                                    ; than length of file (over write EOF)
                Jnc     READY       ; borrow required from CX?
                Dec     CX
        READY:  Mov     AL,0        ; position file relative to beginning
                Mov     AH,42H      ; move file marker
                Int     21H
        ;
        ; end of method 2
        ;
```

Change File Attribute

Function: Hex 43

Registers: AL = Function code

DS:DX = Address of ASCIIZ pathname

CX = New file attribute

Errors: 3, 5

The purpose of the *Change File Attribute* function is to set or retrieve the attributes of a file. The identity of the file is the ASCIIZ pathname addressed by the DS:DX register pair.

The function code in the AL register controls the set or retrieve action of the function. When the AL register is set to zero, the Change File Attribute function returns the file's attribute byte in the CX register. Setting the AL register to one, the attribute value in the CX register is assigned to the file.

This function could be used to give a file the read-only attribute after it had been filled with data.

Each bit in the file attribute byte has a certain significance. The bits are defined in the Create a File function description. When a program is setting the file's attributes, it would be wise to read the attribute byte first, add or delete the appropriate attribute(s), and then reset the attribute byte with this function. In this way, you will preserve the attributes that are not of interest to you.

If there is an error condition detected while the attribute is being read or written, the Carry bit in the Flag register will be set. In this case, the AX register will contain an error code. The errors that can be detected by the Change File Attribute function are:

1 Invalid Function. Check that the access value placed in the AL register was either a 0 or a 1.

3 Path Not Found. Check the spelling of the components of the pathname, and check for a binary zero byte at the end of the name.

5 Access Denied. Check the attribute byte in CX for an attribute that cannot be changed (such as subdirectory or volume name attributes).

I/O Control of Devices

Function: Hex 44

Registers: BX = File Handle

AL = Function value

CX = Number of bytes to be transferred

AX = Number of bytes actually transferred

DX = Returned device information

Errors: 1, 6, 13

The purpose of the *I/O Control of Devices* system call is to allow a program to pass controlling signals to a device and receive status reports from a device. The contents of the AL register controls the action of this system call.

Some functions have restrictions on using a disk file's handle. The functions that allow the use of a disk file handle are numbers 0, 6, and 7, and there is a note in each description restating this restriction.

The values that can be set into the AL register are:

Hex 0 Get device information.   The information word on a device (BX = file or device handle) is returned in the DX register. The format of the device information word is detailed in the following paragraph. Although this function is designed for getting information about a device channel, it can be used for a regular file.

Hex 1 Set device information.   Initial information about a device can be set with this function. Once again, the BX register is loaded with the file handle of the device. The device information word is set in the DX register. In MS-DOS 2.0, the DH register must be set to zero. The DL register is set according to the format of the device information word.

Hex 2 Read bytes from the device control channel.   This function involves the reading of the current controlling configuration of a device. It is not a function that reads data from a device. Use the Read from a File or Device system call for data transfer to a file or device. For instance, if a communications (aux:) device was being controlled by a device driver, this function might be used (depending upon the action of the device driver) to read the current baud, bits per character, and parity statuses. On a video device driver, this function might return the current cursor position, cursor style, or type of graphics being used.

Prior to calling this function, set the CX register to the number of bytes to be read. Set the DS:DX register pair to the address of the buffer that will receive the control bytes from the device driver routine.

Upon return from this function, the AX register will contain the number of characters actually passed by the driver. However, if an error has occurred (the Carry flag is set to 1), the AX register then contains the error code.

Hex 3 Write bytes to the device control channel.   This function is the complement of function 2; it writes bytes of control information to the device driver. Once again, these are control bytes for the control of the device, and not data bytes to be handled by the device. Use the Write to a File or Device system call for data transfer to a file or device. Using the communications driver example again, this function might be used to change the configuration of the communications processor, change the baud, stop bit count, or parity checking scheme.

As in the reading function, the CX, DS and DX registers are used. Set the CX register to the number of bytes to be transferred from a buffer that contains the control sequences. The DS:DX register pair are then set to the address of this buffer.

When this function returns control to the application program, the AX register will contain the number of characters actually accepted by the driver. However, if an error has occurred (the Carry flag is set to 1), the AX register then contains the error code.

Hex 4 Read bytes from a disk drive control channel.   This function is essentially the same as function 2, except that this function is tailored for reading control bytes from a disk drive. With one exception, the register set up is identical to function 2. The exception is: Use the disk drive identifier in the BX register instead of the file or device handle. Setting BX to zero will cause the default drive to be accessed. Otherwise, set the drive identifier in BX (1 = drive A, 2 = drive B, etc.).

Hex 5 Write bytes to a disk drive control channel.   This function is essentially the same as function 2, except that this function is designed for writing control bytes to a disk drive. Once again, use the disk drive identifier in the BX register instead of the file or device handle. Setting BX to zero will cause the default drive to be accessed. Otherwise, set the drive identifier in BX (1 = drive A, 2 = drive B, etc.).

Hex 6 Get input status.   This function permits an application program to check whether a device or file is ready to receive input data bytes. The AL register will contain a Boolean ready/not ready code. When a device is ready, the AL register will contain Hex FF (TRUE) and Hex 00 (FALSE) when the device is not ready. The device driver software makes the appropriate checks and returns the code. Although this function is designed for getting status information about a device channel, it can be used for a regular file.

Hex 7 Get output status.   This function is the complement to function 6 and permits a program to check whether or not a device has a data byte that is ready to be passed to the calling program. The same Boolean values are returned by the device driver. Although this function is designed for getting status information about a device channel, it can be used for a regular file with the device driver returning a Hex 00 (Not Ready) code when the file has reached the end-of-file marker.

Hex 8 Removable media.   This function was added in MS-DOS 3.0. This function permits a program to check whether or not the media type of a device is removable (hard disk versus floppy disk). Place the device designator in question into the BL register. Upon return from the function, the AX register will be set with the status code. If the AX register is set to zero, then the device has removable media. A value of one indicates a fixed media. An error has occurred if the value is Hex FF, indicating that the device designator in the BL register was not valid.

Hex 9 Location of device.   This function was added in MS-DOS 3.1. This function permits a program to check whether a device is a local device or a device on the network. Place the device designator in question into the BL register. Upon return from the function, the DX register will be set with the status code. If the device is local, then the DX register will be set with the attribute word from the device header. If bit 12 is set, the device is on the network. Bit 12 is undefined in the normal attribute word.

Hex 0A Location of Handle.   This function was added in MS-DOS 3.1. This function permits a program to check whether a handle is a reference to a local device or a device on the network. Place the handle into the BX register. Upon return from the function, the DX register will be set with the status code. If the handle is local, then the DX register will be set with the attribute word from the device header. If bit 15 is set, the device is on the network.

Hex 0B Retry control.   This function was added in MS-DOS 3.1. This function permits a program to control the number of retries and amount of delay time that should be attempted when a network or shared device is found to be busy. The number of retries to be attempted is placed in the DX register. The delay time between retries is a count for a loop to be executed to waste time. The count for the loop is placed into the CX register.

MS-DOS default values are a delay of one and retries three times. If your program is expecting to run into busy conditions, reset these values for more successful access.

Hex 0E Check drive assignment.   This function was added in MS-DOS 3.2. This function permits a program to determine whether a block device is being referenced as several logical device names. The number of the drive in question is placed into the BL register. When this function returns, a drive number is carried in the AL register. If the value of the AL register is zero, then only one logical device name is assigned to the drive. If the result is not a zero, the number in the register represents the highest device number assigned to the physical device.

Hex 0F Set logical drive. This function was added in MS-DOS 3.2. This function permits a program to get the next available logical device number and have it assigned to a physical device.

An example of using two logical devices with a single physical device is when MS-DOS is copying files from one diskette to another on systems with a single floppy drive. By prompting you to change diskettes, MS-DOS keeps the diskettes straight because you are swapping them back and forth.

This function removes the need for MS-DOS to prompt for diskettes to be inserted into the drive by assigning a second logical device to the device.

Place the physical drive number in the BL register. The assigned device number is returned in the AL register.

The device information functions use a special word format so that the device driver and an application program can agree on the limits of the driver's capability. This device information word is defined in 16 bits (to fit the DX register). The definitions of these bits are:

ISCIN 0 Console Input Device. This bit is set to one if the device driver controls the standard input device (usually the keyboard, but this can be redirected). This bit is valid only when ISDEV = 1.

ISCOT 1 Console Output Device. This bit is set to one if the device driver is to control the standard output device. The standard output device is usually the video monitor, but the output can be redirected to another device or file. This bit is valid only when ISDEV = 1.

ISNUL 2 Null Device. This bit is set to one if the device driver is either not present or the program wants all of the output to be dumped to the *bit bucket*. This bit is valid only when ISDEV = 1.

ISCLK 3 Clock Device. This bit is set to one to designate the device driver for the system calendar and clock. This bit is valid only when IS-DEV = 1.

SPECL 4 Special Device.   This bit is set to one if this is a special device. This bit is valid only when ISDEV = 1.

RAW 5 Raw/Cooked Mode.   When this bit is set, the device is placed into *raw mode*. This means that all characters will be read and/or written without special processing. The transfers will be in *binary mode*. Characters that may have special meanings (in particular, end-of-file and linefeed) are not to be processed (cooked) by the device driver, but passed as-is in the data stream. Placing a device driver into *cooked mode* allows the device to handle the special character sequences. The end-of-file character (Ctrl-Z) can cause an end-of-file condition. The linefeed character can be expanded to a linefeed and carriage return combination. This bit is valid only when ISDEV = 1.

EOF 6 END-OF-FILE.

ISDEV = 1: When this bit is set to zero, the end of the input stream has been reached.

ISDEV = 0: This bit is set to zero if the channel has been written.

Notice that the descriptions for bits 0–5 are valid if ISDEV = 1. When ISDEV = 0, those bits are used to identify the block (disk) device. A block device driver can control a number of disk drives, so it is necessary to name the channel that was written (0 = A, 1 = B, etc. This is not the same as the drive designations in functions 4 and 5).

ISDEV 7 Device or File Switch.   When the bit is set to one, the associated handle refers to a device channel. When the bit is set to zero, then the handle is a file handle.

RESERVED 8 through 13

CTRL 14 Control String Processing.   If this bit is set by the device driver to one, the device can process the control strings used with functions 2 and 3. If the bit is set to zero, then the control bytes will be ignored. This bit is valid only when ISDEV = 1 and cannot be set through function 1. The device driver must set this bit during its initialization phase.

RESERVED 15   Specific information about writing device drivers can be found in Chapter 12, Device Drivers.

Duplicate a File Handle

Function: Hex 45

Registers: BX = File handle to be duplicated

AX = Duplicated file handle

Errors: 4, 6

The *Duplicate of a Handle* function is a system call that can be used to perform I/O redirection or to copy the characteristics of a device or file to several other handles. The purpose of this function is to request MS-DOS to produce a second handle that refers to the same file or device as an existing handle. The handle of the existing file is passed to MS-DOS through the BX register. The duplicate handle is returned in the AX register.

MS-DOS uses this function to link the standard output device (handle 1) to the standard error device (handle 2). Since the error output device is a duplicate of the original, it cannot be redirected, whereas, the original can.

The next function, Force a Duplicate of a Handle, is the function that causes the actual redirection of I/O from the standard input and output devices to another file.

The utility of the Duplicate a File Handle function is apparently in duplicating the characteristics of a handle before the redirection so the characteristics may be recovered after the redirection is complete. The following narrative will give you an idea of the processes involved:

- Duplicate the handle of the standard input device (save standard input handle characteristics).
- Force standard input device handle to file handle (standard input device handle is closed).
- Perform task with I/O redirection.
- Close file handle.
- Force standard input handle to duplicated handle (restore standard input device).
- Close duplicate handle.

If there is an error detected during the duplication of the handle, the Carry bit in the Flag register will be set. In this case, the AX register will not contain a handle, but the error code instead. The errors that can be detected by the Duplicate of a Handle function are:

4 Too Many Open Files. MS-DOS is handling its maximum number of open files and there are no more available file handles.

6 Invalid Handle. The handle passed to MS-DOS in the BX register was not the handle of an open file.

Force a Duplicate of a Handle

Function: Hex 46

Registers: BX = Original file handle

CX = Second file handle

Errors: 6

The *Force a Duplicate of a Handle* function is a system call that can be used to perform I/O redirection. The purpose of this function is to cause a specific file handle to track with another handle.

For example, one portion of a program may create a data file and establish an associated file handle. This data file can be used to generate input to another portion of the program or to another task that uses the standard input handle of 0001.

Using the Force a Duplicate of a Handle to set the standard input device to track with the input from the file, the second portion of the program can read from the standard input device using the standard input handle, but the source of the input has been redirected to the data file, reading it instead of waiting for input from the keyboard.

When the redirected handle causes a change in the logical positioning in the data file, the internal structure of the original handle will be changed also.

To use this function, the BX register is loaded with the handle of the open file to be duplicated. The CX register is loaded with the handle of the device or file that should track the original file. If the second handle is associated with an open file, the file is closed, disassociating the handle from the file.

If an error is detected during the handle duplication, the Carry bit in the Flag register will be set. In this case, the AX register will contain the error code. The errors that can be detected by the Force a Duplicate of a Handle function are:

4 Too Many Open Files. MS-DOS is handling its maximum number of open files and there are no more available file handles.

6 Invalid Handle. The handle passed to MS-DOS was not the handle of an open file.

The scenario of duplicating a file handle for redirection can be condensed into the following design narrative:

- Open a file for writing.
- Write to file with data for later input phase.
- Close the file.
- Open the file for reading.
- Force the standard input handle to duplicate the file's handle.
- Call routine that reads from standard input, or
- Load and execute a task that reads standard input.
- Close the file.

Create Unique File

Function: Hex 5A

Registers: DS:DX = Pointer to pathname

CX = Attributes

DS:DX = Pathname with filename appended

This function was added in MS-DOS 3.0. In several programming contexts, it becomes necessary to build files that will be read later in the same process and destroyed before the program terminates. Naturally enough, these files are referred to as *temporary files*. One of the problems of creating temporary files is creating a temporary name. Since a temporary name must be a legal name, there is a chance, no matter how slight, that the name may already be in use in the file system. If this was the case, then it is possible to destroy valuable data by opening such a file and writing temporary data into it.

The purpose of the *Create Unique File* function is to generate a filename that is perfectly safe, being unique from any filename in a particular directory.

Prepare for this function by building a pathname in a buffer. MS-DOS will be adding up to 12 characters to this pathname, so allow enough characters in your data structure to accommodate the addition. This pathname must be an ASCIIZ string. The last character before the byte of binary zeroes should be a backslash. Put the address of the buffer into the DS:DX register pair.

It is assumed that there will be some characters in the initial string indicating the pathname to the file. You might suppose that if you had the binary zeroes in the first byte of the structure that the file would be in the current directory.

Select the attributes that you have assigned to the file, and set the binary encoded attributes into the CX register.

MS-DOS will generate a unique filename, and check the directory for this name. If a file exists for this name, MS-DOS will modify the filename and try again. It will continue generating names and checking the directory until it finds one that does not exist. It sort of reminds me of *Rumpelstiltskin* in reverse.

When control is returned to your program from MS-DOS, the unique filename will be found in the prepared buffer. The file will have been created on the disk for you.

Since this function was added in MS-DOS, error codes are handled through the Get Extended Error function.

Create New File

Function: Hex 5B

Registers: DS:DX = Pointer to pathname

CX = Attributes

This function was added in MS-DOS 3.0. It has been added so that a safe way of creating files would be available. If you will remember in the function, Create a File, if the file already existed when the creation was attempted, then the file length was effectively set to zero, destroying the data in the file. This is not always good.

The purpose of the *Create New File* function is to modify the Create a File function so that if a file already exists, no action is taken and an error code is generated to tell you about it. All other aspects of this function are identical to function Hex 3C, Create a File.

The name of the file, with its path (if applicable), is an ASCIIZ string. Put the address of the filename into the DS:DX register pair. Load the CX register with the binary encoded value of the file attributes that you wish to assign to this file.

Since this is a function added in MS-DOS 3.0, error codes are handled through the Get Extended Error function.

Lock/Unlock File Access

Function: Hex 5C

Registers: AL = Lock or unlock command
BX = File handle
CX = Offset high
DX = Offset low
SI = Length high
DI = Length low

This function was added in MS-DOS 3.0. In an environment where several processes could conceivably access the same data from a disk file, it is often necessary to prevent those other processes from changing data in the middle of a critical computation. This usually occurs when you are interested in updating some fast-changing data. Errors will creep in and multiply like wildfire in a heavily accessed file. For instance, if Program A read a record from a public file and started a long process on it, it is possible for Program B to read the same data record, make a fast modification, and rewrite the record. Now, is Program A using the most up-to-date and correct data? It was when it read the record. But it is not, after the modification. What happens when Program A rewrites the record?

Record and file locking helps to prevent this situation.

Is this situation present on an MS-DOS machine? With networking gaining more momentum, the answer is yes.

How about the terminate and stay resident programs in the computer? It is certainly possible to stop a task with a resident editor or debugger, change a data record, and restart the task. Then the change takes on the same problems as the scenario above.

The purpose of the *Lock/Unlock File Access* function is to allow a program to protect certain portions of a file while it alone accesses and processes the data.

To lock a file, the AL register is set to zero prior to using this function. All that is required beyond this is to specify which file is to be locked and what region in the file is to receive the locking.

The file handle for the file to be locked is put into the BX register. Obviously, you must have opened the file to get a handle. And opening a file with an FCB won't be acceptable in this instance.

Specifying the portion of the file to be locked is a little trickier. There are two pieces of information to gather here: starting position in the file, and number of bytes to lock.

It is well known that files can easily exceed 64K bytes in length. This makes using single 16-bit registers out of the question. We will need to use register pairs to get 32-bit numbers for this exercise.

In the CX:DX register pair, set the starting position of the locked region. This value will be a byte offset from the beginning of the file. The CX register gets the most significant portion of the number. The DX register gets the least significant 16 bits. If you are interested in locking a particular record in a binary data file, this number could be calculated from a record number multiplied by the record size to get the offset.

The length of the locked area is placed into the SI:DI register pair. The SI register receives the most significant 16 bits of the length. Remember to set this register to zero if the length is less than 64K. For locking individual records, these registers would always be set to the length of an individual record.

Locking beyond the end of the file is not an error. It may actually be useful to lock past the end of file, if you are going to add to the file or write a random record, expanding the size of the file. You may want to reserve a certain random record location by locking it. You may lock several regions in the same file.

With the successful completion of the MS-DOS function, the records are locked against access from other tasks.

Having locked a file, it is best that you immediately process the required data, update it, and unlock the file. There may be others waiting to use it.

To unlock a region in a file, you prepare the registers in the same manner as you did for locking a region. Since it is possible to lock several areas of a file, you will need to specify which area is being unlocked.

But there is one difference: Set the AL register to one to indicate an unlock operation to MS-DOS.

Do not close a file with locked areas. The references indicate that the results are *undefined*. That word, *undefined*, can be a catchall for all kinds of situations; none of which are good.

Since this is a function that was added in MS-DOS 3.0, error codes are returned through the Get Extended Error function whenever the Carry bit is set.

Set Handle Count

Function: Hex 67

Registers: CX = Number of open files allowed

This function was added in MS-DOS 3.3. The purpose of *Set Handle Count* is to instruct MS-DOS to allow more than the 20 open files, which is the normal maximum. When this function is used, MS-DOS builds a temporary table for the size specified in the CX register and copies the current handle values to it. This table exists only for the process that initiates the call, and presumable, spawned processes. When the initiating process terminates, MS-DOS reverts to the original number of allowable open file handles.

The maximum number of files that can be specified by this function is 64K, the largest number that can be put into a 16-bit register.

This function solves the problem of writing a program that is very intense in its file manipulation, only to have it fail because the user has never set the "FILES =" command in CONFIG.SYS to a reasonable value. With Set Handle Count, the program can perform the equivalent operation without the user having to worry about editing files.

Since this is a function added after MS-DOS 3.0, error codes are handled through the Get Extended Error function. It is possible to get a "Not enough memory" error when the table is being established.

Commit File

Function: Hex 68

Register: BX = File handle

This function was added in MS-DOS 3.3. In the normal flow of operations in MS-DOS, the final buffer is written to a file when the file is closed. File sizes are also calculated and set into the directory at that time. For a system in a network, the information in a file buffer may be very timely and its presence in the physical file may be important for the operation of other systems on the network. The solution in the past was to close and open the file to force the data to the disk.

The purpose of the Commit File function is to bypass the closing and opening of files to force buffers to be written. This function will cause all buffered data for a file to be written to the disk immediately.

Since this is a function added since MS-DOS 3.0, error codes are handled through the Get Extended Error function.

Chapter 8

MS-DOS Memory Management

INTRODUCTION

The topic of this chapter is the memory management functions first appearing in MS-DOS 2.0. This group of functions allows a program to conservatively manage its memory so that it has enough room to operate, load program overlays, and manipulate large data structures, yet leave enough room for starting other tasks. When a program or task is started with MS-DOS, all of the available memory in the system is allocated for the program, starting at its beginning address to the highest user address in the machine. That is, memory reserved for the BIOS, MS-DOS resident code, and any previously executing (and still resident) tasks is not available. Once a program is running, it can manipulate its unused memory through these memory management functions.

MEMORY MANAGEMENT FUNCTIONS

The outstanding feature of memory management functions is the ability to easily load and start the execution of another task. With proper planning, this could provide the support to load and control the execution of several small tasks at the same time.

The functions covered in this chapter are:

Hex 48	Allocate memory
Hex 49	Free allocated memory
Hex 4A	Modify allocated memory blocks
Hex 4B	Load or execute a program

Allocate Memory

Function: Hex 48

Registers: BX = Number of paragraphs requested

AX:00 = Address of allocated memory

Errors: 7, 8

The purpose of the *Allocate Memory* function is to acquire blocks of memory that had been previously released to MS-DOS. Since all of the available memory in the system was allocated to the task when it was loaded, the Allocate Memory function would not be used by the task when it is initially starting and needing to establish some data areas. Rather, this function will allow a program to reclaim memory that was released so that another task could be started. Now that the other program has completed its job, the current program can get back some memory for working space.

To use the Allocate Memory function, the BX register must contain the number of memory *paragraphs* that the program is requesting. Paragraphs are blocks of 16 bytes, where the address of the first byte in the block is evenly divisible by 16.

When the function returns and there were no errors detected, the AX register will contain the paragraph number. If an error was detected (the Carry flag is set), then the AX register will contain either a 7 (memory control blocks destroyed) or an 8 (insufficient memory).

The following code sequence will request 20 blocks (320 bytes) of memory from the DOS:

```
        Mov   BX,20       ; want 20 blocks
        Mov   AH,48H      ; get memory
        Int   21H         ; call DOS
        Jnc   GOTMEM      ; error = carry set
;
;     error handling
;
GOTMEM: Mov   ES,AX       ; set extra segment to new block
```

Free Allocated Memory

Function: Hex 49

Registers: ES = Segment of memory to be returned

Errors: 7, 9

The purpose of the *Free Allocated Memory* function is to release a segment of memory to MS-DOS. Since all of the available memory in the system was allocated to the task when it was loaded, the Free Allocated Memory function would have to be called by the task before requesting that another task or program be loaded above it in memory.

To use the Free Allocated Memory function, the ES register is loaded with the paragraph number at the start of the segment to be released. All allocated memory from that paragraph to the end of the allocated memory block will be released to the MS-DOS memory pool.

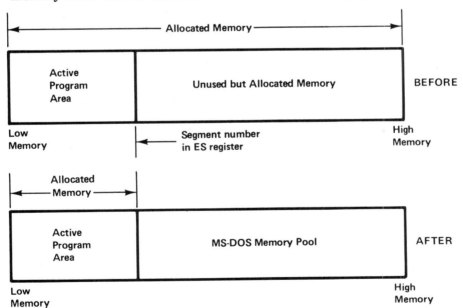

Figure 8-1. Result of Free Allocated Memory.

If an error was detected (the Carry flag is set), then the AX register will contain either a 7 (memory control blocks destroyed) or a 9 (invalid memory block address).

Modify Allocated Memory Blocks

Function: Hex 4A

Registers: ES = Segment of block

BX = New requested size (in paragraphs)

Errors: 7, 8, 9

The purpose of the *Modify Allocated Memory Blocks* function is to provide a smoother interface to the memory allocation functions. This function allows the block of allocated memory to grow and shrink as conditions require. The Allocate Memory function would return the address of the new memory and, given a segment number, the Free Allocated Memory function would remove the segment from the program's allocated memory allotment. This function does not require as much manipulation of addresses and segments. Based upon an established segment, this function requests that memory be appended to the segment or deleted from the end of the segment.

To use the Free Allocated Memory function, the ES register is loaded with the paragraph number of the allocated segment. The BX register should be loaded with the number of paragraphs to be added (positive value) or deleted (negative value).

If an error is detected (Carry flag = 1), then the AX register will contain either a 7 (memory control blocks destroyed), an 8 (insufficient memory), or a 9 (invalid memory block address). If a "growth" request is made and an error occurs, the BX register will return with the value of the maximum allowable block size.

The following code sequence requests 120 paragraphs of memory. If it doesn't receive that many, the program will request whatever it can get.

```
          Assume   ES:NEWSEG
          Mov      BX,120      ; want 120 blocks
ASK:      Mov      AH,4AH      ; grow memory
          Int      21H         ; call DOS
```

```
        Jnc     GOTMEM          ; error = carry set
        Cmp     AX,9            ; check for 'insufficient memory'
        Je      ASK             ; yes...go and ask again
;
;   other error processing
;

GOTMEM:
```

Load or Execute a Program

Function: Hex 4B

Registers: DS:DX = Address of pathname

ES:BX = Parameter block

AL = Command for function

Errors: 1, 2, 5, 8, 10, 11

The purpose of the *Load or Execute a Program* function is to allow a program to read another program's object code from a file, load the object code into memory and, optionally, start its execution.

The loader command is selected and placed into the AL register. The AH register contains the MS-DOS command (Hex 4B). The commands are:

AL = 0 Load and start execution of program

AL = 3 Load overlay

The name of the file to be loaded is contained in pathname form (with a byte of zero at the end of the pathname). The DS:DX register pair must contain the address of the pathname.

Each of the loader commands requires a different parameter block. The ES:BX register pair must contain the address of the parameter block. The parameter block contains information for performing the load. This information includes: the address of the load, relocation offsets, command line messages to be left for the new program, and addresses of default FCBs in the Program Segment Prefix (PSP).

When the command is to load and execute a program, the parameter block is defined as shown in Table 8-1.

Table 8-1. Parameter Block for Load and Execute.

Word	Meaning
0	Segment address of environment string
1–2	Address (Segment:offset) of command line for PSP
3–4	Address (Segment:offset) of first default FCB for PSP
5–6	Address (Segment:offset) of second default FCB for PSP

When the command is to load an overlay, the parameter block is defined as shown in Table 8-2.

Table 8-2. Parameter Block for Overlay.

Word	Meaning
0	Segment address where overlay is to be loaded
1	Relocation factor for relocatable code

Let's take a look at each of the parameters that are needed for this system call. In most instances, the parameters are pieces of data that will appear in the Program Segment Prefix of the new program.

Address of Environment

MS-DOS provides an area in memory, known as the *environment*, which contains a list of strings. These strings define the MS-DOS command processor prompt, set the value of various system switches, and give the user a place to rename lengthy pathname segments with a shorter synonym. This collection is the current environment of the operating system. The environment strings are ASCIIZ strings (characters followed by a byte of binary zeroes), with the ASCII information usually in the form of:

```
parameter = value
```

The location of the environment is passed from program to program so that all programs will know where it is. By passing the address, it also becomes possible to define a custom environment and pass its address in place of the system environment.

The current environment's address is at offset Hex 2C in the Program Segment Prefix of the active program. The value at that offset will automatically be passed to the new program if the environment parameter is set to zero. However, if you wish to designate a new environment, make sure that it starts on a paragraph (segment) boundary. The paragraph number is the value of the parameter for the loader system call.

Address of Command Line

Several programs require certain information to be passed as part of the command line. For instance, to run a specific program in BASIC, the command line might be:

```
MYPROC THISFILE-T
```

The name of the data file to be processed is not a necessary part of loading and starting the processing program MYPROC, but rather is used by the MYPROC program in knowing which data file is to be read and processed. The -T may be a switch for the program to activate a feature, like a procedure *trace*. This parameter is your chance to provide this command line text to the new program. The program segment prefix allows 128 bytes for the command line, so the loader will probably move 128 bytes from the address that gets passed into the PSP.

It is hoped that the new program knows what to do with your command line. The accepted method is to include an initial byte, which will be placed at Hex 80 in the PSP, with the length of the following character string, and then include a carriage return character (decimal 13, Hex 0D) at the end of the valid command line so that the new program can tell where the end of the string is.

The parameter for the command string is an address in the "segment:offset" form.

Addresses of FCBs

As in the case of the command line, some programs require file specifications as input information. One example is a sorting program. A sort utility program could be passed to the File Control Block of the file to be sorted with the results going into a second file described in another FCB.

The Program Segment Prefix has space reserved for two unopened File Control Blocks. The parameters to the loader system call provide for these two FCBs. The address of each is placed into the parameter block.

In the case of file handles, all open files, addressed by their handles, are passed to the new program. This feature allows the current program to establish the standard input, output, and printer files, causing the new program to follow the same file structure. For instance, the current program can create a disk file and before starting the new process, redirect the standard input to that file. Now the new program will think that it's getting information from the standard input (the keyboard), but in reality, be reading a disk file and processing that information.

Segment for Loading

The overlay loader is used to read object code from a file and place it into a specific location in memory. The purpose of the overlay is to provide a temporary segment of program that can be executed as a part of an executing program, and then easily replaced by another overlay with its own purpose. This allows very large programs, broken into overlays, to be executed in very limited areas.

This parameter is the paragraph (segment) number of the memory area where the overlay should be placed. Getting the segment address can be retrieved and placed into the parameter block with the following code:

```
mov ax,seg overlay1
mov es:[bx],ax
```

Relocation Factor

In the case of an overlay, the program segment would have been built independently from the main program. This means that it has no knowledge of the values and offsets of the segment and index registers. This also means that some of the offsets in the overlay need to be modified (relocated) so that their addresses are valid. Not much information is available in the reference material on how to calculate this relocation factor. Following the spirit of MS-DOS, three good guesses would be:

1. Use a value of zero.

2. Use the current value of the Code Segment (CS) register.

3. Use the Code Segment address where the program is being loaded.

This concludes the description of the loader system call, but there are some other things you should know.

When a program is loaded, it is assigned all of the free memory in the machine. If this program is going to spawn other programs, it has to make sure that the memory is available. This is possible by freeing the unused memory with the Free Allocated Memory (Hex 49) or the Modify Allocated Memory Blocks system calls.

The loader mechanism is located in the COMMAND.COM system program. It resides at the high addresses of memory. It is possible to cover COMMAND.COM with your program and destroy the loader process. This isn't serious. However, when you invoke the loader with this system call, MS-DOS will reload COMMAND.COM so that the loader will be present. This reload will damage your program (a maximum of 1,536 bytes). If the current program has overlaid COMMAND.COM and assumed control of the memory with the Allocate Memory system call, MS-DOS will return an error message stating that there was insufficient memory to load COMMAND.COM and the loader.

Chapter 9

Expanded Error Handling

INTRODUCTION

Depending upon which version of MS-DOS you are working with, you can expect a variety of error reporting techniques. In MS-DOS 1.0 and 1.1, an error was usually reported as a nonzero value in the AL register. MS-DOS 2.0 and 2.1 got more sophisticated with more specific error codes that described the cause of the reported error condition.

The directory, device driver, and file-oriented functions of MS-DOS 2.0 provide a status code for the operation. These status codes are returned in the AL register. The codes are only valid if the Carry flag is set. Otherwise, the AX register may contain certain pieces of data being returned from the function, such as a handle identification number. Using the JC (Jump on Carry) and JNC (Jump on No Carry) instructions, the programmer can direct the program flow through the proper error handlers or data collection routines. The programming examples in the chapters that covered these functions illustrated the technique for detecting the error conditions.

ERROR-HANDLING FUNCTION

In the error code listing that is shown in the Get Extended Error function, error codes 1 through 18 are the original MS-DOS 2.0 error codes. These numbers are valid whether you are using MS-DOS 2.0 or 3.0.

MS-DOS version 3.0 introduced even further sophistication to error handling with extended error reporting. These are discussed with the function Get Extended Error.

177

Get Extended Error

Function: Hex 59

Registers: BX = MS-DOS version
AX = Extended code
BH = Error class
BL = Suggested action
CH = Locus

This system call was added in MS-DOS 3.0. The purpose of the *Get Extended Error* function is to return further detailed information about any error conditions that occur in a call to an MS-DOS function. In earlier versions of MS-DOS, error codes were either returned in the AH register when the Carry flag was set, or a value of Hex FF in the AL register indicated a nonspecific error. MS-DOS 3.0 introduced an extended set of error codes, plus processing information that could be used by the application program to interpret and recover from the condition.

When an error occurs during a call to MS-DOS, the Carry flag will be set upon return to the calling program. This can be detected with a JC (Jump on Carry) assembly instruction following the request call to MS-DOS. Instead of finding the error in the AH register, the Get Extended Error function should be immediately called.

Errors that are indicated by Hex FF in the AL register should be ignored, and the extended error code sought with this function.

The Get Extended Error function will return the extended code in the AX register.

The BH register will contain a *class* number for the error. The class of the error gives some indication of the severity and type of error that has occurred.

The BL register will contain a *suggested action* value. This number can be used by the application to help determine some sequence of steps to be taken to correct or evade the error.

The CH register contains a *locus* value. This value tells the application the category of device in which the error occurred.

The extended error codes are shown in Table 9-1 (with their Microsoft names).

Table 9-1. Error Codes

Error Code	Code Name
1	Invalid Function Number
2	File Not Found
3	Path Not Found
4	Too Many Open Files (No Handles Left)
5	Access Denied
6	Invalid Handle
7	Memory Control Blocks Destroyed
8	Insufficient Memory
9	Invalid Memory Block Address
10	Invalid Environment
11	Invalid Format
12	Invalid Access Code
13	Invalid Data
14	Reserved
15	Invalid Drive Was Specified
16	Attempt to Remove the Current Directory
17	Not Same Device
18	No More Files
19	Attempt to Write on Write-Protected Diskette
20	Unknown Unit
21	Drive Not Ready
22	Unknown Command
23	Data Error (CRC)
24	Bad Request Structure Length
25	Seek Error
26	Unknown Media Type
27	Sector Not Found
28	Printer Out of Paper
29	Write Fault
30	Read Fault
31	General Failure
32	Sharing Violation
33	Lock Violation
34	Invalid Disk Change
35	FCB Unavailable
36	Sharing Buffer Overflow
37–49	Reserved
50	Network Request Not Supported
51	Remote Computer Not Listening
52	Duplicate Name on Network
53	Network Name Not Found
54	Network Busy
55	Network Device No Longer Exists
56	Net BIOS Command Limit Exceeded

Table 9-1. Continued

Error Code	Code Name
57	Network Adapter Hardware Error
58	Incorrect Response From Network
59	Unexpected Network Error
60	Incompatible Remote Adaptor
61	Print Queue Full
62	Not Enough Space for Print File
63	Print File Was Deleted
64	Network Name Was Deleted
65	Access Denied
66	Network Device Type Incorrect
67	Network Name Not Found
68	Network Name Limit Exceeded
69	Net BIOS Session Limit Exceeded
70	Temporarily Paused
71	Network Request Not Accepted
72	Print or Disk Redirection Is Paused
73–79	Reserved
80	File Exists
81	Reserved
82	Cannot Make Directory Entry
83	Fail on INT 24h
84	Too Many Redirections
85	Duplicate Redirection
86	Invalid Password
87	Invalid Parameter
88	Network Device Fault

The error classes being returned from MS-DOS are:

1 Out of Resource

2 Temporary Situation   Not an error condition, but a condition which should change with time

3 Authorization

4 Internal Error in the System Software   You may have found a software bug with this one.

5 Hardware Failure Has Occurred   This does not indicate a software error.

6 System Failure Has Occurred   This is a serious internal error not caused by user software.

7 Application Program Error Guess which one is reported the most.

8 Not Found A requested file or device was not found.

9 Bad Format A file or device is of an invalid format or style, which makes it unsuitable for use.

10 Locked File or device has a locked condition attached to it.

11 Media Failure Bad sector or wrong disk was found.

12 Already Exists Creation of an item that already exists.

13 Unknown None of the above.
The severity of the error can suggest various actions that can be taken by the application program to clear the situation. MS-DOS returns a code in the BL register as an action to be taken for the particular error. The action codes are:

1 Retry Attempt function again, since the condition may be temporary. Alert user if there is an error after several attempts. User may elect to abort the task.

2 Delay Retry Pause before attempting the function again. This may occur when a file or device is locked and the passage of time will clear the condition. Alert the user if the error persists after several attempts to determine further action.

3 User Error resulted from input that may have originated with the user. Attempt to get the user to reenter the data. If the program was the originator of the data, you may have to apply some artificial intelligence or take evasive action.

4 Abort Halt the execution of the task immediately with normal cleanup of files and handles. The task cannot proceed, but the internals of the operating system have not been damaged and can take control.

5 Immediate Exit Halt the execution of the task immediately, but without intermediate cleanups.

6 Ignore

7 Retry After User Intervention There is some action that the user can perform that needs to be done before attempting the function again. This might be changing a disk or turning on the modem.

The value returned in the CH gives a general description of the device type causing the error. This value may be of some help when taking the action prescribed by MS-DOS. The locus values are:

1 Unknown

2 Block Device

3 Network

4 Serial Device

5 Memory

Chapter 10

Network Management

INTRODUCTION

MS-DOS 3.0 brings extensions into IBM networking facilities. The functions of the network management functions are based upon the IBM PC Network Program. This program, or one that is compatible to it, must be installed for these functions to operate. With the variety of networking hardware available, it remains to be seen whether these functions gain any popularity in application software.

A networking system affords users at computers on the network the opportunity to share resources found on the other machines. These resources would include files and printers, thereby allowing the community to share data or use the proper printer for a document. That is, a dot matrix printer on one machine could be used to produce draft copies of a document, while final copies could be generated on a laser printer in another part of the office.

One of the changes that becomes apparent when machines are in a network and resources are to be shared is that name or location of a device or file becomes more than the familiar pathname. A way is needed to designate whether a file or device is on the local machine or on the network. This is done by adding the name of a remote machine to the pathname. Pathnames in this network situation are similar to pathnames where all files are on a single machine except a network pathname includes the name of the machine to which the remainder of the pathname is to be applied. A machine name in a path is prefixed with double backslashes. It cannot contain a colon. A network pathname might look something like this:

```
\\groucho\project\readme.doc
```

NETWORK MANAGEMENT FUNCTIONS

The functions in Network Management are:

Hex 5E00 Get machine name
Hex 5E02 Set printer setup
Hex 5E03 Get printer setup
Hex 5F02 Get redirection list entry
Hex 5F03 Redirect device
Hex 5F04 Cancel redirection

Get Machine Name

Function: Hex 5E00

Registers: DS:DX = Pointer to buffer to receive name

CH = Name indicator

CL = NETBIOS name number

This function is a network-oriented function added in MS-DOS 3.1. The purpose of *Get Machine Name* is to return the ASCIIZ string name of the local computer in the network.

The name of the computer will be returned as a 15-byte string, terminated by a byte of binary zero. Place the address of the buffer to receive this string into the DS:DX register pair.

Upon return, if the computer has been assigned a name, the name will be in the buffer whose address was passed to MS-DOS. The CX register should be checked first to indicate the validity of what you find in the string buffer.

If the CH register is zero, then no name has been assigned to the local computer. A nonzero value indicates that a name has been supplied and a NETBIOS number has been assigned to the computer name. This number is supplied in the CL register.

If the Carry flag is set, use the Get Extended Error function to get further guidance for handling the error condition.

Notice that the function number for this function and those that follow is shown as four hexadecimal numbers. In other functions, it has been customary to load the AH register with the function code, and a minor operation code in the AL register. For the network-oriented functions, the entire function number is loaded into the AX register, with no discrimination between major function number and minor operation.

The leading numerals are shared among several somewhat unrelated functions. The functions starting with Hex 5E are hardware network functions. Network redirection functions start with Hex 5F.

Set Printer Setup

> **Function:** Hex 5E02
>
> **Registers:** BX = Redirection list index
>
> CX = Length of setup command string
>
> DS:SI = Pointer to setup command string

This function is a network-oriented function added in MS-DOS 3.1. In a networking situation, one printer may be used by several users who are working at several work stations. This keeps the printer busy and allows everyone to keep working while their reports and listings are being printed.

The problem that presents itself is that one person may want the printer to be configured in one manner, while another person may want something completely different. These differences might be in typeface settings (condensed, expanded, etc.), margins, or quality (rough copy or final draft). The printer will have to be sent a setup command string to make these changes before each printing session. These strings are not always embedded into the text to be printed, so an outside source of setup commands must be used to properly set up the printer for each user's needs.

The purpose of *Set Printer Setup* is to allow the declaration of a printer setup command string for a particular user on the network. This string would be the ASCII character sequence, which should be sent to the printer so that it will configure itself for proper printing.

The command string is placed into a buffer with the calling program. This is not an ASCIIZ string, but will probably have ASCII characters.

Put the address of the string buffer into the DS:SI register pair. Load the CX register with the character count of the buffer.

Load the BX register with the redirection index for the printer that this setup command string is to be assigned. You can find this number with the Get Redirection List Entry function. This value is a more or less temporary handle to the network printer. Since the number can change as redirections are made and canceled, use the Get Redirection List Entry immediately before using the Set Printer Setup function.

Notice that the function code for this function is 16 bits long and is loaded into the AX register as a single value.

If the Carry flag is set up on return from MS-DOS, use Get Extended Error function for the specific error conditions.

Get Printer Setup

> **Function:** Hex 5E03
>
> **Registers:** BX = Redirection list index
>
> ES:DI = Pointer to setup command buffer
>
> CX = Length of setup string

This function is a network-oriented function added in MS-DOS 3.1. The purpose of the *Get Printer Setup* function is to retrieve the printer setup command string that was declared by the *Set Printer Setup* function (Hex 5E02).

Use of this function follows the setup of function Hex 5E02.

The receiving buffer should be large enough to hold the 64 characters that this function is capable of generating. Place the address of the buffer into the ES:DI register pair. This register pair is used, since the buffer will be the destination of a string transfer.

Load the BX register with the redirection index for the target printer. This number is found with the Get Redirection List Index function. Once again, call the redirection function immediately prior to the Get Printer Setup so that the number is current.

The setup string is returned in the designated buffer. The CX register contains the number of valid characters placed into the buffer.

Notice that the function code for this function is 16 bits long and is loaded into the AX register as a single value.

If the Carry flag is set upon return from MS-DOS, use the Get Extended Error function for the specific error conditions.

Get Redirection List Entry

> **Function:** Hex 5F02
>
> **Registers:** BX = Redirection index (0 is first entry)
>
> DS:SI = Pointer to local device name (128 byte maximum)
>
> ES:DI = Pointer to network name (128 byte maximum)
>
> BH (return) = Device Status Flag
>
> BL (return) = Device Type
>
> CX = Stored parameter value

This function is a network-oriented function added in MS-DOS 3.1. The purpose of the *Get Redirection List Entry* function is to retrieve network redirection information for a particular assignment by its index number. That is, given an index number, this function will provide local and network names for devices and files.

The function is called with the requested index number in the BX register. To find a particular device or file in the list, start the BX register at zero and increment it until you find the entry or the end-of-list error is encountered (Get Extended Error code 18).

Supply pointers to buffers so that you receive the local device name and network name in the DS:SI (local device name) and ES:DI (network name) register pairs.

The function returns with the names in the addressed buffers.

The function also uses other registers to report its activity. The BH register is used to indicate validity of the request. A zero in the first bit of the BH register indicates that the device is valid. A one in this bit indicates that the device is not valid.

For a valid device, the BL register holds the device type. The device type indicates a printer (BL = 3) or a file device (BL = 4).

The CX register is supposed to contain a parameter value that was to be set at redirection time. But since the recommended (mandatory) value

for this parameter is zero, it should come as no surprise to you to find a
zero in this register.

Get Redirection List Entry openly acknowledges the fact that it destroys the DX and BP registers. Beware.

Error conditions arising from the use of this function can be investi-
gated through the Get Extended Error function. The error for end-of-list
is 18. This should be an expected condition.

As was seen in the printer setup functions, the index number is required to assign strings to a printer. The printer name was probably
known, but the redirection index wasn't. This function is used to find the
index.

The following scenario could be used to provide that service. The strategy in this sequence is to use brute force and try every index value until
we find the one that matches the printer name.

```
Listing 10-1. Design for Retrieving
Redirection Information.


  Input Parameter  : Pointer to Local Name of Printer
  Output Parameter : Redirection Index


  Load BX register with zero
  Set DS:SI with address of buffer for returned local name
  Loop:
   Set ES:DI with address of buffer for returned network name
   Push BX register (function changes BX)
   Push DX register (function destroys DX)
   Push BP register (function destroys BP)
   Call Get Redirection List Entry
   Pop BP
   Pop DX
   If CARRY is set - error condition
  Call Get Extended Error (error 18 = end of list)
  Exit Loop
   Endif
   If returned BX indicates valid entry
  Set ES:DI with address of passed local printer name
  Compare redirection printer name with passed name
  If match,
   Pop BX
   Return value in BX as index of printer
  Endif
   Endif
```

```
Listing 10-1. Continued

  Pop BX
  Increment BX
EndLoop

Return with invalid printer name error
```

Redirect Device

> **Function:** Hex 5F03
>
> **Registers:** BL = Device type
>
> CX = Value to save for caller
>
> DS:SI = Pointer to SOURCE device name
>
> ES:DI = Pointer to DESTINATION network path

This function is a network-oriented function added in MS-DOS 3.1. The purpose of the *Redirect Device* function is to allow the name of a local device to be used as a reference to another device in a network. All data that would normally flow to or from a local device will be redirected to the device on the network, even though the same device name is used.

For example, you may have a dot matrix printer attached to your computer known as LPT1:. There may be a laser printer on another machine in your local area network. With this function, the name LPT1: can be assigned to the laser printer and the print files redirected to it. This would give you the ability to print rough drafts on a dot matrix printer using the name LPT1:, and then produce a final copy on the laser printer without appearing to change the name of the printer.

To use this function, set the DS:SI register pair to the address of an ASCIIZ string of the local device name. Set the ES:DI register pair to the network path for the redirection. This network path must contain any required passwords needed to gain access to network facilities. The password is an ASCIIZ string that immediately follows the binary zero byte of the network pathname ASCIIZ string. Add a byte of binary zeroes if there is no password.

In the BL register, specify the device type being redirected where:

BL=3 for a printer device

BL=4 for a file device

The CX register is supposed to be used for passing a single value to the device. See Get Redirection List Entry for where this value is accessed. Set the CX register to zero. This is the only value allowed.

Error conditions are indicated by the Carry flag being set upon return from the function. Use the Get Extended Error function to get error information.

Cancel Redirection

Function: Hex 5F04

Registers: DS:SI = Pointer to device name or path

This function is a network-oriented function added in MS-DOS 3.1. The purpose of this function is to remove the network redirection imposed by the Redirect Device function.

The address of the ASCIIZ string with the name of the device whose redirection you wish to cancel and have restored to its local logical assignment is placed in the DS:SI register pair. When the function returns and there is no error condition, the device has to be reassigned to its local assignment.

Disk drives and printers referenced in the cancellation return to their local assignment. If the name in the cancellation is a machine on the network, then the association between the local computer and the named computer is terminated.

Chapter 11

MS-DOS Interrupts

INTRODUCTION

Not all of the functions of MS-DOS are available through the INT 21H software interrupt call. Some of the most primitive functions are available to the programmer through other software interrupts. These functions consist of low-level operations that are used to build the more complex functions already described. Therefore, use of these functions may bypass some checks and bookkeeping that we would normally take for granted. You take upon yourself some extra responsibilities when using these functions. For instance, the disk I/O functions can allow some very creative programs, but you will find yourself outside of the normal file structure of MS-DOS. This means that you must be very careful or you could find out that your program has reorganized the directory and file allocation tables.

There are two types of entries in the portion of the interrupt vector table that is associated with MS-DOS functions. The first type is the normal interrupt vectoring address. This address is the entry point to a routine that accomplishes a specific task. These types of software interrupts are:

Int 20 Program terminate

Int 21 Function request

Int 25 Absolute disk read

Int 26 Absolute disk write

Int 27 Terminate but remain resident

INTERRUPT VECTORS

Two interrupt vectors are available to the programmer for the creation of special error-handling circumstances. MS-DOS maintains a backup copy of these interrupt vectors so that if they are changed in one program, the vector addresses can be restored to their original values when the program terminates. These interrupts are:

Int 23 Ctrl-C and Ctrl-Break handler

Int 24 Critical error handler

The other type of software interrupt vector is not a true interrupt vector, but a storage location for an address which MS-DOS will use during its processing. There is only one of these addresses of interest to the programmer that is not an interrupt address:

Int 22 Termination address

Program Terminate

Interrupt: Hex 20

Registers: None

The purpose of the *Program Terminate* interrupt is to provide a method of invoking an orderly termination of a program. This software interrupt accomplishes the same results as the Program Terminate MS-DOS function discussed in an earlier chapter. As in the MS-DOS function, the program is responsible for:

- All changed files must be closed to remain valid.
- Ensure that the original CS register value is set.

MS-DOS will provide the following services when a program is terminated:

- All disk buffers are flushed.
- Error vector addresses are restored.

- Memory is returned to MS-DOS memory management.
- Return program control to the originating program.

Refer to the description of the Program Terminate function for more discussion on the operations of this interrupt. This interrupt is provided for compatibility with programs written for MS-DOS 1.1 and MS-DOS 1.0. If your program is to operate in an MS-DOS 2.0 (or later) environment, use the Terminate a Process function to terminate the program.

Function Request

Interrupt: Hex 21

Registers: AH = Function identifier

The purpose of the *Function Request* interrupt is to initiate the various MS-DOS functions. The descriptions of the MS-DOS functions are found in previous chapters.

Termination Address

Interrupt: Hex 22

Registers: None

The *Termination Address* vector is the one interrupt entry that is a storage location for MS-DOS. This address represents the address where execution of a parent program should resume when a program is terminated. The calling program should set this value before loading and executing another task. When a program is loaded, the address in the Termination Address is placed into the new program's Program Segment Prefix. Upon termination, this address is retrieved from the Program Segment Prefix and control is transferred to that address.

If the parent process is starting a child process, this address is used to determine the return address upon completion of the child process. If the parent process loads this interrupt vector with a terminating address, it will receive control. If the parent process return address is not stored, the return address of the parent's parenting (grandparent) process will be there and *that* address will be used by the child process as a termination address, bypassing the parent process and returning to the grandparent of the child process. The Termination Address can be set to any reasonable address in the calling program.

The Termination Address is set with the MS-DOS function Set Interrupt Vector (function Hex 25).

ERROR-HANDLING INTERRUPTS

Ctrl-C and Ctrl-Break Handler

Interrupt: Hex 23

Registers: None

The purpose of the *Ctrl-C and Ctrl-Break Handler* is to provide whatever services are required when the Ctrl-C or Ctrl-Break keys are pressed during an MS-DOS Character I/O function. This handler can also be invoked during all MS-DOS functions if the Break Check function (function Hex 33) has activated the checking feature (MS-DOS 2.0 or later). This handler is totally user-defined. Programmers may provide their own interrupt Hex 23 Ctrl-C and Ctrl-Break handling routines by providing the necessary routine and setting the interrupt vector to that routine (using the MS-DOS function Hex 25, Set Interrupt Vector). The interrupt vector address that gets destroyed is restored from the program's Program Segment Prefix when it terminates.

Other than startup code and the return to the MS-DOS function that initiated the interrupt, the contents of the handler are left to the discretion of the programmer. The entry to the handler should preserve all of the registers. This allows the programmer to make full use of all MS-DOS functions and the full instruction set of the computer without damaging the environment of the host program. When the handler has completed its tasks, it should restore the register set to its original contents and return to the MS-DOS function through the use of the IRET (return from interrupt) instruction. The entry and exit code might look like this:

```
Push   AX
Push   BX
Push   CX
Push   DX
```

```
Push   SI
Push   DI
Push   BP
Push   DS
Push   ES
;
;   Ctrl-C Handler Code
;
Pop    ES
Pop    DS
Pop    BP
Pop    DI
Pop    SI
Pop    DX
Pop    CX
Pop    BX
Pop    AX
Iret
```

When the Ctrl-C or Ctrl-Break is detected during one of the buffered output functions (Display Output or Buffered I/O), MS-DOS will display the Ctrl-C and return the following three-character string in the buffered I/O buffer.

1. Ctrl-C (binary value of 3)

2. Carriage return (binary value of 13)

3. Linefeed (binary value of 10)

Critical Error Handler

Interrupt: Hex 24

Registers: DI = Error code
AX = Source of error
AL = Action response

The purpose of the *Critical Error Handler* is to present information to the user concerning or make decisions about the state and fate of a program when a serious error occurs. MS-DOS issues software interrupt Hex 24 when an error occurs during the performance of an MS-DOS function (interrupt Hex 21 type). Programmers may provide their own interrupt Hex 24 error-handling routines by providing the necessary routines (built around the information described here) and setting the interrupt vector to that routine (using the MS-DOS function Hex 25, Set Interrupt Vector). The address that gets destroyed is restored from the program's Program Segment Prefix when it terminates.

Information concerning the source of the error is contained in the AX register. Either the source of the error is a disk drive, or it isn't. The most significant bit of the AH register (bit 7) indicates whether a disk drive was involved. If bit 7 is set to 1, then the error is not a disk error. Some versions of MS-DOS show that the only nondisk error is a bad memory image of the File Allocation Table, with no further data available in this case. In other versions of MS-DOS, the DI register contains a specific error code for an error on a character-oriented device (this is normal for disk errors). Refer to the chart below for the meanings of the error codes found in the DI register.

If bit 7 of the AH register is equal to zero (by far the most common condition), then a disk error has occurred. The following information is available for a disk error:

Identity of the drive
Type of operation being performed when error occurred
Specific problem, if known

The offending disk drive is identified in the AL register. The register identifies the drive by its numeric value (0 = drive A, 1 = drive B, etc.).

The type of operation being performed is stored in the AH register. Bit 7 of the AH register will be zero, but the other bits are available for an operation code. The codes are seen in Table 11-1.

Table 11-1. Types of Operations Causing Errors

AH	Operation
0	System file read
1	System file write
2	File Allocation Table read
3	File Allocation Table write
4	Directory read
5	Directory write
6	Data area read
7	Data area write

Appropriate responses can be retrieved from bits 3 through 5 of the AH register. The value in these bits represents your range of valid choices. The action to the error is put into the AL register. For any of these responses, a zero in the bit means that the response is not valid. A one in the bit indicates a valid response.

Table 11-2. Valid Response.

Bit	Response
3	FAIL (Abort)
4	RETRY
5	IGNORE

The DI register contains more information about the error. Some of the error codes can be used to diagnose nondisk errors.

Table 11-3. Specific Error Conditions.

DI	Error Condition
Hex 0	Attempt to write on a write-protected diskette
Hex 1	Unknown unit
Hex 2	Drive not ready
Hex 3	Unknown command
Hex 4	Data error
Hex 5	Bad request structure length
Hex 6	SEEK error
Hex 7	Unknown media type
Hex 8	Sector not found
Hex 9	Printer out of paper
Hex A	Write fault
Hex B	Read fault
Hex C	General failure

This information is sent to the critical error-handling routine so that an intelligent decision can be made about continuing the progress of the program. The error handler may communicate with the user through the character I/O functions. The use of other functions should be avoided.

There are several options that can be followed after a decision is made. The easiest route is to let MS-DOS handle the situation. By placing a code number into the AL register and returning control to MS-DOS with an IRET (return from interrupt) instruction, MS-DOS will handle the situation. All of the registers are set to operate in this manner (preserve the values of the SS, SP, DS, ES, BX, CX, and DX registers if you are going to do some intermediate processing). All you have to do is decide the course of action. Setting the AL register determines the action. The available actions are:

AL = 0 Ignore the error.

AL = 1 Retry the operation.

AL = 2 Terminate the program (issue INT 23H).

Another alternative is to handle the error within the error-handler and, having recovered from the error, return to the command processor or the offending program. When the error has been successfully handled by your process, the system stack must be restored to its state when the original call to MS-DOS through an INT 21H was made. The structure of the stack (disregarding any additions made by the error handler) appears as:

Table 11-4. Structure of the Stack for Error Handler.

Stack Contents	Origin	Action
IP	INT 24h call	Discard
CS	INT 24h call	Discard
Flags	INT 24h call	Discard
AX	User's register from INT 21H	Pop to AX
BX	User's register from INT 21H	Pop to BX
CX	User's register from INT 21H	Pop to CX
DX	User's register from INT 21H	Pop to DX
SI	User's register from INT 21H	Pop to SI
DI	User's register from INT 21H	Pop to DI
BP	User's register from INT 21H	Pop to BP
DS	User's register from INT 21H	Pop to DS
ES	User's register from INT 21H	Pop to ES
IP	User's register from INT 21H	Pops with IRET
CS	User's register from INT 21H	Pops with IRET
Flags	User's register from INT 21H	Pops with IRET

Performing a POP instruction on all but the last three instructions puts your handler in a position to return to the caller's program with an IRET (return from interrupt) instruction. MS-DOS references suggest that MS-DOS will be slightly unstable until a noncharacter I/O function is used. Presumably, when the I/O function is called, MS-DOS makes some corrections.

Absolute Disk Read

> **Interrupt:** Hex 25
>
> **Registers:** AL = Drive number
> CX = Number of sectors to read
> DX = Beginning logical sector number
> DS:BX = Buffer address

The purpose of *Absolute Disk Read* interrupt is to read full sectors of data to a specific track and sector on a disk. The target sectors of this reading interrupt do not have to be a member of a particular file. This interrupt allows a program to freely read any sector on the disk. This interrupt and the complementary Absolute Disk Write interrupt can be used for some of the following tasks:

- Disk-to-disk copy routines
  read sector(s) from source disk
  write sector(s) to destination disk
- Sector-by-sector byte-level editor
  read a sector
  display contents in hexadecimal and ASCII
  allow changes to sector contents
  write modified sector
- Reconstruct lost files
  read sector with directory entry for lost file
  read File Allocation Table
  use sector editor to find sectors of lost file
  link sector numbers in File Allocation Table
  enter first sector in directory entry
  update file size in directory entry
  write File Allocation Table to disk
  write directory sector to disk

The Absolute Disk Read interrupt causes whole sectors to be read from a particular disk drive and placed into a program-specified buffer.

The AL register contains the identifier of the source disk drive. This interrupt does not search the MS-DOS data structures to find out which disk drive is the default drive, so the program must be sure of what it is doing. This interrupt is expecting the identifiers: 0 = drive A, 1 = drive B, and so on.

The particular sector on the disk is selected by the DX register. The sectors on the disk are numbered (starting at zero). The entire first side (read/write head 0) is numbered, and then the entire second side (for a double-sided diskette) is numbered. This allows easy access to a single-sided disk, where all of the sectors correspond to the first side of a double-sided disk. If the numbering changed sides with every new disk track (for instance, sectors 0 through 7 are on the first side; sectors 8 through 15 are on the second side), there would be all kinds of decoding problems when a single-sided disk was being copied.

The receiving buffer must be a whole multiple of the sector size. If the sector is 512 bytes, then the buffer must be 512, 1,024, 1,536, 2,048, and so on, bytes in length. The DS:BX register pair holds the address of the receiving buffer.

The CX register contains the number of whole sectors that the buffer can hold, and this is the number that MS-DOS will use to determine how many sectors should be transferred to the calling program's buffer.

Be sure that all of the important user registers (nonsegment registers) are saved. This interrupt uses all of the registers and will not save or restore their values.

The flag register will be saved on the stack. This is the normal operation of a software interrupt. However, the flag register will not be restored when the interrupt is finished. The flag register will still be on the stack (don't forget to pop the flags from the stack). The flag register that is current may contain flag settings that indicate error conditions.

Upon return from this interrupt, if the Carry bit in the flag register is zero, then the read operation was successful. If the Carry bit in the flag register is set to one, then an error has occurred and an error code is to be found in both the AL and the AH registers. The AL register will contain the MS-DOS error code. This code is the same as the error codes used in the Critical Error Handler interrupt. The AX register will contain one of the following error codes:

Hex 80 Attachment failed to respond

Hex 40 SEEK operation failed

Hex 20 Controller failure

Hex 10 Bad CRC on diskette read

Hex 08 DMA overrun on operation

Hex 04 Requested sector not found

Hex 03 Write attempt on write-protected diskette

Hex 02 Address mark not found

Hex 00 Error other than those listed

Absolute Disk Write

Interrupt: Hex 26

Registers: AL = Drive number
CX = Number of sectors to read
DX = Beginning logical sector number
DS:BX = Buffer address

The purpose of the *Absolute Disk Write* interrupt is to write full sectors of data to a specific track and sector on a disk. This interrupt is identical to the *Absolute Disk Read* interrupt, except that this interrupt writes a buffer to the disk instead of reading from the disk.

Terminate But Remain Resident

Interrupt: Hex 27

Registers: DX = Segment number of returned memory

The purpose of the *Terminate But Remain Resident* interrupt is to terminate the execution of a program but leave the program's data and instructions in memory. This interrupt provides all of the services of INT 20H and the *Program Termination* function, except that the memory that the program occupies is not returned to MS-DOS. The program becomes a semipermanent member of the system's environment.

When a program is loaded, it is given the responsibility of owning all of the free memory in the machine. Upon terminating, the gracious thing to do is return the unused portion to MS-DOS. This is done by loading the DX register with the segment number of the first segment following the resident part of the program. This can be accomplished with the following code:

```
;
; want to discard everything beyond this point
;
LAST:   Mov DX,Segment LAST   ; last segment in program
        Inc DX                ; first unused segment
        Int 27H               ; bye!
;
; End of program
;
```

This interrupt is provided for compatibility with programs written for MS-DOS 1.1 and MS-DOS 1.0. If your program is to operate in an MS-DOS 2.0 (or later) environment, use the *Terminate and Remain Resident* (Hex 31) function to terminate the program.

CAVEATS

Do not use this interrupt for terminating .EXE type programs that have been loaded into high memory. Not much is said about why this interrupt should not be used, but we can guess at the reasons: (1) Being at the upper end of memory, there is no memory to release upon terminating and all of the memory could be tied up in the program. (2) The command processor (COMMAND.COM) resides at the very top of the user's memory. COMMAND.COM might use the memory itself for data storage and disk transfer areas. If a program is resident there, COMMAND.COM may destroy parts of the program, leaving it worthless (if not dangerous to the rest of the system).

Using this interrupt to permanently install a Ctrl-C or Ctrl-Break handler or critical error-handler is not advised. When this termination interrupt is executed, it restores these handler addresses in the interrupt vector table. This means that the addresses of these new routines are virtually lost. How does anyone (easily) know where the routines are?

This interrupt is capable of creating a resident program with a maximum size of 64K. The Terminate and Remain Resident function should be used for programs of larger sizes.

Chapter 12

Device Drivers

INTRODUCTION

In the previous chapter the primary method of identifying files and devices was through their handles. Using the MS-DOS functions in that chapter, a programmer is able to get input data from and put output data into a file or device with a minimum of programming complexity. The need and ability to read and write files is fairly obvious, but what are these things called *devices* and *device drivers*? This chapter will explain the nature, use, and creation of devices and device drivers.

WHAT IS A DEVICE DRIVER?

To understand the reasons for having device drivers, let's review some of the philosophy of operating systems. An operating system is a collection of software tools that allows application software to take advantage of the computer's resources without having to understand the programming details.

An operating system should provide a standard interface ("environment") so that software that executes on one system will correctly execute on another system with the same operating system (assuming that all file and device operations are conducted by the operating system).

An operating system should provide an application program with uniform interfaces to all of the files and devices on the system. With uniform device interfaces, it is a simple matter to *redirect* the input and output functions of a program. For instance, if a program is written to exploit the uniform interfaces to files and devices through handles, modifying the handle number could change the source of input characters for the console keyboard to a communications port to a text file. Since the interface is identical, the only thing to change is the identification of the source with the handle.

Operating systems are tailored to the computer's hardware configuration. To present a common ground to the application programs, the operating system must account for the configuration differences. For instance, the specific version of MS-DOS that runs on the IBM PC will not work on a Victor 9000. The programs will *see* the same operating system, but the underlying hardware requires that there be two versions of MS-DOS.

The operating system can't possibly account for all of the available hardware configurations and peripheral devices. Each peripheral device requires specific software to support its operation. There are a number of companies that manufacture peripheral devices and there are some cracks. An operating system can't be expected to provide all of this support.

A device driver is a hardware-configuration dependent software tool that controls a peripheral device and presents that control to the application program environment with the operating system's standard interface. The device driver becomes part of the operating system. Since the device driver is hardware-dependent, moving the driver from one system to another similar system could require some minor changes to account for the hardware differences.

SOME USES FOR A DEVICE DRIVER

A device driver can be developed for any peripheral hardware device (or software function) that is used by an application. This statement applies to added devices (joysticks for games, graphic boards, etc.) and standard devices (console keyboard, communications hardware, etc.). If you think that the keyboard is being handled incorrectly for your application, perhaps you want to adapt the keyboard handler to a nonstandard key layout or a foreign keyboard. Then you can replace the standard keyboard handler with your own keyboard driver.

MS-DOS provides these services with drivers that you may choose to replace:

CON: console input (keyboard)

CON: console output (monitor)

AUX: auxiliary I/O (communications)

PRN: standard printer output

Device drivers are developed to provide a service through an established interface. The data passed to and from the device may be unique to the device, but the method of obtaining that data must be standard. The following list of potential device drivers will give you an idea of the number of things that can be accomplished. Some of these drivers will require special hardware (graphics processor or clock/calendar board), but others can be used with an average hardware configuration. These ideas are intended to give creative inspiration:

- Interrupt-driven communications software
- Hardware clock/calendar interface
- Interrupt-driven (background) print spooler
- Random number generator (software device)
- RAM pseudo-disk (software device)
- Interface to external graphics processor
- Special communications protocol handler
- Network interfacing

With the expenditure of some creative energy, you can easily add other device drivers to the list. The important thing is that the driver provides a service through a common interface.

THE STRUCTURE OF THE DEVICE DRIVER

Probably the easiest way to describe all of the functions and structures that are required to create a device driver is to describe each of the integral pieces and their relationships to MS-DOS, the peripheral device, and each other. The major pieces of the device driver and supporting structures are:

- Device header
- MS-DOS request block
- Local pointer to request block
- Strategy code
- Interrupt code

The Device Header

The *device header* is the leading block of information that identifies the device driver. This header occupies the first 18 bytes of the device driver. When a device driver is written (in assembly language), this header is the first group of declarations. The device driver is not a true program, so it will not have a Program Segment Prefix. Therefore, the beginning of the driver should start at relative address zero. For regular programs, the programmer must allow for the PSP and begin the program at offset Hex 100. The fields of the device header are:

Pointer to the next device driver

Driver attributes

Entry address of the strategy code

Entry address of the interrupt code

Name of the device driver

Pointer to the Next Device Driver

When the device drivers are loaded into the computer's memory from the disk, the header blocks of the drivers are linked together to form a chain. Each driver's header contains the address of the next device driver in the chain. If a driver is required to handle a transaction, MS-DOS starts looking for the appropriate driver by checking the name of the first driver in the chain. If it does not find the correct name, MS-DOS gets the address of the next header and continues looking in that header. This searching and skipping continues until either a name match is made or MS-DOS runs out of driver headers to search. In the case of running out of device driver headers, an I/O error exists and an error code ("access denied") is returned to the calling program. To allow room for the chaining address in the header, a double word field is declared for the address. This field should be set to −1 in the original copy of the driver. However, if you are writing several drivers in a single program, the next address field should be set to the relative offset of the next device header in the file. The last header in the file then contains the −1 value, indicating that it is the last driver in the group.

Driver Attributes

A device driver can have several characteristics. The driver attribute word is used to designate some of these characteristics. By setting the various bits in this 16-bit word, you specify the treatment that the driver should receive. Here are the meanings of each of the active bits:

Bit 15 When this bit is set to 1, the device driver is for a block-oriented device. When this bit is cleared to 0, the device driver is a character-oriented device.

Bit 14 By setting this bit to 1, you are telling MS-DOS that this device driver is capable of interpreting or issuing character string commands for better device control. MS-DOS will move these character string commands to and from the driver when the IOCTL operating system function is called.

Bit 13 This is the *non-IBM format* bit. Its setting affects the operation of the build BPB and media check operations. Both of these operations are for block-oriented device drivers. The setting of this bit will be covered in the discussion of these operations.

Bits 5–12 These bits are reserved for later expansion and must be set to zero.

All of the following bit assignments are associated with character devices:

Bit 0 By setting this bit to 1, you designate this device driver as the current *standard input device*. This driver may be a new keyboard handling routine that replaces the MS-DOS-provided routine. Or it might designate an entirely new peripheral as the standard input device (communication board, graphics tablet, electronic mouse, etc.). When this bit is set, this driver overrides the current input device.

Bit 1 By setting this bit to 1, you designate this device driver as the current *standard output device*. You may designate a new set of algorithms for displaying information of the console monitor (the normal standard output device) or direct the output to an entirely different peripheral device (communications board, external graphics processor, logging device, etc.). By separating the declarations of the input and output devices, MS-DOS gives you a chance to control each direction of the data flow. You may designate a device driver as both the standard input and the standard output devices.

Bit 2   This bit is used for designating the NUL device, the *bit bucket*. This device is not available to the programmer for assignment. The bit is in the attribute word as a place-holder for MS-DOS when it designates the NUL device.

Bit 3   By setting this bit to 1, you designate the current clock device for the system. With the abundance of battery-powered clock/calendar boards on the market, it would be foolish to try and provide device drivers within the operating system for all of the clocks. This attribute gives you a chance to customize the clock handler for your specific peripheral clock. It would be a fair assumption that the manufacturer of the board has created this driver (if it is required) and delivered the software driver on a diskette along with the board. This driver will be called whenever one of the clock functions of MS-DOS is called (TIME and DATE). To conform to the system's time and date standards, the time and date should be prepared in the following format:

Bytes 0–1   DATE—The number of days since January 1, 1980.

Byte 2   TIME—Minutes

Byte 3   TIME—Hours

Byte 4   TIME—1/100 Seconds

Byte 5   TIME—Seconds

When the TIME and DATE is read, these six bytes are returned to the operating system. When a write command is issued, the time and date are set from the six bytes sent from the operating system.

Bit 4 Setting this bit to 1 causes the device driver to be labeled as SPECIAL.

Entry Address of the Strategy Code

The purpose of the strategy code will be covered in its own section. However, there is no standard offset from the beginning of the device driver for the start of the strategy code. When MS-DOS is scanning the device headers to find a particular driver and finds it, MS-DOS needs an entry address to the driver's instructions so that it can execute them. This field in the device header gives the offset to the entry of the strategy code. This field is only one word long (most addresses are two words long, a segment and an offset), so the field must contain the offset to the code that must be in the same segment as the header.

Entry Address of the Interrupt Code

The purpose of the interrupt code will be covered in its own section. In the same way as the strategy code entry address, this field in the device header gives the offset to the entry of the interrupt code. This field is also one word long, so the field must contain the offset to the code that must be in the same segment as the header.

Name of the Device Driver

The name of the device driver is placed in the last eight bytes of the device header. For a character-oriented device, this name will be the name that is used to specify the device when transferring data to and from the device during program executions, as in PRN: and CON: filenames in a Pascal program, or MS-DOS utilities, such as the copy utility. For a block-oriented device, only the first byte of the field is used to designate the number of units that the driver can handle. This number is optional since it is filled in, once again, during initialization of the device driver.

Having defined all of the fields of the device header, the actual declaration for a communications handler can be written in assembly language as:

```
           ORG       0
  CODE     SEGMENT   PARAGRAPH
           ASSUME    CS:CODE,DS:NOTHING,ES:NOTHING
  HEADER:
           DD        -1          ; Link field to next device
           DW        8000H       ; Character device
           DW        Strategy    ; Address of strategy code
           DW        Interrupt   ; Address of interrupt code
           DB        'COMM   '   ; Communications handler name
```

The Request Block

The request block is a block of information, formed by MS-DOS, that is used to control the operations of the device driver. MS-DOS passes the request block to the device driver by placing the block's address in the ES:BX register pair. The block has several fields which allow MS-DOS to request actions of and to receive status information from the device driver. The request block for each device operation is slightly different, however the first 13 bytes are standard for each operation. Specific information about the other fields is covered in the discussions on each of the individual operations. The fields for the 13-byte request block header are:

Byte 0   This byte holds the length of the entire request block. This length includes the number of bytes in the request header plus the number of bytes that follow in operation specific fields after the header request block.

Byte 1   This byte identifies the specific unit for which the operation will take place. This byte is meaningful only for block-oriented devices. A block device driver may control several devices. This field identifies which is to be used.

Byte 2   The actual operation to be performed by the device driver is identified in this byte. This command is numeric with a value between 0 and 12. Using this field, the device driver software can index into a *jump table* to find the address of the routine that performs the requested function. The commands are:

0 Initialize the device driver
1 Media check (block-oriented
   devices only)
2 Build BPB
3 IOCTL for input
4 Input
5 Nondestructive input

6 Get input status
7 Flush input
8 Output
9 Output with verify
10 Get output status
11 Flush output
12 IOCTL for output

Bytes 3–4   These bytes represent the status byte of a device driver system. The bits of this two-byte field designate the status of the operation (Done or Not Done, Busy or Not Busy) and whether an error has occurred during the processing. When an error occurs, the device driver uses the lower byte to designate the error number. The definition of the status bits is:

Bit 15   This bit is the Err flag bit. By setting bit 15 to 1, the device driver indicates to MS-DOS and the application program that an error has been detected during processing and an error code is contained in the lower byte of the status word.

Bits 10–14   These bits are reserved by MS-DOS for its own internal use or later expansion.

Bit 9   This bit represents the Busy flag. Its value and interpretation depend upon the operation (input status or output status) that is being requested. This bit is set when a status request (#6 Get input status or #10 Get output status) is made. When an input status request is made, the device driver should set this bit as follows:

0 There are characters in the input buffer and an immediate read request will result in a quick response. MS-DOS assumes that all character-oriented devices have *type-ahead* buffers so that there are characters available when a read is issued.

1 There are no characters in the input buffer and if a read request were to be made at the present time, the calling program would be forced to wait until a character is read from the peripheral device. In most cases, MS-DOS will not issue a read request if this bit is set to one. MS-DOS will continue performing other tasks until a character appears in the buffer and the Busy bit is set to one.

If your device driver does not have a type-ahead buffer, this bit should be set to zero so that MS-DOS will proceed with the read, even though the application program will be forced to wait for the read to be completed. This beats never requesting a read by setting the Busy bit to one.

When an input status request is made, the device driver should set this bit as follows:

0 There is no current output activity at the present time. Any output request would start immediately.

1 There is an output activity currently being handled. Any other output request would be required to either wait or be ignored.

Bit 8   This bit represents the Done flag. This bit is set to one when the device driver completes the requested task. For MS-DOS 2.0, this bit should be set to one when the device driver exits the code. In a multitasking environment (several tasks running at one time), the device driver may receive control and exit several times before the request is completed.

Bits 0–7   This lower byte (eight bits) is used to store the error code when an error is detected and bit 15 (Error flag) is set to one. It is the responsibility of the device driver to set both the Error flag and the error code in the status word. MS-DOS recognizes 13 different error conditions. The error codes and the corresponding codes are:

0 Write protect violation	6 Seek error
1 Unknown unit	7 Unknown media
2 Drive not ready	8 Sector not found
3 Unknown command	9 Printer out of paper
4 CRC error	10 Write fault
5 Bad drive request structure length	11 Read fault
	12 General failure

Bytes 5–8   This field is a double-word area that is used by MS-DOS to store the address of the next request header being handled by MS-DOS. This field should not be altered by the device driver since the next request block may not be a request to the current driver.

Bytes 9–13   This field is a double-word area that may be used by the device driver to link several pending request blocks together. As one request is finished, the next one can be accommodated. For example, a background print spooler might schedule several requests for files to be printed. As the requests arrive, they could be linked to the other pending operations. The actual printing operations would have to be controlled through an interrupt-driven printing routine.

The request block header will not be found at the same place in memory for every request, so the example program segment will not define it as a static data structure, using DB (Define Byte), DW (Define Word) or DD (Define Double word) instructions. Instead, the offsets to the various fields are described as constants with the EQU pseudo-instruction. The offsets are applied to the address passed to the device driver from the operating system. The definition of the request block header is:

```
REQUEST   EQU   0           ; origin of request block
REQLEN    EQU   REQUEST     ; length field = byte 0
REQUNIT   EQU   REQLEN+1    ; driver unit number = byte 1
REQCOMM   EQU   REQUNIT+1   ; command = byte 2
REQSTAT   EQU   REQCOMM+1   ; status word = bytes 3 and 4
DOSLINK   EQU   REQSTAT+2   ; address link for DOS =
                            ; bytes 5,6,7 and 8
REQLINK   EQU   DOSLINK+4   ; address link for device =
                            ; bytes 9,10,11 and 12
```

These values can be added to the base address of the request block (ES:BX register pair) to find the various fields.

Strategy Code

The purpose of the request block is to provide information to the device driver so that the requested function is performed and the correct data is transferred or received. MS-DOS does not send the request block directly to the function. Instead, there are two independent calls to the device driver. The first call (after finding the proper driver through a search of the device headers) is made to the strategy portion of the driver. The entry address to the strategy code is found in the header. The request block is available to the strategy in the SC ES:BX register pair. It is the one and only responsibility of the strategy to capture and save the address of the request block so that the requested function (command field of the request block) can be executed. The code for the strategy portion of the device drive is quite simple and straightforward. The strategy must save the ES and BX registers in a local variable. Since the entire driver is in the same code segment as the header, the variables can be located by the CS register. Typical code for the strategy is:

```
;       The STRATEGY portion of the device driver
;
REQADDR   DD      ?                     ; save area of ES:BX
;
STRAT     PROC    FAR
Strategy:                               ; entry point (address in header)
          Mov     CS:REQADDR,BX         ; Least Significant Word
          Mov     CS:REQADDR+2,ES       ; Most Significant Word
          Ret
STRAT     ENDP
```

Interrupt Code

Immediately following the exit from the strategy code, MS-DOS calls the interrupt portion of the device driver code. There doesn't seem to be any obvious reason for calling this section of the code interrupt, unless entry to this part of the driver is achieved through copying the address to this section from the header block into an interrupt vector address and the corresponding software interrupt generated. Although there are no blocks passed to the interrupt code, the request block contains information that is pertinent to the specified function. This data is stored in the words following the request block header. Details on the exact layout will be covered in the descriptions of the various driver functions. When the interrupt code is entered, the request block (saved by the strategy) is checked for the requested function (command = byte 2). Based upon this value, the proper function is performed. Once again, the functions that can be called are:

0 Init	6 Get input status
1 Media check	7 Flush input
2 Build BPB	8 Output
3 IOCTL for input	9 Output with verify
4 Input	10 Get output status
5 Nondestructive Input	11 Flush output
	12 IOCTL for output

In a pseudo-Pascal narrative, the selection of the proper function is performed in this manner:

```
Save_registers;
Case Request_Block.Command of
```

```
0  : INIT;
1  : MEDIA_CHECK;
2  : BUILD_BPB;
3  : IOCTL_FOR_INPUT;
4  : INPUT;
5  : NON_DESTRUCTIVE_INPUT;
6  : GET_INPUT_STATUS;
7  : FLUSH_INPUT;
8  : OUTPUT;
9  : OUTPUT_WITH_VERIFY;
10 : GET_OUTPUT_STATUS;
11 : FLUSH_OUTPUT;
12 : IOCTL_FOR_OUTPUT;
     End;
     Restore_Registers;
     Return_to_MS_DOS;
```

For an assembly language device driver, a jump table with the entry addresses to the various relevant functions is used to transfer control to the requested function. For any given device driver, it is unlikely that all of the functions will be used. For instance, for a character device, the media check and Build BPB functions are not even valid. So the jump table only has to address the active functions. Unused functions, in case they are requested, should use the exit routine as their entry address. A jump table might look like this:

```
JUMPTBL   LABEL       WORD
   DW     PR_INIT  ; initialize printer
   DW     LEAVE    ; media check not used
   DW     LEAVE    ; build bpb not used
   DW     LEAVE    ; ioctl not used on input
   DW     PR_INPUT ; get list of pending files
   DW     PR_INPUT ; same for non-destruct input
   DW     PR_IN_S  ; input status (always ready)
   DW     LEAVE    ; no input to flush
   DW     PR_OUT   ; add a file name to list
   DW     PR_OUT   ; do same for output w/ verify
   DW     PR_OUT_S ; get printer and list status
   DW     PR_OUT_F ; clear the printer list
   DW     LEAVE    ; ioctl not used on output
```

Initialize (Command = 0)

The *initialization* function of the device driver is called by MS-DOS immediately after the driver is loaded into memory. This function will only be called once. The purpose of the initialization function is to set up any special data areas, initialize addresses and data values, and pass parameters back to MS-DOS about the capabilities of the driver.

The request block, which is sent to the strategy portion of the drive just before this function was called, contains the following fields:

Bytes 0–12   Request block header

Byte 13   Number of units handled by drive (block-oriented devices only)

Bytes 14–17   Ending address for memory recycling

Bytes 18–21   Addresses of array of pointers to device BPB (block-oriented devices only)

The initialization routine prepares the device driver for executing. When the device driver is loaded into memory, it may not be possible to assume the values of some data areas. The initialization function is used to clear buffers and buffer indexes, set counts, and program the programmable hardware devices (communications boards, printers, etc.).

The initialization routine also prepares the operating environment for the device driver. When one of the software routines of the driver is an interrupt handler, the interrupt vector address must be placed into the appropriate address of the vector table, and the interrupt controller hardware must be set to react to those interrupts.

There are two things that the initialization routine must do prior to returning to MS-DOS. One of these things is to set the Done flag (bit 8) in the request header's status word (bytes 3 and 4).

The other chore is to assist MS-DOS's memory management. Technically, the initialization function is going to request MS-DOS to "terminate, but remain resident." This termination is assumed by MS-DOS and should not appear in the initialization function. To properly terminate in this manner, the unused memory must be returned to the MS-DOS memory manager. Normally, a program is given all of the available memory when it is loaded, which it returns when it terminates. However, when a program remains resident in the machine's memory, not all of the memory can be returned (or the program disappears!).

To protect its territory, the device driver must tell MS-DOS where the unused memory starts. The address of this memory boundary is placed in the request block in bytes 14 through 17. Bytes 14 and 15 contain the *offset* of the address, while bytes 16 and 17 contain the *segment* number.

One way to conserve memory resources is to place the code to the initialization routine at the end of the device driver and include its area in the unused memory block. This is done by placing the initialization function entry address into the request block. Using this technique, the memory containing the initialization function, which will never be called again, will be recycled and used in the next driver or as an application program area.

In addition to the preparations shared with a character-oriented device, the block-oriented devices must prepare information concerning the abilities of the device driver for MS-DOS. There are three pieces of information that the driver must provide:

- Number of units that the driver can handle
- Address of BIOS Parameter Block array
- Media descriptor byte

A driver for a block-oriented device may control more than one hardware peripheral. The initialization function must tell MS-DOS how many devices it is going to handle. Since the driver may become resident on machines of various configurations, it may be necessary for the initialization function to check the equipment status word of the host machine before telling MS-DOS what its capabilities are. It is possible that the driver can handle three eight-inch diskette drives, but if the machine only has one eight-inch drive, then MS-DOS should only be told about the single-drive capability.

The number of units that a driver can support is set in the request header in the first byte (offset = 13) after the request block header.

MS-DOS starts assigning logical names to the devices on each driver. The naming starts with *A* and names are assigned sequentially until all of the block-oriented devices are named. For instance, if the next name for a device is *Q* and a driver can support four devices, then the device names are *Q*, *R*, *S*, and *T*. Obviously, the order in which drivers are loaded can affect the names of the logical devices. Keep this in mind when you configure your system with drivers.

Each block-oriented device that is controlled by the device driver will be assigned a BIOS Parameter Block (BPB). The BPB contains parameters for MS-DOS concerning disk sector sizes, number of sectors per track, and directory information. The contents and use of this block will be covered in the *Build BPB function* description.

For the purpose of the initialization phase of the function, however, a BPB should be created that reflects the attributes of the largest media to be used. Since this initial setting of the BPB will affect the size of the buffers used with this driver, the initial request for buffers should be for the maximum that the system will handle. The driver can be written with enough smarts to read the media descriptor byte, thereby allowing the software to determine the nature of the current media and act accordingly.

The device driver must maintain a table of pointers (address offsets) to the BPB of each device. Devices may share a BPB and save memory space by pointing to the same BPB. This table contains a one-word entry for each device. If a driver is handling seven hardware devices, then there will be seven words in this table. Each entry contains an address of a BPB.

Whether the device driver is to control hard disk drives or diskette drives that accept diskettes of various formats (or some other changeable media), MS-DOS provides a means of transferring specific information about a media or device to and from a driver. This allows the software to compensate for various factors. For instance, a single-sided diskette may be replaced by a double-sided diskette on the same drive (same device driver). The device driver must take that fact into consideration when the information of the diskette is accessed. This type of information is available through the media descriptor byte.

The media descriptor byte is maintained by the drivers about each of the block-oriented devices. The media descriptor byte is a field of the BIOS Parameter Block (offset = 20), but the information is also passed in the request block for the Media Check, Build BPB, and the read and write functions. This information is not used by MS-DOS. This byte is merely made available to device drivers so that they will be able to know what type of media is being used on a particular device and modify their actions accordingly. The definition of this byte is:

Bit 0 0 = Not two-sided
       1 = two-sided

Bit 1 0 = Not eight-sectored
       1 = eight-sectored

Bit 2 0 = Not removable
       1 = Removable

All other bits are undefined and set to one.

For the initialization function, the media descriptor byte of the device BPBs should be set to reflect a "good guess" about the media. It will be possible to reliably set the Removable or Not Removable bit. The other bits can be furnished by the *Media Check* and *Build BPB* functions at a later time.

Media Check (Command = 1)

The purpose of the *Media Check* function is to notify MS-DOS whether or not the block-oriented recording media has changed. Notice that this is a block-oriented command.

The request block, which is sent to the strategy portion of the drive just before this function was called, contains the following fields:

Bytes 0–12 Request block header

Byte 13 Media descriptor

Byte 14 Returned media changed response

Bytes 15–16 Pointer to previous volume ID (MS-DOS 3.0 and later)

A change of media occurs when a diskette has been removed from a disk drive and another diskette inserted. Writing to a diskette is not considered a media change. MS-DOS will request a media check to determine whether the diskette's File Allocation Table (FAT) needs to be read into memory before a primary file operation is started. The Media Check function responds with the following values:

−1 The diskette has been changed.

 0 Don't know if the diskette has been changed.

 1 The diskette has not been changed.

To be practical about the whole thing, a safe and easy response would be to always return the IDK (I Don't Know) answer. This will cause MS-DOS to read the FAT frequently, but relieves your function of the responsibility of trying to figure out whether the diskette had been removed. If the disk drive doors cause an interrupt with their openings and closings, you might be able to give a more precise response.

MS-DOS 3.0 and later versions offer additional support for determining a change in media. This support requires that the name of the volume be maintained by the driver. The name of the volume is kept in the root directory of the media. It is indicated by a Hex 08 in byte 11 of the directory record.

Whenever the driver generates a −1 (media changed) result in MS-DOS 3.0, MS-DOS will check the name of the previous volume against the name of the present volume. If the *media changed* result was found to be erroneous, MS-DOS will generate an *invalid disk change* error for the device. It is not obvious what happens if two diskettes containing the same volume name are exchanged, truly changing the media.

If you do not wish to keep track of the volume names of the diskettes being loaded and unloaded in MS-DOS 3.0, use the ASCIIZ string NO NAME as the name of the previous volume ID. This is a name expected by MS-DOS.

Please notice that the only media that concerns this function is the diskette. It is the only removable media with a File Allocation Table. Hard disks and RAM pseudo-disks, with the exception of some of the cartridge disks, can't be changed. Nonchanging media device drivers can always return the *unchanged media* code.

To aid the Media Check in determining its response, the driver should check the media descriptor byte, which is passed in the request block in the byte immediately following the header (offset = 13). By checking the second bit, the Media Check function can decide whether to return the "not changed" code for the Not Removable media or the IDK code for the Removable media.

The request block sent to the Media Check function by MS-DOS contains two extra bytes after the request block header. The first byte (offset = 13) is the media descriptor byte for the media in question. The second byte (offset = 14) is the byte where the Media Check response is to be stored.

The last thing that the Media Check function of the device driver must do is to update the status word in the request block header. The minimum action required here is to set the Done flag. If there is cause to report an error, then the Err flag should be set and the appropriate error code set in the lower byte of the header.

Build BPB (Command = 2)

The *Build BPB* function is applicable for block-oriented devices only. The purpose of this function is to form a BIOS Parameter Block (BPB) from information that is resident on the device's media or synthesized by the device driver itself.

The request block, which is sent to the strategy portion of the driver just before this function is called, contains the following fields:

Bytes 0-12   Request block header

Byte 13   Media descriptor

Bytes 14-17   Address of transfer area

Bytes 18-21   Address of device BPB

The BPB is a table that contains information about the currently active disk media. This table can be formed in two ways. The first way to be discussed is to read the BPB from the *boot sector* of the diskette. The second method of forming the table is for the device driver to create its own BPB. This option would be used when the driver is operating a device with a very limited configuration (e.g., a RAM-based pseudo-disk or a hard disk).

Regardless of which method is used to form the BPB table, the definition of the table's fields remains the same. The fields of the BPB are:

Bytes 0-1   Number of bytes in each sector

Byte 2   Sectors per allocation unit

Bytes 3-4   Number of sectors reserved for use by DOS

Byte 5   Number of File Allocation Tables

Bytes 6-7   Maximum number of root directory entries

Bytes 8-9   Total number of sectors on the media

Byte 10   Media descriptor

Bytes 11-12   Number of sectors per File Allocation Table

Reading the BIOS Parameter Block from the diskette is the most reliable method of forming the BPB to be returned to MS-DOS. Since it was placed on the disk by the FORMAT utility, the disk resident BPB contains the field values that exactly describe the media.

To read the BPB from the media, it is necessary for the device driver to know what the current media is. This is true because the BIOS Parameter Block is located in the boot sector of the disk, which may vary from media type to media type. The boot sector is the first sector on a diskette.

It is read by the ROM (Read Only Memory)-based startup routine when power is applied to the computer. The contents of the boot sector are read into memory and given control of the machine. The code contained in the boot sector completes the loading of the operating system.

This is where the IBM format attribute bit in the device header block is used. If the attribute bit is set to one, the media is not IBM format. In this case, there may not be a boot sector on the diskette and the BPB will have to be created manually. This would happen when the device driver is written to retrieve files from a diskette that was formatted by a different operating system or when eight-inch diskettes are used (MS-DOS formatted eight-inch diskettes do not have a standard boot sector).

When the media is IBM format, the media descriptor can be used to determine where the boot sector is located on the diskette or hard disk.

If there is a reason to suspect the validity of the media descriptor, such as when a diskette may have been changed, the device driver can use another method for determining the media type. One of the parameters of the request block (offset = 14) contains the address to a sector-size buffer. For IBM format media, this buffer holds the first sector of the File Allocation Table (FAT), which may be read, but not modified. The first byte of the FAT is the ID byte, and it is also a media descriptor. Since this byte was set by the format utility, there should be no suspicion about its validity. By the way, for not IBM format media, the buffer can be used as a scratch area.

For a diskette, the boot sector is located in the first sector of track 0 on side 0.

CAUTION: The following information may be only applicable to the IBM PC and compatible machines. For the hard disk, the boot sector is more difficult to find. The first sector on the hard disk contains a boot record and a partition table. A hard disk may be divided into one to four partitions, with each partition acting as an independent disk. Only one partition may contain bootable sectors. The partition table is located at the end of the boot record at offset Hex BE. Each of the 4 entries in the partition table are 16 bytes long and are defined as:

Byte 0   Boot Indicator

Hex 00 = NOT bootable

Hex 80 = Bootable

Byte 1 Start of Partition—Read/write head

Byte 2 Start of Partition—Sector number

Byte 3 Start of Partition—Cylinder (track)

Byte 4 System Indicator

Hex 00 = Unknown

Hex 01 = MS-DOS

Byte 5 End of Partition—Read/write head

Byte 6 End of Partition—Sector number

Byte 7 End of Partition—Cylinder (track) number

Bytes 8–9 Number of sectors preceding this partition (LSW)

Bytes 10–11 Number of sectors preceding this partition (MSW)

Bytes 12–13 Number of sectors allocated to this partition (LSW)

Bytes 14–15 Number of sectors allocated to this partition (MSW)

The boot sector for the hard disk partition is the first sector of the partition. This sector is located at the position defined by bytes 1 through 3 of the partition table entry. These values can be used in conjunction with BIOS routines to read the sector into memory. Read the boot sector from the media into a 512-byte buffer.

Whether the boot sector is read from a diskette or a hard disk, the format of the sector remains the same. The BPB is not the only item in the sector. The following table is the map of the boot sector:

Bytes 0–2 Jump instruction to boot code at end of sector

Bytes 3–10 Name of OEM (MS-DOS distributor) and version number

Bytes 11–23 BIOS Parameter Block

Bytes 24–25 Number of sectors per track

Bytes 26–27 Number of read/write heads

Bytes 28–29 Number of hidden sectors

Bytes 30–511 Bootstrap code

The Build BPB function must pass the address of the BPB to MS-DOS through the request block (offset = 18) and set the request block header status to DONE before returning to MS-DOS.

On the other hand, creating a BPB for a block device is simply a matter of setting up the fields of the BIOS Parameter Block in your program code and assigning values to the fields. The declarations in the example that follows can be used to set up a default BPB. The parameters used in the fields correspond to the normal values used by MS-DOS. These values can be used by the initialization function since it requires that a BPB be created so that MS-DOS can set up buffers of the proper size for later use. The address to this block of parameters is placed in the last field (offset = 18) of the request block.

```
;
; BIOS Parameter Block
;
BPB_Sector_Size    DW    512
BPB_Alloc_Units    DB    1
BPB_Reserved       DW    1
BPB_FATs           DB    2
BPB_Dir_Entries    DW    64
BPB_Image_Size     DW    8*80   ; 8 sectors x 80 tracks
BPB_Media_Descr    DB    0FFH   ; 2 sided 8 sectors
BPB_FAT_Sectors    DW    2
```

INPUT/OUTPUT FUNCTIONS

The *input* and *output* functions of the device driver are the routines that perform the bulk of the work. They are responsible for the delivery to and from the application programs and the peripheral device. Since all of the functions share a common interface with MS-DOS through the request block, and the only differences involve the direction of data flow, they are going to be described together. The IOCTL functions will involve some independent discussion.

IOCTL for Input (Command = 3)

Input (Command = 4)

Output (Command = 8)

Output with Verify (Command = 9)

The request block, which is sent to the strategy portion of the driver just before this function is called, contains the following fields:

Bytes 0–12   Request block header

Byte 13   Media descriptor (block-oriented devices only)

Bytes 14–17   Address of transfer area

Bytes 18–19   Byte or sector count

Bytes 21–22   Starting sector number (block-oriented devices only)

The purpose of the input and output functions is to transfer data between a transfer area buffer and the peripheral device. Input functions fetch bytes of information from the device and place them into the next available location in the buffer, while output functions reverse the flow, writing information to the peripheral.

The address of the transfer buffer is located in the request block (offset = 14).

The amount of data to be transferred is also contained in the request block (offset = 18). The data volume depends upon the device type. For character-oriented devices, the count in the request block is measured in single bytes. For block-oriented devices, the count refers to the number of whole sectors that are to be transferred. Whatever the requested value is, the device driver must return the count (in the appropriate units) of the actual transfers completed. This information replaces the requested count in the request block (offset = 18).

Block-oriented devices will not be concerned with filenames and pathnames, since these details are handled by MS-DOS. The basic information that the block-oriented driver needs to have is: What kind of media is being accessed, and where should the media be accessed? These pieces of information are also available in the request block.

The media descriptor (offset = 13) informs the driver about the nature of the recording media and allows the driver to make some decisions when address calculations are performed.

The starting sector number for the I/O operation is also available in the request block (offset = 21). Using the information available in the media descriptor (number of sectors per track and number of sides to the media), the driver can calculate the proper track and sector address for the operation. Information is also available in the local copy of the BIOS Parameter Block.

Character-oriented output devices may use interrupts to control their operations.

For example, some communications processors will send an interrupt to the main processor whenever the transmitter buffer is not full. The interrupt handler would move characters from an intermediate buffer to the communications buffer until the buffer was full. When the intermediate buffer is emptied, the *buffer is not full* interrupt is disabled by the interrupt handler. The output function of the device driver is only responsible for inserting characters into the intermediate buffer and enabling the *buffer is not full* interrupt.

Another example: Background printing can be accomplished by interrupting the main processor whenever the printer is ready to receive more characters to print. The interrupt handler is responsible for reading the contents of the file being printed, deciding if the file is completely written, and whether or not there are more files to be printed. The output function has the responsibility of maintaining a list of files that are ready to be printed. The device driver gets called only to add or delete filenames on the print list. Design ideas for both of these drivers can be found in a later section.

IOCTL for Output (Command = 12)

The *IOCTL Input* and *Output* functions involve the one-way flow of data from the application program to the device driver. The data that is found in the transfer buffer is not data to be written to the peripheral. It is data which is to be interpreted by the IOCTL routines and used as a source of device control commands. For instance, a communications program will have the requirement to change its baud (rate of transmission), parity (error checking) conventions, and the structure of the transmitted character. For example:

```
B=300/P=E/N=8/S=1//
```

might be interpreted by the IOCTL Input or Output routines as:

Set baud to 300.

Set parity to even.

Set number of bits per character to eight.

Set number of stop bits to one.

In any case, this information is not data to be sent out through the peripheral. Instead, it is intended to be used to control the peripheral. The controlling program would assemble the command stream (as dictated by the IOCTL specifications) in a buffer in a manner identical to preparing data, and send it to the device driver by the IOCTL option.

IOCTL input is control sequences for an input device, and IOCTL output is used to control an output device.

Nondestructive Input (Command = 5)

The purpose of the *Nondestructive Input* function is to send the next available character in the device's input buffer back to the application program or MS-DOS without moving the index pointer away from the character. Therefore, when a "for-real Input" function is finally requested, the character returned from this function will also be returned with the Input function. This gives a program a chance to look ahead in the buffer by one character.

The request block, which is sent to the strategy portion of the drive just before this function was called, contains the following fields:

Bytes 0–12 Request Block Header

Byte 13 Returned character

To put the idea into a more visual form, the following Pascal and C sequences show how a normal Input function would fetch the next character and increment the index so that it points to the next character.

```
Character  := Buffer [Next_Index];
Next_Index := Next_Index + 1;

c = buffer[next_index++];
```

In contrast to the normal Input function, the Nondestructive Input function would not increment the index after fetching the character. Any subsequent fetch will retrieve the very same character.

```
Character := Buffer [Next_Index];

c = buffer[next_index];
```

Using C or Pascal to actually write a device driver is not a very good idea, but using it to describe a function makes the operation easier to understand.

The request block which initiated the Nondestructive Input function contains a single byte following the request header. The character that has been fetched by this function is to be placed in that byte (offset = 13).

The Nondestructive Input function should update the input status word and place it into the status word in the request block header prior to leaving the function.

Get Input Status (Command = 6)

Get Output Status (Command = 10)

The purpose of the *Get Status* functions is to set the appropriate current status word into the request header. A separate status word is kept for both the input status and output status. The requested status (determined by the value of the command) is placed into the request block.

It is not the responsibility of these functions to actually form the status word. That task is the ongoing responsibility of the Input functions, Output functions, and peripheral interrupt handlers.

The request block does not contain any information, besides the data within the request block header, that is used by these functions.

Flush Input (Command = 7)

Flush Output (Command = 11)

The purpose of the flush commands is to immediately empty the appropriate buffer of all characters or pending requests.

For example, the *Flush Input* function for a new keyboard handler would be required to reset the pointers to the input buffer so that they indicate an empty buffer. A keyboard buffer will normally have two index pointers: one that indicates where the next character from the keyboard is to be placed, and the other indicates where the next character to be passed to the application program is located. The *characters in the buffer* condition exists when the pointers are different. When the pointers are equal, there are no more characters to pass from the buffer. The flush function would merely set both index pointers to the same value, typically the value of zero.

If the device driver was a background print utility and the *Flush Output* function was issued, the appropriate action would be to delete all of the filenames in the pending list.

The request block does not contain any additional information that is needed by the flush functions. However, the flush function must set the appropriate status into the status word of the request header and set the Done flag.

Device Drivers as a Part of MS-DOS

Device driver software is loaded into the computer's memory whenever the power is turned on or MS-DOS is rebooted. At that time, the driver becomes a part of MS-DOS.

The question is: How does MS-DOS know where to find the device driver software in the first place? You tell it.

When MS-DOS is being loaded into memory, one of the things that the loading software does is to check for a software configuration file named CONFIG.SYS. This configuration file is supposed to contain commands for setting up MS-DOS. This file is created by the user. One of the commands that can be executed is the naming of the device driver files.

You can find additional information about the other available commands in the MS-DOS reference manual for your particular machine.

To designate a device driver to be installed, a DEVICE = command must be added to the CONFIG.SYS file for each device driver that you wish to include in the operation system. A DEVICE = command might look like this:

```
DEVICE=a:support\drivers\print.com
```

The command, DEVICE = is followed by:

- The name of the drive, if the file is not on the default drive
- The intermediate pathname (if necessary)
- The name of the file
- The filename extension (as required)

Using the list of DEVICE = commands as a guide, MS-DOS loads the device drivers and puts the loaded memory under its control.

Device Driver Design Examples

The following section contains the preliminary interrupt code designs for a background printing utility (prints files while other programs are running) and an interrupt-driven communications I/O device drivers.

The first device driver is designed to provide a background printing capability.

Once this device driver is installed, a program can use the MS-DOS Write to Device function to send a filename to this print spooling utility. The device name is placed in the device header and might be called SPOOLER.

The purpose of the device driver is to place that filename into a list of files that are ready to print. An interrupt-driven routine moves characters from the file to the printer whenever the printer signals that it can receive more characters. When a file has been completely printed, its entry is removed from the list and the next file in the list is prepared for printing. This sequence continues until the list is emptied, at which time the printer interrupt will disable itself and the printing will halt. When a new file is added to the list, the device driver will enable the interrupt routine and everything starts all over again.

```
Listing 12-1. Design of the Print Spooler
Device Drive.

    INIT :
            initialize data
            initialize printer
            set interrupt vector address interrupt processor mask
                FOR IBM-PC:
                    Printer-is-ready interrupt is:
                        Interrupt Request 7
                        Interrupt Vector OF
                        Vector Address 3C through 3F
```

Listing 12-1. Continued

```
        set 'break' address in request block
        disable the printer interrupt

MEDIA CHECK: N/A

BUILD BPB: N/A

IOCTL FOR INPUT: N/A

INPUT:
NONDESTRUCTIVE INPUT:
        for each filename on waiting list
        copy filename to buffer as ASCIIZ

GET INPUT STATUS: N/A

FLUSH INPUT: N/A

OUTPUT:
OUTPUT WITH VERIFY:
        find next open position in print queue
        move filename to print queue
        enable printer interrupt

GET OUTPUT STATUS:
        move current status word to buffer
        BUSY = list is full
FLUSH OUTPUT:
        for every position in waiting list
          mark as empty
          clear pointer to waiting list
          close current file
          disable printer interrupt

IOCTL FOR OUTPUT:
        (to remove a particular file from list)
        get name from request buffer
        find name in list
        relink the list around removed file
        set position to available

PRINTER INTERRUPT:
        save registers
        if current file handle = 0
          get filename from list
          call DOS to open file
```

Listing 12-1. Continued

```
        set internal buffer to empty
        set appropriate pointers
        send FORMFEED if required
    if internal buffer is empty
    call DOS with file handle to read sector into buffer
    get actual count of characters
    mark for EOF if input count <> buffer size
    while printer is willing to accept characters and
        buffer contains characters to send:
        send character to printer
    reset interrupt
    if EOF is reached
        mark current file as finished
        remove from active chain
        get next entry for current file
        set file handle to zero
        if not more files to do
            disable printer interrupt
    restore registers
```

The second device driver is a communications driver.

There are two methods of transmitting and receiving characters in a communications environment. The first method is called *polling*. In the polling method, the communications processor is checked at regular intervals to see if a character is ready to be read, or if the transmitter buffer has room for another character. If the polling is done frequently enough, there are no lost characters from the communications receiver, and there is a steady output through the transmitter. However, when high-speed communications are used, the polling method may lose a couple of characters when the program is involved in a lengthy I/O sequence, such as turning on a diskette drive, waiting for the proper speed, finding a certain track and sector, reading a record and turning off the drive, and not being able to actively poll the communications device.

The other technique is the *interrupt-driven* method. Using the interrupt method, the communication processor sends an electronic signal to the central processor, asking the CPU to interrupt (stop) whatever it is doing, read the character from the communications device, and place the character into a buffer so that it is not lost when the next character arrives. The time that it takes to perform this operation is so short that a disk operation hardly notices it. The interrupt can also signal the CPU that the transmitter is empty and is ready to send the next character. In this case, the CPU stops, fetches the next character from a transmission buffer, sends it to the communications processor, and restarts the interrupted task. The following listing details the activity of a device driver that controls the activities of the communications interrupt handler.

```
Listing 12-2. Design of Communications Device
Driver.

    INIT :
            initialize data
            initialize communications port
            set interrupt vector address interrupt processor mask
                FOR IBM-PC:
                Communication interrupt is:
                  Interrupt Request 4
                  Interrupt Vector 0C
                  Vector Address 30 through 33
            set 'break' address in request block
            enable interrupt


    MEDIA CHECK: N/A

    BUILD BPB: N/A

    IOCTL FOR OUTPUT:
    IOCTL FOR INPUT:
            get command bytes from request buffer
            load registers for call to BIOS to set communications
                parameters (baud, stop bits, etc.)

    INPUT:
            if communications buffer contains characters
              get next character from input buffer
              move character to program buffer
              update communication buffer index to next character
                  -or
            if communications buffer contains characters
              move characters to program buffer
              until buffer size is reached (CX register value) or
              all characters are moved from communications buffer.

    NONDESTRUCTIVE INPUT:
            if input buffer contains characters
              get next character from input buffer
              move character to program buffer
```

```
Listing 12-2. Continued

GET INPUT STATUS:
        fill in proper bits if there are characters in the buffer

FLUSH INPUT:
        set the pointers into the input queue to zero
        set status to no characters ready

OUTPUT:
OUTPUT WITH VERIFY:
        get count of characters in the buffer
        move characters to output buffer
        stop when count is reached or buffer filled
        enable transmit interrupt to send the buffer

GET OUTPUT STATUS:
        move current status word to buffer

FLUSH OUTPUT:
        set pointers in output buffer to zero
        disable the transmit interrupt

COMMUNICATIONS INTERRUPT:
        save all registers
        check communications status for interrupt type
            (character received vs. transmitter buffer empty)
        if received character (highest priority)
          read character from processor
          if character is XON or XOFF
            XOFF :  disable transmit interrupt
                    set XOFF flag
                    set BUSY bit in status word
            XON  :  enable transmit interrupt if characters in
                    buffer
                    clear XOFF flag
                    clear BUSY bit in status word
          if there is room in buffer
            put character in buffer
          else
            set buffer overflow status bit
            reset interrupt
        if ready for transmit interrupt
          while communication buffer is not full and
              there are characters in output queue
              get character from output queue
              send to output port of communications processor
```

Listing 12-2. Continued

```
        if no more characters in output queue
          disable transmit interrupt
        else
          reset interrupt
    restore registers
```

Open (Command = 13)

Close (Command = 14)

These functions were added in MS-DOS 3.0. These calls are used to control the opening and closing of devices on the system. This should not be confused with opening and closing files on a device.

The action of this call is generally determined by the type of device being accessed. Block-oriented devices will have a different interpretation of this call than will character-oriented devices.

For block-oriented devices, this call is used to record a reference count as an activity measure of the device. Every use of the *Open* command increments an activity counter. As long as the counter is greater than zero, then there is some ongoing activity. The *Close* command would decrement the same counter. A value of zero while the Close command is active shows that the last file or activity has halted. This may signal the end-of-use of files on this device and that the media is to be removed. The close that clears the activity counter should take it upon itself to flush any buffers that may still be partially filled. This insures that all data is safely written.

Some program execution time may be saved if the attribute byte is checked for the device. If the device is nonremovable media (bit 11), it would not be necessary to map the activity of the device and second guess the user about the use of the media.

For character-oriented devices, the Open command can be used to send initialization strings. The Close command could be used to send a closing command, such as a page feed to the printer so that the last page printed is ejected.

Removable Media (Command = 15)

This function was added in MS-DOS 3.0. This call internally sets the media descriptor byte to indicate that a device is removable media. This information is required by the FORMAT utility in determining how to deal with the media.

Set bit 11 in the attribute byte of the request header to one prior to using this call.

Get Logical Device (Command = 23)

This function was added in MS-DOS 3.2. The action of this function is to report the identity of the last logical device number that was assigned to the block device. Several logical drives may be assigned to a single physical device. This function reports the range of assignments that have been made.

The device being requested is found in byte 13 of the request block. The result of the request is returned in the same block. Return a zero if there are no assignments beyond the basic device number.

The layout of the request block is:

Byte 0–12 Request block header

Byte 13 Unit code (input)

Byte 13 Last device referenced (output) .

Byte 14 Command code

Byte 15–16 Status

Byte 17–20 Reserved

Set Logical Device (Command = 24)

This function was added in MS-DOS 3.2. This function is for setting additional logical device numbers to a block device. This will allow MS-DOS to address a single physical device through a number of logical references.

The request block holds the block device identification seeking a logical assignment. The device identifier is in byte 13 of the request record. Place the last logical assignment number made into the same location.

The layout of the request block is the same as the one for the Get Logical Device command.

It is quite apparent that the creation and use of a device driver can be a complicated process. Breaking down the complete driver into its individual sections helps simplify the matter, somewhat. Then there is the putting-it-back-together-again process.

To aid you in creating a working device driver, the following assembly code is a complete working device driver. This driver is for a communications interface, and it only handles the reception of characters. However, it does illustrate the layout of the driver code.

Notice that the initialization section is at the end of the driver. Its memory location is returned to MS-DOS when the initialization phase is completed.

There is also an extra routine included in the code. There is an interrupt handler. This routine is activated through the interrupt vector table whenever a character has been received by the communications processor and the processor interrupts the main processor. The address of the interrupt handler is loaded into the vector table by the initialization routine using an MS-DOS system call.

This driver could easily be expanded to:

- Transmit characters using the output entry point

- Control the communication parameters (baud, character length, etc.) using the IOCTL input and output entries

- Use multiple communication ports using IOCTL to designate which port is being used.

This particular device driver was written for the NEC APC. The use of specific BIOS codes and hardware devices may not be applicable for other computers. This driver can be used for a guide in creating other drivers, however. The ideas and designs are the same on other machines.

Listing 12-3. Communications Device Driver.

```
DEVICE  SEGMENT  BYTE
        ASSUME   CS:DEVICE,DS:Nothing,ES:Nothing
;
; DEVICE = COMM
;
; start offset of code from 0
;
        ORG      0
;
; standard device driver header
;
```

Listing 12-3. Continued

```
COMMHDR:
          DW        -1,-1
          DW        8000h
          DW        Strategy
          DW        Entry
          DB        "COMM    "
;
; definition of request block
;
LENG     EQU       0
UNIT     EQU       LENG+1
CMD      EQU       UNIT+1
STATUS   EQU       CMD+1
DOSLINK  EQU       STATUS+2
MYLINK   EQU       DOSLINK+4
BREAKER  EQU       MYLINK+5
MEDIA    EQU       MYLINK+4
DTA      EQU       MEDIA+1
COUNT    EQU       DTA+4
CHAR     EQU       MYLINK+4
;
; interrupt storage area
;
; QUEUE   --> storage for received characters
; QUEIN   --> index into QUEUE for next received character
; QUEOUT  --> index into QUEUE for next character to be
;                 sent to application program
;
QUEUE    DB        2048 DUP (?)
QUEIN    DW        0
QUEOUT   DW        0
;
; communications interrupt handler
;
HANDLER PROC      FAR
INTERRUPT:
          Push      AX
          Push      BX
          Push      CX
          Push      DX
          Push      SI
          Push      DI
          Push      DS
          Push      ES
          Push      BP
;
; having saved the environment of the application
; read the status port of the communications processor
;
```

Listing 12-3. Continued

```
            In      AL,STATUS_PORT
            Test    AL,2
            Jz      INTOUT
;
; if a character has really been received
;   get character
;
            In      AL,COMM_PORT
;
; calculate address of next location in buffer
; use the AND instruction to force address to 0
;  if there is an overflow of the index value
;
; an AND instruction with an immediate operand will only
; function with the AX register, so save that register for a bit
;
            Push    AX
            Mov     AX,CS:QUEIN         ; get input index
            Inc     AX                 ; point to next position
            And     AX,2047           ; mod 2048
            Mov     CS:QUEIN,AX        ; put it back
            Mov     BX,AX             ; save index
            Pop     AX                ; recover character
            Mov     CS:QUEUE[BX],AL   ; store byte
INTOUT:
            Mov     AL,20h            ; code to clear interrupt
            Out     20h,AL            ; in interrupt hardware processor
            Sti                       ; allow interrupts
            Pop     BP
            Pop     ES
            Pop     DS
            Pop     DI
            Pop     SI
            Pop     DX
            Pop     CX
            Pop     BX
            Pop     AX
            Iret
HANDLER ENDP
;
; jump table for incoming commands
;
JMPTBL:
            DW      COMMINIT
            DW      EXIT
            DW      EXIT
            DW      EXIT
            DW      GETCHAR
            DW      LOOKCHAR
            DW      GETSTAT
            DW      FLUSHER
```

Listing 12-3. Continued

```
        DW      EXIT
        DW      EXIT
        DW      EXIT
        DW      EXIT
        DW      EXIT
;
; Strategy Area == save ptr passed by MS-DOS
;
SAVPTR  DD      0
STRATP  PROC    FAR
;
; save address in ES:BX registers for later use
;
Strategy:
        Mov     CS:WORD PTR SAVPTR,BX
        Mov     CS:WORD PTR SAVPTR+2,BX
        Ret
STRATP  ENDP
;
; normal operations entry
;
OPS     PROC    FAR
ENTRY:
;
; save the caller's environment
;
        Push    SI
        Push    AX
        Push    CX
        Push    DX
        Push    DI
        Push    BP
        Push    DS
        Push    ES
        Push    BX
;
        Lds     BX,CS:DWORD PTR SAVPTR   ; get ptr left by MS-DOS
        ASSUME  DS:Nothing
        Xor     AX,AX
        Mov     AL,DS:BYTE PTR CMD[BX]    ; get command
        Mov     SI,Offset JMPTBL          ; base of jump table
        Add     SI,AX                     ; add command offset
        Add     SI,AX
        Cmp     AL,11                     ; command out of range?
        Ja      EXIT                      ; forget it
        Mov     CX,DS:WORD PTR COUNT[BX]  ; get number of byte to xfer
;
; get address of transfer buffer from block
; put into ES:DI registers
;
```

Listing 12-3. Continued

```
        Les     DI,DS:DWORD PTR DTA[BX]   ; addr of buffer
        Push    CS                        ; copy CS register
        Pop     DS
        ASSUME  DS:DEVICE
        Jmp     [SI]                      ; goto processor
EXIT:
        ASSUME  DS:NOTHING
        Or      AH,01h                    ; set done flag
        Lds     BX,CS:DWORD PTR SAVPTR    ; get packet addr again
        Mov     DS:WORD PTR STATUS[BX],AX ; store flag
        Pop     BX
        Pop     ES
        Pop     DS
        Pop     BP
        Pop     DI
        Pop     DX
        Pop     CX
        Pop     AX
        Pop     SI
        Ret
;
; individual functions of the communications driver
;
GETCHAR:
        Mov     AX,CS:QUEOUT              ; get output index
        Cmp     AX,CS:QUEIN              ; check with input index
        Je      GETCHAR                  ; no char yet, wait
        Mov     DX,0
GETONE:
        Inc     DX                       ; keep count of actual xfer
        Inc     AX                       ; incr output index
        And     2047                     ; index mod 2048
        Mov     BX,AX                    ; where index will do some good
        Mov     AL,CS:QUEUE[BX]          ; get char from input list
        Stosb                            ; put char into applic buffer
        Mov     AX,BX                    ; restore that index for loop
        Cmp     AX,CS:QUEIN             ; caught up with input?
        Loopne  Getone
GOTLAST:
        Mov     CS:QUEOUT,AX             ; Update index for later
        Lds     BX,CS:DWORD PTR SAVPTR
        Mov     DS:WORD PTR COUNT[BX],DX ; save final count
        Xor     AX,AX                    ; no errors
        Jmp     EXIT                     ; all done
;
LOOKCHAR:
;
; want to look at next character without moving index
; 1. get current index
; 2. increment to next location (wrap around if req)
```

Listing 12-3. Continued

```
; 3. return char at that position
;
        Mov     AX,QUEOUT               ; get index
        Inc     AX                      ; need next value
        And     AX,2047                 ; wrap around index mod 2048
        Mov     SI,AX                   ; now it's a real index
        Mov     AL,QUEUE[SI]            ; get char
        Push    DS                      ; save for a moment
        Lds     BX,DWORD PTR SAVPTR     ; get addr of MS-DOS packet
        Mov     DS:[BX].CHAR,AL         ; put char in special place
        Pop     DS                      ; restore
        Xor     AX,AX                   ; no error
        Jmp     EXIT                    ; go back
GETSTAT:
;
; set BUSY flag if both indexes are set to the same value
;
        Mov     AX,QUEOUT               ; get output ptr
        Cmp     AX,QUEIN                ; how do they stack up?
        Je      SETBUSY                 ; no chars avail
        Xor     AX,AX                   ; not BUSY -- chars avail
        Jmp     EXIT
SETBUSY:
        Mov     AX,0200h                ; set BUSY bit
        Jmp     EXIT
FLUSHER:
;
; flush the contents of the interrupt buffer
; set both indexes to the same thing (0)
;
        Xor     AX,AX                   ; get a zero
        Mov     QUEIN,AX                ; set indexes
        Mov     QUEOUT,AX
        Jmp     EXIT
;
; the part that will not stay resident
;
point3  db      13,10,"communications device driver loaded",13,10,"$"
COMMINIT:
;
; use IBM PC BIOS !!! communications setup
;
        Mov     DX,0                    ; first serial port
        Mov     AH,0
        Mov     AL,10011010b            ; 1200 baud
                                        ; even parity
                                        ; 1 stop bit
                                        ; 7 data bits
        Int     14h                     ; BIOS RS-232 function
;
```

Listing 12-3. Continued

```
; set vector for communications (vector 11 / 0Ch)
;
        Push    DS                      ; will destroy this soon
        Push    DX                      ; this too
        Mov     AX,Seg INTERRUPT        ; function needs interrupt
        Mov     DS,AX                   ; address in DS:DX pair
        Mov     DX,Offset INTERRUPT
        Mov     AL,0Ch                  ; this is vector 11
        Mov     AH,025h                 ; set vector
        Int     21h                     ; DOS does it
        Pop     DX                      ; restore..DS later
;
; tell MS-DOS what code can be released to MS-DOS
; ... all memory after COMMINIT
;
        Lds     BX,DWORD PTR SAVPTR     ; leave addr in packet
        Mov     DS:[BX].BREAKER,Offset COMMINIT
        Mov     DS:[BX].BREAKER+2,CS
        Pop     DS                      ; restore DS now, it's safe
;
; all done .... no error
; print message
;
        Mov     DX,Offset point3        ; addr of msg
        Mov     AH,9                    ; display msg thru MS-DOS
        Int     21h
;
;
        Xor     AX,AX                   ; no error
        Jmp     EXIT
OPS     ENDP
DEVICE  ENDS
        END
```

Now you have a device driver for your computer. To use the driver in a real situation, the following steps should be accomplished:

- Build a CONFIG.SYS file that designates the driver program as a device.
- Assemble the device driver program:
  Link the device driver program.
  Convert the .EXE program file to a .COM program file. This is done with the EXE2BIN or LOCATE utilities.
  Move the .COM version of the program to your BOOT disk, or at least to the disk with the CONFIG.SYS file (which must be bootable).

- Reboot the system. The device driver is loaded during the boot process. If you included the little message in the initialization routine, you will be able to see when the installation occurs.

What you now need is a program that uses the device driver. The following code is taken from a file transfer program. What is shown here is the opening of the device driver and the reading of characters from the communications port. To build a complete file transfer program, you would add the opening of a file, the writing to the file, a method of getting out of the read and write cycle, and the closing of the file. Every book should have at least one of these; it should be intuitively obvious to the reader how these steps are done.

Listing 12-4. Communications Program Segment.

```
        Mov     DX,Offset COMM  ; addr of device name
        Mov     AL,0            ; open for reading
        Mov     AX,3Dh          ; open device driver
        Int     21h
        Jc      HELPME          ; handle the error
        Mov     HNDL2,AX        ; save device HANDLE
;
; get byte from comm -- this goes inside of read/write loop
;
        Mov     BX,HNDL2        ; identify device w/HANDLE
        Mov     CX,BUFSIZE      ; number of char expected
        Mov     DX,Offset BUFFER ; addr of buffer
        Mov     AH,3FH          ; read from a device
        Int     21h             ; call MS-DOS
        Jc      HELPME          ; oops! error
;
;
; and further in the program, the data segment
;
;
DATAX   SEGMENT PARA 'DATA
COMM    DB      "COMM",0        ; asciiz string of device name
HNDL2   DW      0
BUFSIZE EQU     256
BUFFER  DB      BUFSIZE Dup (?)
DATAX   ENDS
```

Chapter 13

Expanded Memory Management

INTRODUCTION

It certainly isn't a formal part of MS-DOS, but since it carries, in part, the Microsoft name, the Intel/Lotus/Microsoft Expanded Memory Specification (EMS) will become part of the programmer's stable of tools in the coming years. This chapter deals with the concepts of expanded memory, the programming interfaces, and some ideas for using expanded memory.

In the very early days of microcomputing, you were a fortunate individual (hacker extraordinaire) if your personal computer had 8K bytes of RAM. 1K or, more likely, 256 bytes of RAM was normal. The 16K memory chips were still a dream, an inconceivable possibility. The 16K chips did appear, and 64K machines sprang up everywhere. Here was enough computing power and memory to do just about anything. If it wasn't enough memory, you should be doing the job on a mini or mainframe.

Such were the reasonings when the first MS-DOS prototypes were developed. It was certainly true that the 8088 microprocessor could address much more memory than the 64K of the 8080, Z80, or 6502. It was decided to set an upper bound to the user-accessible memory at a place that would represent more memory than the user would ever need; 640K looked good. To date, everything was done in one-tenth of the area, so 640K looked like a safe limit. We programmers certainly fooled them.

Expanded memory was introduced to supply the programmer with more data storage area. I suppose that you could shove program segments or overlays into the expanded memory, but this looks like a chancy thing. Let's take a look at what expanded memory is and how it works.

Expanded memory, physically speaking, is a collection of random-access memory chips wired with data, address, and control signals. There can be several million (mega-) bytes of memory in expanded memory. This memory is organized into 16K *pages*. One megabyte of memory consists of 64 pages—remember this.

Although there are all of these bytes on the memory board, they have no fixed address in the sense that the memory in the 640K MS-DOS user area has fixed addresses. They are electronically floating around as phantom memory. Actually, they are addressed independently through a controller on the expanded memory board.

In a typical MS-DOS microcomputer, the user is allowed to use 640K of the memory space. This has to be shared with the operating system, interrupt handlers, device drivers, and resident utilities. Above the 640K barrier, there are other things. The video buffers for the monochrome and color adapters, bootstrap code, ROM BIOS, and ROM BASIC all reside in this area.

Fortunately, there are some holes in the memory used above 640K. There are six pages of 64K above the 640K barrier. The use of these pages varies with your configuration, however, there will undoubtedly be open pages to be used.

In an addressing scheme known as *bank switching*, the 16K pages of the expanded memory can be made to appear in the open portions of the address space above the 640K limit. Using the EMM (Expanded Memory Manager) through a software interrupt, you can request for a specific page to be made available for access, use it, and then replace it with another page in the EMM address space. When you are ready to use the unpaged memory, you can bring it back into the window with all of your data intact.

The hardware and software drivers make the memory directly accessible to you. There is no copying of data to and from the memory board into and out of the address space above 640K. The hardware actually assigns the hardware address to the floating memory, giving it a fixed and usable address.

Your responsibility lies in remembering which page contains which data.

The expanded memory manager is not a part of MS-DOS, but should be on a software diskette accompanying your hardware memory board. The manager is installed as a device driver in the CONFIG.SYS file at *boot* time.

You can access the memory manager through the software interrupt Hex 67, supplying the function number in the AH register. That sounds familiar. The code would look like this:

```
; All other registers are set for the function
;
        Mov AH,function
        Int 67H
;
; Check the AH register for the return status
```

The functions available to you in the Expanded Memory Manager are:

Hex 40	Get memory status
Hex 41	Get segment address of page area
Hex 42	Get page counts
Hex 43	Get EMM handle and allocate memory
Hex 44	Map memory into page area
Hex 45	Release handle and memory
Hex 46	Get EMM version
Hex 47	Save mapping context for handle
Hex 48	Restore mapping context
Hex 4B	Get number of assigned handles
Hex 4C	Get number of pages for handle
Hex 4D	Get number of pages for all handles

MEMORY MANAGEMENT FUNCTIONS

For each of these functions, the return status code is placed into the AH register.

Get Memory Status

Function: Hex 40

Registers: AH = Function code

AH = Status

Error Codes: Hex 0 = EMM is present and functioning

Hex 80 = EMM internal software error

Hex 81 = Hardware error

Hex 84 = Request for invalid function was made

The purpose of the *Get Memory Status* function is to initialize and check on the operation of the expanded memory features. This function is to be used only in the event that the expanded memory is known to exist on the user's computer. It is not a function for testing the availability of expanded memory.

Before this function can be used with any validity, the existence of expanded memory must be verified. This verification can be done in one of two standard methods.

First, we could examine the addresses in the interrupt vector table for an address for the Hex 67 interrupt. If this vector has been assigned, we can be sure that something will handle the software interrupts that we will issue. However, there is no guarantee that the address in this vector is being used for expanded memory. This is to say that there is nothing to keep some software company that hasn't gotten the word to leave Hex 67 interrupt-free for expanded memory to use this interrupt. To really make sure that the proper driver is in place, we will carry the inspection another step and check the installed name in the device driver header.

Trusting that all is okay in the system, the following code will allow you to check for the expanded memory driver before you get the memory status. This code sequence uses the MS-DOS Hex 35 Get Interrupt Vector function to see if the vector table has been set for expanded memory. Setting the vector is the task of the expanded memory driver, which the operating system installs during system initialization.

```
Use the MS-DOS function 35 (Get Interrupt Vector)
   to get driver base address.
This function returns the entry address of the driver in
   the ES:BX register
Check the ES:BX register pair for ZERO.
There is no driver if the register pair is zero.
The standard device driver header contains the name of
   the driver at offset Hex 10
Compare the name of the driver to "EMMXXXX0" to verify
   that the driver is truly the expanded memory driver.
```

This sequence should confirm the existence of the expanded memory driver.

The second method is to use the IOCTL functions for device drivers to check the existence of the expanded memory driver. This involves attempting to open the device driver and check the status. Here is the code sequence for using the IOCTL method:

Listing 13-1. Initializing EMM.

```
int ioctl(handle,func,xfer,status)
int          handle;
int          func;
int          xfer;
int          *status;
{
  union REGS  regs:

  regs.h.ah = 0x44;
  regs.h.al = func;
  regs.x.cx = xfer;
  regs.x.bx = handle;
  int86(0x21,&regs,&regs);
  if (status) *status = regs.x.dx;
  return (int) regs.h.al;
}
init_mem()
{
```

Listing 13-1. Continued

```
int         tmp_handle;
int         status;
union REGS  regs;

/* find out if EMM exists */
tmp_handle = open ("EMMXXXX0",O_RDONLY);
if (tmp_handle == -1)
  {
  printf("Expanded Memory Not Found -- Process Ends\n");
  exit(1);
  }
status = iotcl(tmp_handle,7,0,NULL);
close (tmp_handle);
if (!status)
  {
    printif("Expanded Memory Not Ready -- Process Ends\n");
    exit(1);
  }
regs.x.ax = 0x4000;
int86(0x67,&regs,&regs);
}
```

Now is the proper time to issue the Get Memory Status function. A return code of zero in the AX register indicates that everything is ready to go in the expanded memory.

Get Segment Address of Page Area

Function: Hex 41

Registers: AH = Function code

BX = Segment number of page area

Error Codes: Hex 0 = Successful completion

Hex 80 = EMM internal software error

Hex 81 = Hardware error

Hex 84 = Request for invalid function was made

The purpose of the *Get Segment Address of Page Area* is to provide the segment number that has been designated as the bank switching address

for the local system. The unused portion of memory above 640K may be
different from machine to machine. Depending upon which hardware extensions have been installed in the local system and which other software is resident, the location of the open area for the expanded memory
bank switching window may be affected. Therefore, it is necessary that
you get this segment address for a base for further addressing of the paging area.

The paging area is 64K in length, being divided into four 16K byte
areas (pages). The segment number returned by this function is the base
address of the first 16K page. Other pages are at 16K offsets from this
point.

The following C code is highly MS-DOS-dependent. If your programs
are supposed to be transportable to other non-MS-DOS C environments,
make sure that you surround this code with plenty of comments to explain what you are doing.

Listing 13-2. Get Address of Paging Area.

```
/* a single page of EM is 16K long */
   typedef char  page[0x4000];

/* this is a table of pointers into each */
/* of the pages */
   page  *page_area[4];
   union REGS  regs;

/* get the base segment of the paging area */
   regs.x.ax = 0x4100;
   int86(0x67,&regs,&regs);
   base = reg.x.bx;

/* this looks like a kludge ... maybe it is ... */
/* get the address of the pointer to the page area */
/* load the base address plus the offset to the page */
/* remember to put the offset into segment format */
/* which is incremented by 16 byte paragraphs */

*((int *)&page_area[0] + 1) = base;
*((int *)&page_area[0]) = 0;
*((int *)&page_area[1] + 1) = base + 0x0400;
*((int *)&page_area[1]) = 0;
*((int *)&page_area[2] + 1) = base + 0x0800;
*((int *)&page_area[2]) = 0;
*((int *)&page_area[3] + 1) = base + 0x0c00;
*((int *)&page_area[3]) = 0;
```

In the other function descriptions, we'll see what to further do with this information.

Get Page Counts

Function: Hex 42

Registers: AH = Function code

BX = Unallocated pages

DX = Total pages in memory

Error Codes: Hex 0 = Successful completion

Hex 80 = EMM internal software error

Hex 81 = Hardware error

Hex 84 = Request for invalid function was made

The purpose of the *Get Page Counts* function is to get the total number of pages available in the expanded memory and the number of those pages that are available (unallocated). You can use this function to determine whether there is enough memory left for your application, or how much to request without causing allocation problems.

This function can be used without first requesting an initial allocation and opening a handle.

The following C code can be used to extract this information:

```
regs.x.ax = 0x4200;
int86(0x67,&regs,&regs);
avail_pages = regs.x.dx;
total_pages = regs.x.bx;
if (avail_pages < MIN_REQUIRED)
{
 printf("Task ends -- Not enough expanded memory\n");
 exit(1);
}
```

Get EMM Handle and Allocate Memory

Function: Hex 43

Registers: AH = Function code
BX = Page count requested
DX = Handle

Error Codes: Hex 0 = Successful completion

Hex 80 = EMM internal software error

Hex 81 = Hardware error

Hex 84 = Request for invalid function was made

Hex 85 = No handles are available

Hex 87 = Requested more memory than physically available

Hex 88 = Not enough pages unallocated to fill request

Hex 89 = Request for zero pages is invalid

To actually use the expanded memory, a handle must be assigned by the memory manager to the memory that is allocated to you. The purpose of the *Get EMM Handle and Allocate Memory* is to process your request for an initial memory allocation and provide a handle through which you may reference this allocation.

You may request several handles, each with its own allotment of expanded memory. It may be easier to keep certain memory usages separated by handle and page rather than trying to maximize memory usage by interleaving everything within the same handle.

The following data structure may help to keep things in perspective:

```
/* number of EMM pages planned for allocation */
#define  PAGE_COUNT 12;

int  i;
```

```
int   handle;
union REGS  regs;

{
 /* allocate 12 pages and a handle */
 regs.x.aX = 0x4300;
 regs.x.bX = PAGE_COUNT;
 int86(0x67,&regs,&regs);
 handle = regs.x.dx;
}
```

The contents of the page manager matrix would reflect the page location of any given page. A value of 0 through 3 shows an active page in the paging area. If the value is −1, then the page is in the floating condition.

Map Memory into Page Area

Function: Hex 44

Registers: AH = Function code

DX = Memory manager handle

BX = Number of logical memory page

AL = Page number (0–3)

Error Codes: Hex 0 = Successful completion

Hex 80 = EMM internal software error

Hex 81 = Hardware error

Hex 83 = Invalid handle

Hex 84 = Request for invalid function was made

Hex 8A = Page number requested is outside of handle's pages

Hex 8B = Illegal page area requested. Must be 0–3.

The effect that we want out of the expanded memory manager is for 16K pages of memory to appear in a window of memory upon request. When the usefulness of this page is done, it can be sent to never-never land until it is needed for some reason. The purpose of the *Map Memory into Page Area* is to perform the bank and page switching that causes the requested page to appear in the window of memory.

This will be the most often used function in the expanded memory group.

To use this function, load the following register to make the swap request:

DX Handle assigned for page allocation

BX Page number to be switched into page area

AL Page area (0–3) for this page

```
int get_page(handle,page,area)
int     handle;
int     page;
int     area;
{
union REGS    regs;

    regs.x.ax = 0x4400 + area;
    regs.x.dx = handle;
    regs.x.bx = page;
    int86(0x67,&regs,&regs);
    return regs.h.ah;
}

/* reference data in page with this structure */

*(page_area[page]+data_offset)
```

Release Handle and Memory

Function: Hex 45

Registers: AH = Function code

DX = Assigned handle

Error Codes: Hex 0 = Successful completion

Hex 80 = EMM internal software error

Hex 81 = Hardware error

Hex 83 = Invalid handle

Hex 84 = Request for invalid function was made

Hex 86 = Error in saving or restoring page map context

The expanded memory manager is a resident device driver in the operating system. Its lifetime is beyond that of any one program. Therefore, when a program or task terminates, it is necessary for the task to relinquish control of the expanded memory that was allocated for it.

Normally, a terminating task will automatically release its memory and file allocations since these are being tracked by the operating system. But since the EMM is outside of the scope of MS-DOS, you cannot count on MS-DOS to release the expanded memory that you have acquired. You are responsible for closing the handle.

The purpose of the *Release Handle and Memory* function is to notify the EMM that you will have no further use of the memory allotted to a given handle. This function can be used to close out the expanded memory acquisitions before terminating the program, or just allowing the EMM to recycle the memory so that it can be used for another purpose within your program.

Load the DX register with the assigned handle that controls the memory pages that are to be released.

If you left the handle open when a task is terminated and somehow passed the identity of the handle to another task, you might suspect that all kinds of data structures could be passed from one program to another.

I don't know if this is within the bounds of EMM or breaking the rules. It falls into the I-wonder-what-would-happen-if category.

Here is a little C routine to do the memory and handle release:

```
int release_EMM (handle)
int    handle;
{
union REGS  regs;

  regs.x.ax = 0x4500;
  regs.x.dx = handle;
  int86(0x67,&regs,&regs);
  return regs.h.ah;
}
```

Get EMM Version

> **Function:** Hex 46
>
> **Registers:** AH = Function code
>
> **Error Codes:** Hex 0 = Successful completion
>
> Hex 80 = EMM internal software error
>
> Hex 81 = Hardware error
>
> Hex 84 = Request for invalid function was made

As with MS-DOS, different versions of the software will contain different functions. Before trying to perform some of the more extensive functions with EMM (especially in the future), check to see that the version on the user's computer is correct for the things you want to do.

The purpose of the *Get EMM Version* function is to return the version of the EMM that the target computer is using.

The version number is returned in the AL register.

The following code will get the function number:

```
int get_EMM_version()
{
union REGS regs;

    regs.x.ax = 0x47;
    int86(0x67,&regs,&regs);
    return regs.x.ax;
}
```

Save Mapping Context for Handle

Function: Hex 47

Registers: AH = Function code

DX = Handle

Error Codes: Hex 0 = Successful completion

Hex 80 = EMM internal software error

Hex 81 = Hardware error

Hex 83 = Invalid handle

Hex 84 = Request for invalid function was made

Hex 8C = Page mapping save area is full

Hex 8D = Mapping context for handle already saved

When an interrupt driver or a resident software takes control of the computer, the context or environment (data registers, address registers, status registers, and instruction registers) of the currently active task (that is, before it was temporarily stopped) must be saved. This will allow the context (registers) to be restored at a later time and the application program to continue as if nothing had happened.

The *Save Mapping Context for Handle* function works in much the same way. When a program interrupts an active task and needs to use the expanded memory, it can get a handle and save the context of the EMM before starting to use the memory for its own needs.

The interrupting program using this function must acquire an extra handle to be used for saving the context. After the handle is acquired, set the handle value into the DX register and initiate this function.

Obviously, as in popping registers from the program stack to restore the environment of an active task, the interrupting program must restore the EMM context for the active program to proceed as if nothing had happened to it.

Use the Restore Mapping Context before leaving the interrupt handler to return the EMM to its original state.

It can be assumed that the program using this function will be written in assembly language, since it will be in a device driver or interrupt handler.

```
; Get handle to identify the context

        mov     ax,4400h
        mov     bx,4           ; ask for 4 pages
        int     67h
        or      ah,ah          ; check for errors
        jnz     problem

; Handle is in DX
; save context with this handle

        mov     handle,dx  ; use the new handle
        mov     ax,4800h
        int     67h
        or      ah,ah          ; check for errors
        jnz     problem
```

Restore Mapping Context

Function: Hex 48

Registers: AH = Function code

DX = Handle

Error Codes: Hex 0 = Successful completion

Hex 80 = EMM internal software error

Hex 81 = Hardware error

Hex 83 = Invalid handle

Hex 84 = Request for invalid function was made

Hex 8E = Context restore failure

Popping the stack of registers will restore the environment for an active task. Restoring the mapping context for the EMM puts it back to the state that it was before the interrupting task was activated.

The purpose of the *Restore Mapping Context* function is to restore the EMM context to its original state before being saved.

The restoration is connected with a handle assigned to the interrupting task, not with the program handles. Load the handle used to save the context into the DX register.

```
; Handle needs to be in DX
; restore context with this handle

    mov    ax,4900h
    mov    dx,handle
    int    67h
    or     ah,ah
    jnz    problem
```

Get Number of Assigned Handles

Function: Hex 4B

Registers: AH = Function code

BX = Number of handles

Error Codes: Hex 0 = Successful completion

Hex 80 = EMM internal software error

Hex 81 = Hardware error

Hex 83 = Invalid handle

Hex 84 = Request for invalid function was made

The purpose of the *Get Number of Assigned Handles* function is to allow the EMM to report the number of handles in use. A value of zero indicates that the EMM is idle.

The following code will report the number of handles being used by the EMM:

```
int get_EMM_handle_count()
{
union REGS regs;

   regs.x.ah = 0x4b00;
   int86(0x67,&regs,&regs);
   return regs.x.bx;
}
```

Get Number of Pages for Handle

Function: Hex 4C

Registers: AH = Function code

DX = Handle

BX = Number of pages owned by handle

Error Codes: Hex 0 = Successful completion

Hex 80 = EMM internal software error

Hex 81 = Hardware error

Hex 83 = Invalid handle

Hex 84 = Request for invalid function was made

The purpose of the *Get Number of Pages for Handle* function is to get the number of pages of expanded memory that are currently owned by a handle.

This number should agree with the number of pages requested when the handle was opened. One could guess that this function could be used to find the size of expanded memory when the handle is passed to a library routine or other task.

Set the DX register to the handle of the allocated memory of the request.

The number of allocated pages is returned in the BX register.

```
int get_page_count(handle)
int     handle;
{
union REGS  regs;
  regs.x.ax = 0x4c00;
  regs.x.dx = handle;
  int86(0x67,&regs,&regs);
  return regs.x.dx;
}
```

Get Number of Pages for All Handles

Function: Hex 4D

Registers: AH = Function code

ES:DI = Address of page table

BX = Number of active handles

Error Codes: Hex 0 = Successful completion

Hex 80 = EMM internal software error

Hex 81 = Hardware error

Hex 83 = Invalid handle

Hex 84 = Request for invalid function was made

For the very curious, page counts for all of the handles can be fetched with the *Get Number of Pages for All Handles*. This function builds a table with 256 entries (maximum) showing the number of pages assigned to each of the handles.

Put the address of the 256-entry table into the ES:DI register pair. The table is constructed of 32-bit (2-word) entries. The maximum size of the table will be 1,024 bytes.

The number of active handles is returned in the BX register. This value will give you some idea of how many valid table entries have been put into the table.

The following code will allow this table to be built. The code segment assumes that a *large*, *compact*, or *huge* memory model is being used so that the segment and offset portions of the address of the table are passed to the function.

```
long  table[256];
get_all_page_counts(table);

get_all_page_counts(t)
int   *t;
{
union REGS  regs;
struct SREGS  sregs;
```

```
  regs.x.ax = 0x4D00;
  regs.x.di = FP_OFF(t);
  sregs.es  = FP_SEG(t);
  int86x(0x67,&regs,&regs,&sregs);
  return &regs.x.bx;
}
```

Chapter 14

BIOS Programming

INTRODUCTION

The commands covered in the earlier chapters dealt with the services provided by the MS-DOS software. These DOS functions are available to any user who is operating a computer that uses MS-DOS. However, there are commands that are available only on the IBM PC and some of the *compatible* and *work-alike* computers on the market. These commands control the BIOS (Basic Input Output Services) functions. On the IBM PC, BIOS commands are included with the computer when you purchase it. They are written in machine code and *burned* into ROM (Read Only Memory), so that the BIOS functions are a permanent part of your computer system. This ROM-based software is also known as *firmware*.

The BIOS functions provide the basis for the functions available through MS-DOS, and are, therefore, very similar to MS-DOS. However, despite the similarities, they should be considered for general programming usage because some of the services are more straightforward than MS-DOS. And, in some cases, the BIOS functions are more flexible than MS-DOS. However, the trade-offs for flexibility in programming are taking the responsibility for ensuring program correctness and error handling, and a decrease in transportability. A program that is dependent upon certain machine characteristics may not be usable on machines of other brands.

SOFTWARE INTERRUPTS

This chapter will not cover all of the BIOS functions, since some are used only when the computer is being turned on (*booted*). However, the functions that are useful to the systems and application programmer will be covered. These functions are (identified by the hex value of their software interrupt):

Int 10   The video I/O function

Int 11   Equipment check

Int 12   Memory check

Int 14   RS-232 I/O

Int 16   Keyboard I/O

Int 17   Printer I/O

Each of these function types has many subfunctions that perform specific actions. Selecting the subfunction is done by placing the numeric code for the desired subfunction into the AH register. Other registers may be used to control the behavior of the selected subfunction. The program segments in the detailed explanation of each function will illustrate the use of the registers.

If you should decide to use these functions, please be aware that not all computers that use MS-DOS will recognize these functions, since the functions are presumably unique to the IBM PC. Once again, there are certain compatible computers that will also use these BIOS commands. Check the technical reference that comes with your machine. For the IBM PC, you can get more information about these functions in Section 3 and Appendix A of the *IBM PC Technical Reference Manual*.

The Video I/O Function

BIOS Interrupt: 10

BIOS Functions: Set video mode

Set cursor type

Set cursor position

Read cursor position

Read light pen position

Select active display page

Scroll active page up

Scroll active page down

Read attribute/character at cursor position

Write attribute/character at cursor position

Write character only at cursor position

Set color palette

Write dot

Read dot

Write teletype

Get current video state

On the IBM PC, the video adapter cards contain the video buffer memory. Everything that is seen on the screen is resident in that memory. The video generator and the main microprocessor can both access the video buffers so that a program can directly manipulate the contents of the video buffer. One of the big advantages of managing your own video output is that you can write characters to the screen at any location without disturbing the position of the cursor. Recall that the MS-DOS character I/O functions would only write characters to the current cursor position. It is distracting to watch the cursor, which should be marking an input position for text, racing around the screen as you update other material (such as the time). For instance, in a communications program, there may be a lot of activity on one part of the screen as information is received and displayed, but if you are not entering anything, the cursor should just be sitting there waiting for your input, not directing the location of each character coming into the system.

The first thing that you need to know is the address of the screen buffer so that you can properly display your information. And the first problem you encounter is that the address of the monochrome buffer and the address of the color buffer are not the same. This is not too difficult a problem to solve, since the monochrome buffer starts at address B000:0000 (Hex) and the color buffer starts at address B800:0000 (Hex). The real problems start when your program has to run on *any* IBM PC. The proper address must be used or else your data does not show up on the screen. One solution is to use the *equipment check* BIOS call to tell you which adapter card is mounted in the computer. Knowing which card is being used, your program can adapt its video addressing to the correct buffer.

The next hurdle involves gaining an understanding of screen attributes. When using characters (alpha mode), each position on the screen is described by a 16-bit word. The ASCII character to be displayed is stored in the first byte of the word. This byte always has the even-numbered byte address of the two bytes. It is also the least significant byte when the two bytes are manipulated as a word. The second byte is the attribute byte. It occupies the odd-numbered byte address of the word, and is the most significant byte of the word. The attribute byte describes how the character is to be displayed. For the monochrome display, the attribute controls character intensity, underlining, reverse video, and blink. The bits of the monochrome attribute byte are defined in Table 14-1.

Table 14-1. Video Attribute Bits (B&W)

Bits	Meaning
0–2	Character characteristics
3	Character intensity
4–6	Background characteristics
7	Character blinking

These attribute bits respond according to the diagram in Table 14-2. When none of the configurations appear as an attribute, the character is displayed in normal intensity. Attributes may be combined, as long as their characteristics are not mutually exclusive. For instance, you can have a highlighted, underlined, and blinking character, but you cannot have an underlined and invisible character.

Table 14-2. Attribute Bit Map.

7	6	5	4	3	2	1	0	
x	0	0	0	x	0	0	0	Invisible character
x	x	x	x	x	0	0	1	Underlined character
x	x	x	x	1	x	x	x	Highlighted character
1	x	x	x	x	x	x	x	Blinking character
x	1	1	1	x	0	0	0	Reverse video
x	1	1	1	x	1	1	1	Masked character

0 bit is set to 0

1 bit is set to 1

x don't care

On the color displays, the attribute byte defines character color, blinking, and background color. The bits of the color attribute byte are defined in Table 14-3.

Table 14-3. Video Attribute Bits (Color).

Bits	Meaning
0–2	Character color
3	Character intensity
4–6	Background color
7	Character blinking

Both the character color and the background color codes are derived from the same set of color values. The three bits of the color value, used in determining the color, control the display of the three primary colors (RGB = red, green, and blue) on the screen. When the bit for red is set to 1, red becomes a component of the displayed color. The various colors are determined through the presence and intensity of the primary colors. The color of the character can be brightened slightly by setting the *char-*

acter intensity bit to 1. The color codes and the corresponding colors are defined in Table 14-4.

Table 14-4. Color Bit Map.

R	G	B	Color
0	0	0	Black
0	0	1	Blue
0	1	0	Green
0	1	1	Cyan
1	0	0	Red
1	0	1	Magenta
1	1	0	Brown
1	1	1	Light gray

When the intensity bit is set to 1 for brown the displayed color is yellow. Light gray becomes white when the intensity is turned on. The other colors display a slightly brighter and lighter shade of the base color.

An interesting exercise in manipulating attribute values is to form attributes that carry the same significance for both the monochrome and color monitors. If you are writing a program that can run with either monitor, it would simplify the program (and minutely speed up the execution) if the same attribute value is used in both cases. For instance, to grab the attention of the user of the program, you might want a highlighted and blinking warning sign on the monochrome monitor. For the color monitor, you might want a blinking warning sign in red letters. Can you find an attribute value that will provide both display criteria?

Using a color monitor presents another problem: The program must either turn the video off before writing to the screen buffer and then turn it on again when it is finished, or wait for the vertical and horizontal retraces (when the video processor turns off the scanning beam) to write into memory. Why? Remember that the microprocessor and the video processor share the video buffer. If you start modifying the contents of the buffer while the video processor is actively using the memory, the microprocessor takes priority and makes the modification. The video generator can't stop painting characters on the screen just because it can't get to the buffer, so it generates garbage (GIGO) or *sparkles* on the screen. This doesn't seem to be much of a problem on the monochrome display.

The following algorithm gives the steps in producing your video screen:

```
get segment address of current buffer
calculate offset from beginning of buffer
  from row and column data
if color
then
  wait for retrace
  turn off video
  endif
put character into video buffer
if color
then
  turn on video
  endif
```

If these benefits aren't worth the extra programming but you want a better interface to the video monitor than MS-DOS can offer, you will want to use the *Video I/O* BIOS function. The Video I/O function allows a program to manipulate the screen of the video monitor without regard to the type of video adapter or monitor being used.

AH = 0 Set Video Mode

The purpose of the *Set Video Mode* subfunction is to configure the video adapter processor to the various operating modes available. There are a number of modes for the color adapter. The mode is selected by placing the numeric code for the mode into the AL register prior to executing the BIOS interrupt. This routine is not required for the IBM-PC monochrome displays. The mode is set automatically at power on (AL = 7). The modes are shown in Table 14-5.

Table 14-5. Video Modes.

Alphanumeric Modes

Code	Color or B&W	Screen Size
AL = 0	Black & white	40 × 25 (power on default)
AL = 1	Color	40 × 25
AL = 2	Black & white	80 × 25
AL = 3	Color	80 × 25

Graphics Modes

Code	Color or B&W	Screen Size
AL = 4	Color	320 × 200
AL = 5	Black & white	320 × 200
AL = 6	Black & white	640 × 200

The following code sequence shows how to set up the video processor for 80 × 25 color alphanumerics:

```
                    ; video i/o with color 80x25
     Mov   AX,3 ; set AH=0 and AL=3
     Int   10H
```

AH = 1 Set Cursor Type

The purpose of the *Set Cursor Type* subfunction is to control the shape of the hardware-controlled cursor. The blinking cannot be stopped, but you can define the size of the cursor. The cursor is made up of multiple short horizontal lines. With this subfunction, you can set the starting and ending lines of these horizontal lines. The cursor can be a full-block cursor, underline cursor, overline cursor, or through-the-character cursor. The definition of the cursor is placed into the CX register prior to calling the BIOS function. The CH register defines the starting line of the cursor. On the monochrome display, the top of the cursor is line 0 and the bottom is line 13. The defaults are 11 and 12 for the top and bottom of the cursor. On the color display, the top of the cursor is line 0 and the bottom is line 7. The defaults are 6 and 7 for the top and bottom of the cursor.

The following code sequence shows an assembler routine that is callable from Pascal for setting the type of the cursor.

```
;   Set Cursor Type
;   Stack Frame:  Start : Value     Offset = 8
;                 End   : Value     Offset = 6
;                 Return            Offset = 0
;
CURSTYPE          PROC    FAR
                  ASSUME  CS:CODE
                  PUBLIC  CURSTYPE
                  Push    BP              ; save frame pointer
                  Mov     BP,SP
                  Mov     CH,[BP+8] ; get start line of cursor
                  Mov     CL,[BP+6] ; get end line of cursor
                  Mov     AX,100H
                  Int     10H
                  Pop     BP
                  Ret     4
CURSTYPE          ENDP
```

AH = 2 Set Cursor Position

The purpose of the *Set Cursor Position* subfunction is to move the cursor to a specific screen location. Cursor positioning is critical when using the Video I/O routines because the character and attribute reads and writes use the cursor location as their base addresses. The cursor position is specified by its row and column on the screen. The upper left corner is row 0 and column 0. To move the cursor, the row number is placed in the DH register, and the column in the DL register. If you are using multiple pages in alphanumeric mode, you must specify the page number in the BH register. For most applications, the BH register should contain a zero. The BH register must be set to zero for graphics. The following code sequence shows routines for moving the cursor to the *home* position and to a general position. Both routines are callable from Pascal.

```
        ; Home Cursor
        ; Procedure Home; External;
        ;
HOME      PROC      FAR
          ASSUME    CS:CODE
          PUBLIC    HOME
          Push      BP
          Mov       BP,SP
          Mov       BH,0  ; active page
          Mov       DX,0  ; home = (0,0)
          Mov       AH,2  ; video i/o to move cursor
          Int       10H   ; video i/o BIOS
          Pop       BP
          Ret
HOME      ENDP


        ;
        ; Move Cursor
        ; Procedure MoveCurs (Row, Col : Integer); Extern;
        ;
MOVECUR   PROC      FAR
          ASSUME    CS:CODE
          PUBLIC    MOVECUR
          Push      BP
          Mov       BP,SP
          Mov       BH,0       ; active page
          Mov       DL,[BP+8]  ; get row
          Mov       DH,[BP+6]  ; get col
          Mov       AH,2       ; move cursor
```

```
                Int       10H          ; video i/o
                Pop       BP
                Ret       4
      MOVECUR   ENDP
```

AH = 3 Read Cursor Position

The purpose of the *Read Cursor Position* subfunction is to get the current screen location of the cursor. The cursor position is specified by its row and column on the screen. When the subfunction is complete, the row number will be found in the DH register, and the column in the DL register. This subfunction also gets the current cursor type and places it into the CX register (see Set Cursor Type). If you are using multiple pages in alphanumeric mode, you must specify the page number in the BH register. For most applications, the BH register should contain a zero. The BH register must be set to zero for graphics. The following code sequence shows a routine for reading the current position of the cursor. The routine is callable from Pascal.

```
      ;
      ; Get Cursor
      ; Procedure GetCurs (Var Row, Col : Integer); Extern;
      ;
      GETCUR    PROC      FAR
                ASSUME    CS:CODE
                PUBLIC    GETCUR
                Push      BP
                Mov       BP,SP
                Mov       BH,0         ; active page
                Mov       AH,3         ; get cursor
                Int       10H          ; video i/o
                Push      BP           ; save for a time
                Mov       BP,[BP+8]    ; get row address
                Mov       [BP],DH      ; store row value
                Pop       BP           ; get BP back
                Mov       BP,[BP+6]    ; get col address
                Mov       [BP],DL      ; store col value
                Pop       BP
                Ret       4
      GETCUR    ENDP
```

AH = 4 Read Light Pen Position

A light pen is a wandlike, hand-held instrument that allows a person to point to position on the video monitor's screen, select various menu items, set points of a line, or mark an object (picture or text) for some action (such as moving or deleting). The light pen contains a light-sensitive cell that senses the light which is emitted by the video display. The light pen is activated by a small switch on the side of the pen or an internal switch that is activated when the pen is pressed against a hard surface (presumably the face of the CRT). When the light pen switch is activated and the scanning beam of the display enters the light pen, sensitizing the light cell, the video hardware controller will receive a signal. Upon arrival of this signal, the controller saves the current position of the scanning beam. The application program can check the status word of the controller for a light pen reading.

The purpose of the *Read Light Pen Position* subfunction is to completely handle all of the hardware-related interactions with the video controller pertaining to the light pen. When an application program uses this function, it is told whether the light pen had been used, and if the light pen had been used, the screen coordinates of the pen's activation.

This function goes one step further and converts the screen position into the current graphics mode. This means that if the program is using alpha mode, the screen position will be returned in character row (0 to 24) and column (0 to 79) coordinates; if the current mode is high-resolution graphics, the position will be converted to current scan line (0 to 199) and approximate horizontal pixel position (0 to 639).

There are no register setup requirements to use this subfunction. However, the BX, CX, and DX registers will be used to return coordinate values. The contents of these registers will be changed, even though the light pen had not been activated. It might be wise to save the current values of these registers if they contain important information.

When the light pen subfunction has completed its work, the AH register will contain the status of the light pen's activity. If the AH register is set to zero, there has not been a light pen selection. A value of one in the AH register indicates that the light pen has been used. The subfunction resets the video controller so that it can detect the next light pen activation.

The positioning data is then extracted from the BX, CX, and DX registers. In all display modes, the DH register holds the row (0–24) number, while the column (0–79) position is in the DL register.

In the graphics modes, the location of the light pen selection is better defined. The CH register (notice that the entire CX register is not used) contains the scan line with a value between 0 and 199. The BX register is used to return the horizontal pixel position.

Depending upon the current graphics resolution, the BX register will contain a value between 0 and 319 (medium resolution) or 0 and 639 (high resolution).

The details of the subfunction give the impression that the positioning accuracy of the light pen is somewhat less than the resolution of medium or high resolution graphics. This means that if any of a number of neighboring pixels are selected with the light pen, the video controller will consistently indicate the same one of those pixels as being selected. For example, the following code segment shows a program waiting for a light pen event, moving the cursor to the location of the light pen:

```
;
;       assume that the graphics mode = alpha
;
;       wait for light pen
;       could also branch around if no light pen
;
LIGHT:  Mov   AH,4   ; read light pen
        Int   10H    ; video bios
        Cmp   AH,0   ; check for strike
        Beq   LIGHT  ; 0 = no light pen
;
;       have :DX = row and column of light pen
;       need :DX = row and column of cursor
;             BH = display page (0)
;
        Sub   BH,BH  ; clear page register
        Mov   AH,2   ; set cursor position
        Int   10H    ; video bios
;
;       cursor should be a light pen position
;
```

AH = 5 Select Active Display Page

The color adapter card for the IBM PC is capable of displaying 640 pixels (picture elements) or dots in each of 200 horizontal lines. Since each dot requires one bit of memory, the adapter card must contain 640 × 200 bits (128,000 bits or 16,000 bytes) of video data.

On the other hand, when the adapter card is placed into alpha mode, it requires two bytes (one for the character and one for the character's attributes) for every screen position. The 40 × 25 alpha mode needs 2,000 bytes for a complete screen, and the 80 × 25 alpha mode requires 4,000 bytes for each screen.

Since the graphics adapter has to have 16,000 bytes, it has room for eight 40 × 25 screens or four 80 × 25 screens. It becomes obvious that it would be nice if a program could be displaying one screen while it is preparing another, and then switch from one screen to the other at some critical point in the program.

The purpose of the *Select Active Display Page* subfunction is to activate a selected screen (display page) and display its contents. This subfunction is only valid when one of the alpha modes is selected.

To select a display page, the page is identified through the AL register prior to calling this subfunction. The page number is dependent upon the current alpha mode. In alpha modes 0 and 1 (40 × 25 displays), pages 0 through 7 are valid. In modes 2 and 3 (80 × 25 displays), only pages 0 through 3 are valid.

The following instructions cause display page 0 to be selected:

```
;
; select page 0
;
PAGE0:  Mov AH,5    ; make display page active
        Mov AL,0    ; select page 0
        Int 10H     ; video bios
;
; page 0 is now displayed
;
```

AH = 6 Scroll Active Page Up

AH = 7 Scroll Active Page Down

The purpose of the *Scroll Active Page* subfunctions is to vertically move a section of the display (*window*) and add blank lines to the vacated areas.

Both subfunctions work in the same manner, with the exception that the scrolling motions are in opposite directions. Scrolling a window using the *up* subfunction causes the material displayed in the window to move toward the top of the screen. Blank space at the bottom of the window is replaced by spaces. Scrolling a window using the *down* subfunction causes the material displayed in the window to move toward the bottom of the screen. Blank space at the top of the window is replaced by spaces.

These subfunctions are capable of scrolling graphics. Since the scrolling subfunctions can operate within a window of the screen, there are several function parameters that have to be loaded into registers. These parameters are:

- Number of lines to scroll
- Definition of the window
- Attributes of the blanked area

The number of lines to be scrolled is defined through the AL register. If you want to scroll the display up by one line to allow the inclusion of a new line at the bottom of the screen, then the AL register would be set to one. Scrolling several lines would involve loading the AL register with the appropriate number. Setting the AL register to zero will cause the window to be cleared. When the graphics mode is active, the amount of scrolling is still relative to character lines.

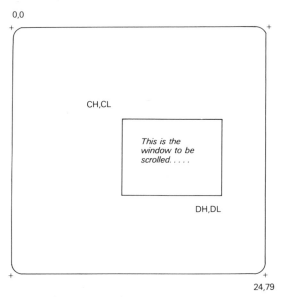

Figure 14-1. Scrolling a Portion of the Screen.

The scrolled window is defined by naming the rows and columns that make up the boundaries of the screen area. This is done in alpha mode coordinates (even when graphic mode is active). Whether you use 40 × 25 or 80 × 25 coordinates depends upon the current video mode. For graphic modes, use 80 × 25 coordinates. Two sets of row and column coordinates are required: the upper left-hand corner of the window and the lower right-hand corner. These coordinates are loaded as follows:

CH register   Upper right-hand row coordinate

CL register   Upper right-hand column coordinate

DH register   Lower left-hand row coordinate

DL register   Lower left-hand column coordinate

Probably the least obvious of the parameters to the scrolling subfunctions is this last parameter, attributes of the blanked area. When the contents of the window are moved, there is no doubt about the identity of the characters that are to replace them. It will be replaced by spaces.

But what of the attributes? Should the area be in reverse video, highlighted, or a certain color? This parameter gives the program a chance to define the characteristics of the blanked area. Place the new attribute into the BH register.

When all of the parameters are set, calling the subfunction will move the contents of the window in the specified direction. For an application where a new line of text is to appear in the blanked area, it is the responsibility of the application to write the new line onto the screen.

If the program scrolls off a line of text at the top of the screen and then scrolls down to make room at the top of the screen, the original text is gone and will not be redisplayed unless you put it back there.

AH = 8 Read Attribute/Character at Cursor Position

The purpose of the *Read Attribute/Character at Cursor Position* subfunction is to retrieve the character and its attributes, which is currently stored at the current cursor's position. This is a *screen read*.

The only parameter to this subfunction is the page number from which the character is to be read. The page number must be placed in BH register. The page number is only required during operations in alpha mode. This subfunction will return the character and its attributes in the AX register. The ASCII character will be in the AL register, and its attributes in the AH portion of the register.

AH = 9 Write Attribute/Character at Cursor Position

The purpose of the *Write Attribute/Character at Cursor Position* sub-function is to place a character and a set of attributes at the current cursor's position. This subfunction is a *screen write*.

A number of parameters are required to write to the screen with this subfunction. Naturally, the character and its attributes are required. The character is placed in the AL register and its attributes are placed in the BL register.

NOTE: When the graphics mode is active, the Write Dot subfunction is used to create the images of characters on the screen. The contents of the BL register will then be transferred to the AL register (the color register for Write Dot) and the selected color attribute used. Setting bit 7 of the color attribute register (BL, in this case) will cause some extra operations to be executed. Review the description of the Write Dot subfunction before writing characters in the graphics mode.

For the alpha mode, a page number must be specified. This parameter allows a program to prepare text on several nondisplayed pages at one time. The page number that is to be used is placed in the BH register. This subfunction also includes a *repeating* feature: a character that may be written several times on a single line. This feature could be very useful in filling a line with spaces from the cursor position. This subfunction will not continue writing characters to the next line. It is therefore possible to set the repeat factor to a high number so that no matter how far the cursor is from the left edge of the screen, it can clear the line from the cursor position to the end of the line. The number of times that the character should be written is placed in the CX register.

To put them all in one place, the parameters to this subfunction are:

AL register   ASCII character to be written

BL register   Attribute or color of character

BH register   Alpha mode page number

CX register   Repetition factor

You can design your own characters for reading and writing when the graphics adapter is in graphics mode. The problem is that your characters must have internal (numeric) values that are greater than 127.

Each character must be designed within an eight-bit by eight-bit area and all 128 (128–255) values should be defined.

Probably the easiest way to design the character is on graph paper. Darken the graph paper squares in an 8 × 8 area to define the character. When the characters are designed, translate the dark and light areas to a binary code with each line making a byte of information. The eight bytes from each character become the data to be placed into your program for the creation of your alphabet.

Put the address of your first character into address Hex 0:007C. The Video I/O BIOS will look at that address whenever it encounters a character value greater than 127. If Hex 0:007C is not zero, the BIOS routines will follow the address to your character definitions and display the appropriate image.

The following figure shows the definition of the Greek letter pi. The first grid shows the formation of the character using graph paper to form the shape. Using the Xs to mark the character, a binary code is derived for each line. This is the character generator code for each line of the letter. For ease of reading and data entry, the binary code is converted to hexadecimal.

0									= 00000000 = 00h
1		X	X	X	X	X	X		= 01111110 = 7Eh
2	X		X			X			= 10100100 = A4h
3			X			X			= 00100100 = 24h
4			X			X			= 00100100 = 24h
5			X			X			= 00100100 = 24h
6			X			X			= 00100100 = 24h
7									= 00000000 = 00h

Figure 14-2. Creating a Custom Character.

The definition of this character in the application program would look like this:

```
; the Greek Pi (no label required)
  DB 000H,07EH,0A4H,024H,024H,024H,024H,000H
```

The other characters in the 128-character sequence would be defined in the same way.

AH = 0A Write Character Only at Cursor Position

The purpose of the *Write Character Only at Cursor Position* subfunction is to place a character at the current cursor's position. This subfunction is a *screen write* that will not modify the current value of the position's attribute byte.

This subfunction is identical to the Write Attribute/Character at Cursor's Position subfunction with the exception that the attribute value in BL is not used.

AH = 0B Set Color Palette

When the color video processor is operating in *medium-resolution* graphics mode (320 × 200), the program has a limited number (8) of colors that can be painted. Further limiting the number of colors is the fact that only four of the eight colors may be painted on the screen area at one time. The four colors are comprised of three foreground colors and one background color.

Furthermore, there are two color palettes with three of the colors fixed to each. Which group of three foreground colors is being painted is determined by the *current palette*. The background color is displayed whenever the foreground color is set to zero.

The purpose of the *Set Color Palette* subfunction is to select which group of colors may be painted at any time. The color groups are:

Palette 0 Green (1), Red (2), Yellow (3)

Palette 1 Cyan (1), Magenta (2), White (3)

The background color may be one of 16 colors. Colors 8 through 15 are intensified colors. If the monitor running the program does not have the capability of intensifying colors, then colors 0 through 7 will be the only ones displayed. Intensified colors will appear as though they were the corresponding unintensified color.

The background colors are given in Table 14-6.

Table 14-6. Color Values.

Value	Color
0	Black
1	Blue
2	Green
3	Cyan
4	Red
5	Magenta
6	Brown
7	Light gray
8	Dark gray
9	Light blue
10	Light green
11	Light cyan
12	Light red
13	Light magenta
14	Yellow
15	White

The palette selection process uses the BH and the BL registers. The value of the BH register controls the action of the subfunction.

BH = 0 Select a Background Color   This background color will be displayed whenever the foreground color code is set to 0. The value of the background color (0–15) is placed into the BL register prior to calling this subfunction.

BH = 1 Select a Color Palette   Selecting a color palette establishes which group of three colors may be painted. The groups are given above. The value of the color group is placed into the BL register.

For example:

```
;
; set background to light red
;
      Mov     BH,0      ; set background
      Mov     BL,12     ; select light red
      Mov     AH,0BH    ; set color palette
      Int     10H       ; video i/o
;
; activate color group 0
;
      Mov     BH,1      ; select palette
      Mov     BL,0      ; activate green, red and yellow
      Mov     AH,0BH    ; set color palette
      Int     10H       ; video i/o
```

By cleverly picking the background color and then using the proper color palette to paint the same color in foreground, a program would fill the screen with a solid color. Then by changing either the background color or the color palette (or both), the painted information would suddenly be visible.

AH = 0C Write Dot

In computer graphics, the basic data structure is the picture element or pixel. On the monitor's screen, a pixel is a single dot. The purpose of the *Write Dot* subfunction is to paint a screen pixel with a color (on or off with a black and white format). Two pieces of information are required to use this subfunction: the location (row and column) and color of the pixel. The current video mode determines the range that these pieces of data can have.

Table 14-7. Screen Resolutions.

Resolution	Row	Column	Colors
Medium	0–199	0–329	0–15 background
			1–3 foreground
High	0–199	0–639	Black and white only

There is a low-resolution mode for the video processor, but BIOS does not support its use. Refer to the *IBM PC Technical Reference Manual* for more details.

The DX register is used to pass the row coordinate to the subfunction. While the CX register is used with the column coordinate to the subfunction, the AL register contains the color. For medium resolution, the valid values are 0 through 3. Using the zero value allows the background color to be visible.

For the high-resolution mode, a zero in the AL register will write a black dot, and a one will write a white dot.

Setting bit 7 in the AL register will cause the value of the register to be *XOR*ed with the current value. This could cause some fancy color flashings, but in the high-resolution mode it will have a profound effect. If the value of the AL register is one, then every bit written will reverse itself from white to black and black to white (reverse video).

Since the pixel is the basic building block of computer graphics, a number of primitive graphic routines can be built up around this subfunction. The first primitive would be to draw a line from one screen location to another. The line would be written as a group of dots. Patterned or dashed lines would mean that some of the dots in the line are not drawn. Several books are available that cover the algorithms for line drawing and other graphic forms.

AH = 0D Read Dot

The purpose of the *Read Dot* subfunction is to get the color of a specific pixel. This subfunction is the reverse of the Write Dot subfunction. Given a row and a column for a pixel, get the color.

The DX register is used to pass the row coordinate to the subfunction. While the CX register is used with the column coordinate to the subfunction, the AL register returns with the color. For medium resolution, the valid values are 0 through 3. For the high-resolution mode, the AL register will contain a zero (black) or a one (white).

AH = 0E Write Teletype

The purpose of the *Write Teletype* subfunction is to let the video processor and the monitor simulate a dumb teletypewriter style terminal.

The character being placed on the screen will appear at the cursor, and the cursor will advance. If the cursor is at the left edge of the screen, it moves to the right side of the screen and down to the next line. If the current line is the last line of the screen, then the screen will be scrolled and the bottom line cleared for the new line.

The Write Teletype subfunction will respond to the backspace, line-feed, carriage return, and bell characters without displaying them on the screen.

For the Write Teletype subfunction to be called, the character to be written must be in the AL register. This subfunction uses the Write Character Only at Cursor Position subfunction to write the character to the screen, so the character will still appear in graphics mode.

However, if the graphics mode is active, this subfunction will need a color. Place the color in the BL register. Be mindful of bit 7 in the BL register. In the high-resolution mode, setting the AL register to 129 will write the character in reverse video. In alphanumeric mode, the BH register must be set to the current page. It must be set to zero for graphics.

```
; write a msg to the screen
; Procedure TTY (Vars Msg : String; Count : Integer);
;
TTY      PROC      FAR
         ASSUME    CS:CODE
         PUBLIC    TTY
         Push      BP
         Mov       BP,SP
         Les       DX,DWORD Ptr [BP+8]
         Mov       CX,[BP+6]
         Mov       SI,0
WRYT:    Mov       AL,ES:[DX+SI]
         Inc       SI
         Mov       AH,0EH
         Mov       BH,0
         Mov       BL,1
         Int       10H
         Loop      WRYT
         Pop       BP
         Ret       6
TTY      ENDP
```

AH = 0F Get Current Video State

The purpose of the *Get Current Video State* subfunction is to get the configuration of the video adapter and return it to the calling program. This subfunction echoes information entered through other Video I/O subfunctions. Specifically, the video state information includes:

• Current video mode

• Number of character columns

• Active video page

The video mode is the code described in the Set Video Mode subfunction. The mode is returned in the AL register.

The number of character columns is defined by the current video mode, and is set to either 40 or 80. The number of characters in a column is returned in the AH register.

The active video page is set with the Select Active Display Page subfunction (see *AH = 5 Select Active Display Page*). The active page number is returned in the BH register.

Equipment Check

BIOS Interrupt: Hex 11

BIOS Functions: Get equipment configuration

The *Equipment Check* function allows the programmer to fetch an encoded list of options currently attached to the IBM PC. This function is useful because it lets a program know what the configuration of the host machine is so that it can make adjustments for the equipment. For instance, the video buffer address of a monochrome display is different than the address of a color monitor video buffer. Using the Equipment Check function, a program can check for which type of video display is being used, and use the appropriate address in its Video I/O routines.

Equipment Check returns the data word found at address 40:10 (Hex) in the AX register. The equipment configuration is determined by which bits are set in the register. The following table gives the meaning of the equipment word.

Table 14-8. Equipment Bit Map

Bit	Equipment
15,14	Number of Printers Attached (0–3)
13	Not Used
12	Game I/O Attached
11,10,9	Number of RS-232 Cards Attached (0–4)
8	Not Used
7,6	Number of Diskette Drives 00 = 1, 01 = 2, 10 = 3, 11 = 4 only if bit 0 is set to 1
5,4	Initial Video Mode 00 = Unused 01 = 40 × 25 BW using color card 10 = 80 × 25 BW using color card 11 = 80 × 25 BW using BW card
3,2	Motherboard RAM Size (PC Only) 00 = 16K 01 = 32K 10 = 48K 11 = 64K

Table 14-8. Continued

Bit	Equipment
1	Math Co-processor (AT only) 0 = Not installed 1 = Installed
0	Diskette Drives Installed 0 = No diskette drive(s) 1 = Diskette drive(s) installed (see bits 6 and 7)

```
; Pascal called routine
; Equipment Check from BIOS
; Function Equip : Word;
; no parameters
;
EQUIP      PROC    FAR
           ASSUME  CS:CODE
           PUBLIC  EQUIP
           Push    BP
           Mov     BP,SP
           Int     11H
           Pop     BP
           Ret
EQUIP      ENDP
```

Memory Check

BIOS Interrupt: Hex 12

BIOS Function: Get size of memory

The purpose of the *Memory Check* function is to return to the calling program with the number of contiguous 1K (1,024 byte) blocks of memory that are installed in the computer.

This returned count may be inaccurate if there are boards with extended memory installed in the machine without the memory area of the motherboard being filled (or the switches properly set).

This function could be used by a large program that requires a large amount of memory for its data area. By calling this routine, the program could determine if the host computer was big enough to accommodate the program and its data. If the host computer was too small, the program could signal the user that the machine was too small and then abort.

This function fetches the system memory size word at address 40:13 (Hex). The following assembler routine can be used to get the system memory size and return the value to the calling program through a Pascal function:

```
; Memory Size Check from BIOS
; Function Memory : Word;
; no parameters
;
MEMORY      PROC    FAR
            ASSUME  CS:CODE
            PUBLIC  MEMORY
            Push    BP
            Mov     BP,SP
            Int     12H     ; get memory size in Ks
            Pop     BP
            Ret
MEMORY      ENDP
```

RS-232 I/O

BIOS Interrupt: Hex 14

BIOS Functions: Initialize the communications processor

Send character over the comm. line

Receive a character from comm. line

Return comm. line status

The subfunctions of the *RS-232 I/O* BIOS function control the actions of the RS-232 asynchronous communications boards. The async board is used for sending and receiving information to and from other computers (not necessarily other IBM PCs). When the computer is attached to a modem, the communications may take place using the telephone system, giving your computer access to national computer networks and services, electronic mail, and file-transfer capabilities between computers.

There are four subfunctions associated with this BIOS function:

- Setting up the communications board so that the communications processor will understand and agree with the incoming signals from another source
- Checking the status of the communications process
- Sending characters
- Receiving characters

Setting the AH register determines the action of the function.

For all RS-232 I/O subfunctions: The DX register must be set to 0 or 1 to indicate which RS-232 card is to be activated by the function. If there is only one card in the system, DX should be set to zero.

AH = 0 Initialize the Communications Processor

This subfunction will set up the communications processor so that it will properly communicate with other computer systems. The criteria for this initialization involve:

Baud   Rate of transmission; roughly the number of bits sent in one second.

Parity   An error-checking scheme to ensure that the data was not damaged during transmission and reception.

StopBit   The number of bits used at the end of the data to tell the receiving processor that the character has been finished (this is analogous to a caboose at the end of the train).

Word Length   The number of bits in a transmitted character
There are a limited number of settings for each of these pieces of information. And there are a few common, standard settings to make the task of figuring out what the settings should be fairly easy. This information is encoded into the AL register prior to calling the function.

Table 14-9. RS-232 Interface Values.

Bit	Criterion	Usage
7,6,5	Baud	Transmission/Reception Rate
		000 = 110 Baud
		001 = 150 Baud
		010 = 300 Baud (standard)
		011 = 600 Baud
		100 = 1200 Baud (common)
		101 = 2400 Baud
		110 = 4800 Baud
		111 = 9600 Baud (common with direct connect)

Table 14-9. Continued

Bit	Criterion	Usage
4,3	Parity	Error Detection 00 = No parity checking (common) 01 = Odd parity 11 = Even parity (most common)
2	Stop Bits	0 = 1 stop bit 1 = 2 stop bits
1,0	Char Size	10 = 7 bits (standard ASCII) 11 = 8 bits

When this subfunction is completed, the AX register will contain the status bytes from the line control status port and the modem status port of the communications processor. The contents of these status bytes are detailed in the last subfunction description.

AH = 1 Send a Character Over the Communications Line

This subfunction will send the character in the AL register over the RS-232 communications line.

Prior to calling the RS-232 I/O function, the character to be sent should be placed in the AL register and the subfunction code in the AH register. When this subfunction is given control, it will wait until the communications processor is able to accept the character to be sent. Control will then return to the calling procedure.

If something should happen that prevents the acceptance of the character, this subfunction will return with the most significant bit (bit 7) of the AH register set to 1.

The function returns with the AX register containing the communications status words.

The following code sequence could be used for sending characters:

```
;
; Pascal interface to RS-232 I/O - Send Character
; Function SendChar (C : Char) : Word; status returned
; Example:    Status := SendChar(Ch);
;
SENDCHAR PROC      FAR
         ASSUME    CS:CODE
```

```
        PUBLIC    SENDCHAR
        Push      BP
        Mov       BP,SP
        Mov       AL,[BP+6] ; get char to send
        Mov       AH,1      ; set send command
        Int       14H       ; call RS-232 I/O
        Pop       BP
        Ret       2
SENDCHAR ENDP
```

AH = 2 Receive a Character from the Communications Line

This subfunction will receive a character from the RS-232 communications processor.

When this subfunction receives control, it will wait until a character is received from the communications line or approximately one-half second of waiting occurs (time out). If this is too long for your program to be idle (it could be sending characters during this waiting time), you should plan on using the status word from the last subfunction to determine whether or not a character is ready to be read.

When the status word indicates that a character is ready, use this subfunction to retrieve it. The received character is placed in the AL register. The AH register contains the line control status byte.

You will have to remove (or mask) the status word to get the returned character. The status word has already been partially masked so that only the error bits are active. Therefore, if the status word is not equal to zero, then an error has occurred during the receiving function and should be checked.

```
; Function GetChar : Char;
; Example: Status := GetChar;
;          Ch := Chr(Status);
;          Status := Status Div 256;
GETCHAR      PROC     FAR
             ASSUME   CS:CODE
             PUBLIC   GETCHAR
             Push     BP
             Mov      BP,SP
             Mov      AH,2      ; set recv command
             Int      14H       ; call RS-232 I/O
             Pop      BP
             Ret
GETCHAR      ENDP
```

AH = 3 Return the Communications Line Status

This subfunction will get the current communications status bytes from the line control and modem control registers in the communications processor. By fetching the status of the communications processor, a program can optimize its interface to that processor. The subfunctions that send and receive characters will wait until the communications processor is ready for the activity.

For example, the sending function will not be able to write the character into the communications processor buffer until it is empty, and so will continue checking the buffer status until the buffer is empty. If your program takes the responsibility of doing the *buffer is empty* check, the program can be doing other things until the processor is ready for another character.

This subfunction returns the status work in the AX register. This status word is also returned after the other communications subfunctions. The status word is defined in Table 14-10.

Table 14-10. RS-232 Status Codes.

Register	Bit	Meaning
AH	7	Time out has occurred
AH	6	Transmit is idle
AH	5	Transmit buffer is empty
AH	4	Break detected
AH	3	Framing error (stop bit problem)
AH	2	Parity error (data bits changed)
AH	1	Overrun error (reading too slowly)
AH	0	Data is ready
AL	7	Incoming carrier detected
AL	6	'Telephone ringing' detected
AL	5	Data Set Ready
AL	4	Clear to Send
AL	3	Change in incoming carrier detect
AL	2	Trailing edge ring detector
AL	1	Change in Data Set Ready
AL	0	Change in Clear to Send

The AH register contains the *line control status*. The AL register contains the *modem status*.

Keyboard I/O

BIOS Interrupt: Hex 16

BIOS Functions: Read an ASCII character from keyboard

Check for available character to be read

Get the current shift status

It was mentioned during the discussion about the MS-DOS traditional character I/O functions that the DOS functions provided a service that had to be compatible with the most primitive I/O device that might be used with the system. Subsequently, the character I/O routines were primitive to match the abilities of the teletypewriter. To escape this problem, the programmer can use the keyboard services directly available through the use of this BIOS function.

What really makes this function attractive is the ability to check for the availability of an ASCII character prior to committing the program to reading the character. Both MS-DOS and this function's *Keyboard Read* will cause the program to wait until a character is typed on the keyboard. However, the Keyboard I/O function provides a suitable *Check Before Reading* subfunction.

Now, MS-DOS provides a *Check Before Reading* capability, but it does some other checking you might not want to do. For instance, the MS-DOS check will cause a program halt if Ctrl-C is detected. For a communications program where a host sees your computer as a dumb terminal, the Ctrl-C signal can be very important in controlling your programs running on the host. If MS-DOS siphons off the Ctrl-C (and kills the communication program), you are forced to go out of your way and program some alternate way of sending the Ctrl-C signal. This function does not tamper with the ASCII characters read from the keyboard.

The Keyboard I/O function provides the following services:

- Read the next character from the keyboard

- Indicate if a character is ready

- Get the shift status code

These functions are selected by setting the proper command code in the AH register prior to calling the Keyboard I/O function with the software interrupt.

AH = 0 Read the Next ASCII Character from Keyboard

This keyboard subfunction will read the next character entered from the console keyboard and return it to the calling program in the AX register. The character is returned in two parts: the ASCII code and the internal scan code.

In most situations, the AL register is the only register of importance, containing the ASCII code corresponding to the key that was pressed on the keyboard. The AH register contains the scan code for the same key. The scan code usually corresponds to the number of the key on the keyboard. The keys on the keyboard are all electronically numbered. The numbering scheme can be found on pages 2–16 and 2–17 of the *IBM PC Technical Reference Manual*.

The scan code becomes very important when a non-ASCII key or key combination is pressed. For instance, the 10 function keys to the left of the main keyboard can be very useful for controlling a program, but they do not have a corresponding standard ASCII code. When these function keys are pressed, the AL register will contain a zero, and the scan code in the AH register will tell the program which function key, cursor key, or ALT key combination was pressed.

The following tables show the various keys and the contents of the AH register (shown in decimal values) when this function is done (AL register is always zero).

Table 14-11. Function Key Assignments.

AH Register	Key(s) Pressed
59	Function Key 1
60	Function Key 2
61	Function Key 3
62	Function Key 4
63	Function Key 5
64	Function Key 6
65	Function Key 7
66	Function Key 8
67	Function Key 9
68	Function Key 10
84–93	Shift and Function Key 1–10
94–103	Ctrl and Function Key 1–10
104–113	Alt and Function Key 1–10

The keys found on the keypad to the right of the main keyboard are shown in Table 14-12. The Num Lock key controls the way in which the keystroke is interpreted.

Table 14-12. Cursor Key Assignments.

AH Register	Key(s) Pressed
71	Home
72	Up Arrow
75	Left Arrow
77	Right Arrow
80	Down Arrow
73	Page Up
81	Page Down
79	End
82	Ins (Insert)
83	Del (Delete)

The codes in Table 14-13 are formed by pressing the Alt key on the main keyboard and simultaneously pressing one of the regular keyboard letters or numbers.

Table 14-13. Main Keyboard Assignments.

AH Register	Key Pressed
16–25	Q,W,E,R,T,Y,U,I,O,P
30–38	A,S,D,F,G,H,J,K,L
44–50	Z,X,C,V,B,N,M
120–131	1,2,3,4,5,6,7,8,9,0,-,=

Other scan codes are listed in the *IBM PC Technical Reference Manual* on pages 3–14.

The use of the Alt key while pressing a letter or number can be a powerful tool. Since the AL register is set to zero, there is no chance of confusing the entry of a regular ASCII character and a command to the program. The Alt key can be used to designate commands in a program.

```
Repeat
  Get a character from the keyboard
  If AL = 0
  Then
    Call command processor using scan code in AH
  Else
    Call text processor using ASCII character in AL
  Endif
Until 'QUIT' command is entered
```

Here is a word of caution about using a QUIT command by looking for an Alt-Q. There seems to be a bug in the IBM PC which appears when the Alt-Q combination is pressed. The value of 16 is not returned as you might expect. Instead, the printer (if you have one and it is on; otherwise you get a print error message) will echo each of the lines appearing on the video display. The Alt-Q and the Ctrl-PrtSc keystroke are identical.

AH = 1 Indicate If an ASCII Character Is Ready

This Keyboard I/O subfunction will indicate whether a character is ready to be read from the keyboard. In reality, the character is not read directly from the keyboard, but from a keyboard buffer. The occurrence of a character being entered on the keyboard will cause an interrupt. The interrupt handler is responsible for reading the scan code from the keyboard and making the necessary translations to the proper ASCII code. When the interrupt handler is finished with its task, it places the translated character and scan code into the keyboard buffer.

The location of the characters in the keyboard buffer is controlled by two markers or indexes. One index shows the location of the next character to be removed from the buffer, while the other index shows the location where the interrupt handler should place its next character in the buffer. If these two indexes refer to the same location (they are equal), then there are no characters to be read from the buffer.

By testing the values of the two indexes for equality, this subfunction can determine whether a character is ready to be read. The results of the test are preserved in the Zero Flag (ZF) bit of the flag register. Using a Jump on Zero instruction after the control returns to the calling program, the program can determine the readiness of the keyboard buffer.

This subfunction makes no judgment about the value of the ASCII code. That is, it does not take any action on the Ctrl-C code or any other code. This subfunction will, however, return the ASCII value of the next character in the buffer in the AL register. It does not advance the index when it fetches the character, so that when the reading subfunction is used, no characters are lost.

The following code sequence shows how this subfunction can be called and the results used:

```
;
; Function KEYRDY : Boolean;
; Example:    While Not KEYRDY Do
;                Begin
;                {do necessary things while waiting}
;                End;
;             C := GetChar;
;
KEYRDY      PROC    FAR
            ASSUME  CS:CODE
            PUBLIC  KEYRDY
            Push    BP
            Mov     BP,SP
            Mov     AH,1
            Int     16H
            Jz      ISRDY
            Mov     AL,0
            Jmp     KEYBYE
ISRDY:      Mov     AL,1
KEYBYE:     Pop     BP
            Ret
KETRDY      ENDP
```

AH = 2 Get the Current Shift Status Code

This Keyboard I/O subfunction will inform a program about the state of the shift keys when the last key was pressed. Determining the state of the shift keys could be vital to properly interpreting the meaning of the pressed key.

The shift keys have no associated scan codes. Therefore, if it is a responsibility of the program to determine the state of the shift keys in making some value judgment, then using this subfunction is the only way in which the identity of the pressed keys can be determined.

Notice that the status is so specific as to show the difference between the left and right shift keys. This could lead to something like this:

```
If the right shift key is pressed, highlight the character
```

The status byte is returned in the AL register. The definition of the bits is shown in the following table.

Table 14-14. Keyboard Status.

Bit	Meaning (when set to 1)
7	Insert state is active
6	Caps lock state has been toggled
5	Num lock state has been toggled
4	Scroll lock state has been toggled
3	ALT shift key is being pressed
2	Ctrl shift key is being pressed
1	Shift key at left of keyboard is pressed
0	Shift key at right of keyboard is pressed

Printer I/O

BIOS Interrupt: Hex 17

BIOS Functions: Print a character

Initialize a printer port

Read the printer status

The *Printer I/O* functions provide access to all of the printers attached to the computer system. The fact that there may be multiple printers (dot matrix and letter quality) associated with a single machine may make this function slightly more useful than the corresponding MS-DOS function. The MS-DOS function does not allow the selection of which printer is to be used. For a single printer configuration, the MS-DOS *Printer Output* function is the reasonable choice.

The Printer I/O function provides for all aspects of printer control:

- Sending of a character to a specific printer
- Initializing a printer
- Checking the status of the printer

These subfunctions are selected by placing the appropriate code into the AH register prior to calling the function. The specific printer is identified by placing a 0, 1, or 2 into the DX register.

In Pascal, you may want to set up a printer type to assign the proper values to the DX register for the printers:

```
Type
    Printer = (Dot_Matrix, Letter_Quality, Laser_Printer);
```

The BIOSPRNT procedure would be declared as:

```
Procedure BIOSPRNT (     Device : Printer;
                         C      : Char;
                     Var Status : Byte); EXTERN;
```

And the BIOSPRNT procedure is used in this way:

```
For I := 1 to STR.Len Do
  Begin
  BIOSPRNT (Dot_Matrix, STR[I], Status);
  If Status <> 0 Then Send_Err (Prt_Error, Status);
  End;
{send carriage return and line feed - end of line}
BIOSPRNT (Dot_Matrix, Chr(13), Status);
BIOSPRNT (Dot_Matrix, Chr(10), Status);
```

AH = 0 Print a Character

This Printer I/O subfunction will send a character to the designated printer. The character to be printed must be placed in the AL register prior to the function call. The function will wait until the printer is not busy and then print the character or, having waited for a preset time, return to the calling program with a time out error.

In the case of the time out error, the AH register will be equal to one, all other status bits having been cleared to zero.

The BIOSPRNT procedure previously described could provide the service of printing a character.

```
;
;      Procedure BIOSPRNT (     Device : Printer;
;                               C      : Char;
;                           Var Status : Byte); EXTERN;
;
BIOSPRNT PROC        FAR
         ASSUME      CS:CODE
         PUBLIC      BIOSPRNT
         Push        BP
         Mov         BP,SP
         Mov         DX,[BP+6]       ; get id of printer
         Mov         AL,[BP+8]       ; get character to print
```

```
         Mov     AH,0            ; select print function
         Int     17H             ; BIOS print function
         Mov     BP,[BP+10]      ; get address of status byte
         Mov     [BP],AH         ; put status byte
         Pop     BP
         Ret     6               ; bye
BIOSPRNT ENDP
```

AH = 1 Initialize a Printer Port

This Printer I/O subfunction will reset a selected printer to its initialized state. Initializing a printer will usually reset the internal settings of information to the power-up values. This initialization will cause the top-of-page to be located at the current position of the paper. You will have to readjust the paper so that the position of the paper agrees with the printer's internal line counter. The printer is initialized when the computer is turned on (using this subfunction) and when the printer is turned on (to its own default values), so there should no reason for a program to reset the printer.

AH = 2 Read the Printer Status

This Printer I/O subfunction will inform a program about the state of the designated printer. When a program is performing many tasks, it may not be able to wait for a printer to be ready to accept a character. In this case, a program may want to interrogate the status of a specific printer before sending a character. If the printer is ready, then send the character. Otherwise, move on to the next task (sending a character to another printer?).

The following table defines the bits used in the printer status byte. This byte is returned in the AH register.

Table 14-15. Printer Status.

Bit	Meaning (when set to 1)
7	Printer is Busy
6	Acknowledge to Last Character
5	Out of Paper
4	Printer is Selected
3	I/O Error
2	Unused
1	Unused
0	Time Out Error

Adapting the code sequence from the Keyboard I/O function, we get the following program segment that prints text files while the program waits for a key to be pressed on the keyboard.

```
While Not KEYRDY Do
  Begin
  {do necessary things while waiting}
  If PRNTRDY (Dot_Matrix)
  Then
    Begin
    Get (Text_File);
    BIOSPRNT (Dot_Matrix, Text_File^, Status);
    End;
  If PRNTRDY (Letter_Quality)
  Then
    Begin
    Get (Textual_File);
    BIOSPRNT (Letter_Quality, Textual_File^, Status);
    End;
  End;
C := GetChar;
```

Chapter 15

Trying It Out

INTRODUCTION

Computer science is not computer programming. It is the art and science of solving problems that require a computer to prove the correctness of the solutions. Programming is a skill that provides you with a means of describing your solution to the computer. We're going to wrap up with some problems, some solutions that utilize the MS-DOS functions, and a program that you can use.

Throughout this text, you have seen the numerous functions that MS-DOS can perform for you in your programs. With these functions, you have encountered examples of code that utilize them. Now let's quickly bring some of these concepts together.

The following discussion will revolve around the development of a simple assembly language program that you may find useful. This development is handled in several steps:

1. Describing a problem that is often encountered

2. Finding an interesting solution to the first problem

3. Finding a second problem in the solution

4. Outlining the attack at the second problem

5. Showing the evolution of the program to solve the problem

6. Proving that it works

PROGRAMMING STYLES

It is my experience that there are several styles of programming. This is probably also your experience. What I have noticed is that the extremes of the programming style spectrum are two interesting styles.

At one end is the programmer who fully develops a program before it is ever compiled, with an eye for detail that rivals that of an eagle; compiles it with few, if any, errors; and the program works the first time. This person knows (to a very high degree of understanding) and uses proven programming practices and doesn't want to get into the unknown areas of computers. A lot of attention to details. Very methodical. I said that this was at the edge of the spectrum; it doesn't happen very often that a programmer with this ability comes along.

The other end of the spectrum is certainly more familiar to me. Here lives the programmer that follows my first rule of program development and modification:

It is easier to modify a program that is working properly than to modify one that is broken.

Sounds reasonable to me. These people will start with the bare bones of a program, becoming satisfied that one section works before moving on to the next chunk of work. There is a lot of trial and error (you learn a lot by doing the wrong things) and you crash the machine a couple of times while you *push the edge of the envelope.*

The program development that is presented here is the trial-and-error form: a group of little experiments showing us the way to the final program. Build a simple little program that works. Add a feature, get it working, and add another feature. The program is shown in five steps of development with the time, wrong paths, and heartbreaks removed.

On with the story!

The Global Problem

Since I mostly use the trial-and-error techniques in program development, I make mistakes. Sometimes I find that I have been making the same mistake in several program modules (separate files). The problem is: How can I make all of the changes in these files without calling each with my programming editor and fixing each one?

The Global Solution

Believe it or not, the solution is to use the much criticized EDLIN editor that comes with MS-DOS to solve this problem. This may sound like a strange solution, but I have used it several times with great results. Let's look at the situation.

The major reason for using EDLIN is that the input can be redirected in such a way that it can come from a file instead of the keyboard. This allows us to activate EDLIN with a command line, such as:

```
edlin mytext.doc < fixes
```

This command would tell EDLIN to edit the file "mytext.doc" and to use the commands in the file known as FIXES instead of receiving the commands from the keyboard. The less than symbol is used to redirect or transfer the source of input from the standard input device (keyboard) to another device or file. A greater than symbol would redirect the output that would normally go to the standard output device (screen) to another device or file.

The solution is not concerned with inserting or deleting text, just the modification of text. EDLIN does this very well with:

```
1,9999rold text^Znew text
```

You will have to have an editor to create this command that will allow the Control-Z to be entered. I may be lucky; I've got one.

And you must not forget the command at the end of the command stream to save the results and exit the editor. The command is the letter *e.*

A command sequence to start converting a Pascal program to a C program might look like this:

```
1,9999rprocedure^Zint
1,9999rbegin^Z{
1,9999rend^Z}
1,9999r:=^Z??
1,9999r=^Z==
1,9999r??^Z=
1,9999r<>^Z!
1,9999rnot^Z!
e
```

This sequence will not make a complete conversion, but you can see how it might help on the mundane editing chores.

So for each program module that you have, you would enter:

```
edlin myfile.pas <pas2c
```

This brings up a little problem that sets the stage for the second problem, the one that we're trying to get to. If this editing process is to be performed on several files, it will still take some time to enter each EDLIN command to activate the editing.

For a little problem, a simple solution. Build a Batch file that activates EDLIN for each file. With a batch stream running, you can walk away while it is editing each file. In a file whose filetype is .BAT, enter an EDLIN activation command for each file that is to be processed. Save the file and run it as a batch stream. In the long run, you use as much time doing this as if you had just activated EDLIN for each file.

The Program Problem

Is there an easier way to create this batch file than entering each name as a parameter to the EDLIN command with an editor?

The Program Solution

If we could find something that would generate the names of the files to be edited, we could add the EDLIN command and the redirection file-name to each name and have the batch file.

For a source of filenames, nothing beats the DIR command in MS-DOS. In fact, the exact files that need to be edited can be selected through the use of wildcards (the "*" and "?" notations). For instance, DIR *.PAS would show only the Pascal source code files. If this list were saved in a file, the list could be edited to form a batch file. With a little redirection of output, we get the command:

```
dir *.pas >ed.bat
```

And when we look into the ED.BAT file, we see:

```
Volume in drive B has no label
Directory of B:\

MATCH       PAS     285     1-27-83     4:19p
NEXTTOKE    PAS     504     9-07-82     6:55p
WRITEBLO    PAS    1461     3-14-83    12:21a
RETURNBL    PAS     193     8-21-82     7:34p
UPDATELI    PAS     116     7-02-82     4:39p
REPLACE     PAS    2011     3-07-83     4:30p
TEXTUAL     PAS    1864     3-14-83    12:11a
DETAB       PAS     497     3-14-83    12:48a
CHANGELI    PAS     818     1-27-83     2:03p
DELETEBL    PAS     705     7-02-82     4:43p
DELETELI    PAS     695     7-02-82     4:44p
JOINLINE    PAS    1444     7-02-82     5:01p
MARKCHAN    PAS     255     7-02-82     5:02p
MOVELINE    PAS     604     7-02-82     5:04p
INSERTFI    PAS    1016     3-14-83    12:40a
SPLITLIN    PAS     818     3-08-83     7:46a
FIND        PAS    1298     3-07-83     3:00p
TOKENDUP    PAS     668     3-14-83    12:59a
BLOCKDEF    PAS    1863     3-14-83    12:45a
DUPLICAT    PAS     509     3-14-83    12:51a
INSERT1     PAS     660     3-14-83    12:54a
SHRINKLI    PAS     917     3-14-83    12:57a
WRAPAROU    PAS     882     3-14-83    12:59a
       26 File(s)     112128 bytes free
```

Notice the dates in the listing. It's been a long time since I've written any Pascal code. This was all that I had around.

Several things are striking: There are header lines with no valid filenames in them. Sometimes there are files known only as "." and ".." (directory references) and a last line with remaining disk space; these have got to go. And there are problems on the filename lines. For starters, the name of the file starts in column one. There is little foothold for adding the EDLIN command to the line. Looking farther to the right, there are spaces between the filename and the filetype. There isn't a period to separate the fields, either. Beyond the filetype field, you will find the file size and the time and date stamp for the file. These will serve no purpose to us, so they will have to be removed.

This all boils down to a lot of editing that still has to be done.

One saving grace of the DIR command is that it is consistent. We know where the fields are going to be, and we can do something about it.

Suppose that we could build a very special editor that would do all of the editing and rearranging of a DIR output to produce the necessary batch file. The input to the program would be lines from the DIR command, and the output would be the formed batch file. BEB (Build Edlin Batchfile) would automate all of the manual editing that would have to be done.

To build a batch file, we would get the proper directory listing in a file, use that file as input to BEB, and redirect the output of BEB to the waiting batch file.

Oh, yes, remember that file of editor commands that is used as input for EDLIN? It has to be known by BEB to add to the output lines.

```
dir *.pas > beb.in
beb pas2c < beb.in > ed.bat
```

This form of redirection is used so often that MS-DOS uses a simpler method of notation to show data flow. Adopted from UNIX, it is called *piping* or *pipelines*. Programs that appear in the flow of data are called *filters*, since they perform some process on the data to change it. When using pipes and filters, the processes (programs) are entered on a single command line, separated by the vertical bar ("|") to show piping sequence. The output of the filter to the left of the bar becomes the input for the filter to the right of the bar. The following command string would perform the same thing as the earlier command sequence:

```
dir *.pas | beb pas2c > ed.bat
```

Adding some other filters to the pipe can make the output even nicer. Adding the SORT command to the pipe produces a batch file that will modify the files in alphabetical order.

```
dir *.pas | sort | beb pas2c > ed.bat
```

To start the editor process, submit the batch file and relax.

If you really want to show your knowledge of pipes and batch files, you can take the pipeline command one step further. You don't have to produce a batch file if you pass the output of the pipe directly to the MS-DOS command processor. You can do this by activating a second command processor at the end of the pipe. BEB will have to generate an EXIT command to leave the secondary command processor.

```
dir *.pas | sort | beb pas2c | command
```

Enough on pipes, filters, and how BEB is going to work for us. Let's turn to how BEB is going to work.

Just going through the manual tasks that preparing the batch file requires can give us a good idea of what will be involved in creating BEB. Here they are in one place:

- Get name of EDLIN command file.
- Read a directory line from input (until done).
- Remove the filesize, time, and date information.
- Add a period between the filename and the filetype.
- Remove spaces between the filename and the filetype.
- Write a proper EDLIN command line.
- Add an EXIT command if you are using the command processor in the pipeline.
- Return control to MS-DOS.

Not to leave anything to chance, the first program in the development of BEB was a simple program that did nothing (except let me know that it was there). If it manages to do this well, I have a program that works and is therefore easy to modify. If it doesn't do nothing well (Do you like the proper (??) use of the double negative?), then something is wrong with my simple program and I can fix it now before is blossoms into something disastrous.

Listing 15-1. A Simple Program.

```
DATA      segment
hello     db       "Hello, world",13,10,"$" ; a little message
DATA      ends

CODE      segment
          assume   cs:CODE,ds:DATA  ; default registers
START:
          mov      ax,seg DATA      ; establish addr of DATA
          mov      ds,ax            ; and into the register

          mov      dx,offset hello  ; get addr of message
          mov      ah,09h           ; DOS display command
          int      21h              ; MS-DOS does it

          mov      ah,4ch           ; DOS termination command
          int      21h              ; Bye!
CODE      ends
```

Listing 15-1. Continued

```
STACK    segment  stack
         assume   ss:STACK
         dw       64 dup (?)
STACK    ends
         end      START
```

When a program starts, the Data segment (DS) register is not addressing the data segment. It and the ES register are addressing the Program Segment Prefix (PSP). The register must be changed to address the data in the Data segment.

The second program in the series isn't much different than the first. You will notice that the program sections that call MS-DOS have been moved to *macros*. This is a good way of organizing often-used pieces of code that are too simple to be in a subroutine.

Knowing that I might have the address of a message buffer and not the buffer itself in my possession, I wanted to try passing an address to the DX register in the *display* macro instead of using the *offset* operator to produce the address as in the first example. Why? The parameter to BEB, indicating the name of the file with the EDLIN commands, will be in the PSP, and I will want to know if I can display it from there. I couldn't, but not because this macro didn't work. The DS register wouldn't cooperate.

Listing 15-2. Check Output Capabilities.

```
display  MACRO    msg
         mov      dx,msg
         mov      ah,09h
         int      21h
         ENDM

exit     MACRO    exitcode
         mov      al,exitcode
         mov      ah,4ch
         int      21h
         ENDM

DATA     segment
m1       db       "message1",13,10,"$"
m2       db       "message2",13,10,"$"
addr1    dw       offset m1
addr2    dw       offset m2
DATA     ends
```

Listing 15-2. Continued

```
CODE        segment
            assume      cs:CODE,ds:DATA
START:
            mov         ax,seg DATA
            mov         ds,ax
            display     addr1 ; print first message
            display     addr2 ; print second message
            exit        0
CODE        ends


STACK       segment     stack
            assume      ss:STACK
            dw          64 dup (?)
STACK       ends
            end         START
```

The next experiment was written to find out what it was going to take to handle redirected input. The biggest problem that I ran into with this program is detecting the end of the input. Since the input is from the standard input device, there is no FCB or status word to indicate the end-of-file. I tried the Buffered Input command. As it turns out, MS-DOS retains control until a carriage return and linefeed are seen. This is great for all of the input except the end-of-file marker. This is generally a Ctrl-Z character. It is not followed by the carriage return and linefeed. Therefore, MS-DOS captures the end-of-file line and never comes back.

The method of detecting the end-of-input used in this example follows another line of reasoning. If the input is redirected and originates in a file, then isn't it fair to say that whenever a character is not available from the standard input device, we can be pretty sure that the input stream is finished? The example program uses this idea. Getting the input status from MS-DOS, the program can decide its action. When a character is available, there must be another line to fetch and process. With no characters available, the program terminates.

Other changes in the output portion of the program were made to facilitate the output of several messages on the same line. To do this, the carriage return and linefeed characters were removed from the internal messages and placed into a separate message area. A special *macro* was added just for the occasion of needing the carriage return and linefeed characters.

Listing 15-3. Read a Line, Show a Line.

```
display     MACRO      msg
            mov        dx,msg
            mov        ah,09h
            int        21h
            ENDM


crlf        MACRO
            display    <offset linefeed>
            ENDM


exit        MACRO      exitcode
            mov        al,exitcode
            mov        ah,4ch
            int        21h
            ENDM


getline     MACRO      buffer,eof
            LOCAL      top
            LOCAL      out
            mov        di,0             ; start at beginning of buffer
top:
            mov        ah,08h           ; get char no echo
            int        21h              ; call DOS
            cmp        al,1ah           ; is character = ^Z (EOF)
            je         eof              ; jump to passed EOF address
            cmp        al,0dh           ; is character = <CR>
            je         top              ; skip it - don't save it
            cmp        al,0ah           ; is character = <LF>
            je         out              ; end of line -- leave
            mov        buffer[di],al    ; put character into buffer
            inc        di               ; ready for next character
            jmp        top              ; get another
out:
            mov        buffer[di],"$"   ; add $ as end-of-line for DISPLAY
            ENDM


putchar     MACRO      char
            mov        dl,char          ; proper place for character
            mov        ah,02h           ; show this character on screen
            int        21h              ; call DOS to show it
            ENDM


DATA        segment
linefeed    db         13,10,"$"
inline      db         80 dup (?)
DATA        ends


CODE        segment
            assume     cs:CODE,ds:DATA
START:
            mov        ax,seg DATA
```

Listing 15-3. Continued

```
        mov     ds,ax
READ:
        mov     ah,0bh          ; is a character ready?
        int     21h             ; ask DOS to find out
        or      al,al           ; generate a flag for comparison
        jz      EOF             ; 0 = no more characters
        getline inline,EOF      ; read the next line
        display <offset inline> ; show it
        crlf
        jmp     READ            ; do it again, do it again
EOF:
        exit    0               ; back to MS-DOS
CODE    ends

STACK   segment stack
        assume  ss:STACK
        dw      64 dup (?)
STACK   ends
        end     START
```

Almost There

The next step in the program was to add a subroutine that would check a line from the input device and decide if it was a filename line or other extraneous line from the DIR process. The FIND subroutine checks the first letter of the input buffer against a list of characters. If the input buffer character matches one of the characters in the list, the AL register returns with all ones. If AL is zero, then no match was found. Specifically, the letters in the STOP list are: space, period, and dollar sign. These are the characters that appear in DIR output lines that are not used by BEB. The dollar sign appears when the *getline* macro finds an empty input (blank) line.

The keyboard status code was promoted to macro status.

The output now inserts the EDLIN command at the front of the filename and the less than symbol after the filename (for redirection) in anticipation of the output of BEB.

Listing 15-4. Almost BEB.

```
display MACRO   msg
        mov     DX,msg
        mov     ah,09h
        int     21h
        ENDM
```

Listing 15-4. Continued

```
crlf        MACRO
            display    <offset linefeed>
            ENDM

kbhit       MACRO      eof
            mov        ah,0bh
            int        21h
            or         al,al
            jz         eof
            ENDM

exit        MACRO      exitcode
            mov        al,exitcode
            mov        ah,4ch
            int        21h
            ENDM
getline     MACRO      buffer,eof
            LOCAL      top
            LOCAL      out
            mov        di,0
top:
            mov        ah,08h
            int        21h
            cmp        al,1ah
            je         eof
            cmp        al,0dh
            je         top
            cmp        al,0ah
            je         out
            mov        buffer[di],al
            inc        di
            jmp        top
out:
            mov        buffer[di],"$"
            ENDM

putchar     MACRO      char
            mov        dl,char
            mov        ah,02h
            int        21h
            ENDM

DATA        segment
m1          db         "edlin $"
m2          db         "< $"
linefeed    db         13,10,"$"
```

Listing 15-4. Continued

```
edlin      dw       offset m1
redirect   dw       offset m2
inline     db       80 dup (?)
stops      db       " .$",0
DATA       ends


CODE       segment
           assume   cs:CODE,ds:DATA
START:
           mov      ax,seg DATA
           mov      ds,ax
           xor      sp,sp
READ:
           kbhit    EOF               ; if nothing ready, quit to EOF
           getline  inline,EOF        ; read the ready line
           call     find              ; is this a valid filename line?
           or       al,al             ; generate a comparison flag
           jnz      READ              ; no good -- read another
           mov      inline+15,"$"     ; throw away filesize etc with early $
           display  edlin             ; produce the line:
           display  <offset inline>   ; EDLIN filename <
           display  redirect
           crlf
           jmp      READ              ; do again
EOF:
           exit     0                 ; bye


FIND       PROC
           mov      al,inline         ; get first character from input
           mov      di,0              ; reset index to first in STOPS
here:
           mov      ah,stops[di]      ; get char to check against
           or       ah,ah             ; generate flag
           jz       nomatch           ; binary zero is end of list - no match
           cmp      ah,al             ; check char against input char
           je       match             ; got one!
           inc      di                ; no match - try next
           jmp      here              ; do again
nomatch:
           xor      al,al             ; no match -- return 0
           ret
match:
           mov      al,0ffh           ; matches -- return all ones
           ret
FIND       ENDP
```

Listing 15-4. Continued

```
CODE      ends

STACK     segment   stack
          assume    ss:STACK
          dw        64 dup (?)
STACK     ends
          end       START
```

BEB

There was a bit of a jump to this next listing, but here is BEB. There were several minor adjustments to get to this point. The major step here is the retrieval of the parameter from the command line. MS-DOS edits the command line and leaves the parameters of the command line in the PSP starting at offset 128 (Hex 80). The byte at the first location is a character count of the number of characters in the parameter buffer starting in the next byte. This number should be used to count the transfer of characters to a program buffer.

When the program begins, the DS and ES registers are both pointing to the beginning of the PSP. Since the DS register is used as the SOURCE base register in byte moves by the microprocessor, it must remain pointing at the PSP. The ES register is reset to point to the data area of the program as the Destination base register.

Using the count from the PSP, the DS:SI (source index) register pair and the ES:DI (destination index) register pair move the command parameters to a local buffer for use in the output line. Remember to put a "$" at the end of the name so that when it is written, MS-DOS has a termination character.

The only other important code that was added to the program was the function that shrinks the filename and filetype fields of the directory line into a single string.

Listing 15-5. Build EDLIN Batch.

```
display   MACRO     msg
          mov       DX,offset msg
          mov       ah,09h
          int       21h
```

Listing 15-5. Continued

```
                ENDM

skip            MACRO   reg,char            ; macro to skip characters
                LOCAL   out                 ; and position REG to first
                LOCAL   again               ; instance of not equal to CHAR
again:
                cmp     BYTE PTR [reg],char ; is REG pointing to a CHAR?
                jne     out                 ; no - we are done
                inc     reg                 ; yes, check next
                jmp     again               ; check it out
out:
                ENDM

copy_to         MACRO   buffer,char         ; macro to copy from [SI to a
                LOCAL   do_again            ; buffer until CHAR is found
                LOCAL   out
                mov     di,offset buffer    ; get address of buffer
do_again:
                cmp     BYTE PTR [si],char  ; is char to move a CHAR?
                je      out                 ; yes - we are done
                movsb                       ; move the character
                jmp     do_again
out:            mov     BYTE PTR [di],"$"
                ENDM

crlf            MACRO
                display linefeed
                ENDM

kbhit           MACRO   eof
                mov     ah,0bh
                int     21h
                or      al,al
                jz      eof
                ENDM

exit            MACRO   exitcode
                mov     al,exitcode
                mov     ah,4ch
                int     21h
                ENDM

getline         MACRO   buffer,eof
                LOCAL   top
                LOCAL   out
                mov     di,0
```

Listing 15-5. Continued

```
top:
                mov     ah,08h
                int     21h
                cmp     al,1ah
                je      eof
                cmp     al,0dh
                je      top
                cmp     al,0ah
                je      out
                mov     buffer[di],al
                inc     DI
                jmp     top
out:
                mov     buffer[di],"$"
                ENDM

putchar         MACRO   char
                mov     dl,char
                mov     ah,02h
                int     21h
                ENDM

PSP             segment
                db      128 dup (?)
len             db      ?
params          db      127 dup (?)
PSP             ends

DATA            segment
exit_dos        db      "exit$"
edlin           db      "edlin $"
redirect        db      " < $"
linefeed        db      13,10,"$"
inline          db      80 dup (?)
stops           db      " .$",0
parameter       db      40 dup (" ")
DATA            ends

CODE            segment
                assume  cs:CODE,ds:PSP,es:DATA
START:
                mov     AX,seg DATA         ; establish addressing
                mov     es,AX               ; use ES for now
                xor     sp,sp

                mov     cl,ds:len           ; length of parameter area
```

Listing 15-5. Continued

```
                xor       ch,ch                      ; in PSP -- sets loop count
                mov       si,offset DS:params        ; establish buffer addresses
                mov       di,offset ES:parameter     ; DS still points to PSP
get_param:
                movsb                                ; move parameter to buffer
                loop      get_param                  ; do until done
                mov       BYTE PTR ES:[di],"$"       ; add $ for display purposes

                mov       AX,es                      ; get DS pointing to right
                mov       ds,AX                      ; place
                assume    cs:CODE,ds:DATA,es:DATA

READ:
                kbhit     EOF                        ; is input ready? NO -> EOF
                getline   inline,EOF                 ; get input line
                mov       al,inline                  ; pass first char to qualifier
                push      AX
                mov       AX,offset stops            ; pass address of disqualifying
                push      AX                         ; characters
                call      is_there                   ; call checking routine
                or        al,al                      ; generate comparison flag
                jnz       READ                       ; found line with no filename
                mov       AX,offset inline           ; pass address of input line
                push      AX
                call      shrink                     ; routine to shrink filename
                display   edlin                      ; construct the output line
                display   inline
                display   redirect                   ; EDLIN filename < edits
                display   parameter
                crlf
                jmp       READ
EOF:
                display   exit_dos                   ; for leaving COMMAND in pipeline
                crlf
                exit      0                          ; bye


;
; this procedure will check a single character
; against a list of characters
; TRUE = found one
; FALSE = not in list
; the comparison list ends with binary zero to
; identify end
;
; parameter stack:   character      offset 6
;                    addr of list   offset 4
```

Listing 15-5. Continued

```
;                  return addr    offset 0
IS_THERE   PROC
           push    bp
           mov     bp,sp
           mov     BX,[bp+4]          ; get address of char list
           mov     di,0               ; set index to beginning
here:
           mov     al,[BX][di]        ; get char from list
           or      al,al              ; 0 means end of list -- no match
           jz      nomatch
           cmp     al,[bp+6]          ; compare input character
           je      match              ; found one?
           inc     di                 ; get next char from list
           jmp     here               ; keep going
nomatch:
           xor     al,al              ; none found, return 0
           pop     bp
           ret     4
match:
           mov     al,0ffh            ; found one -- return all ones
           pop     bp
           ret     4
IS_THERE ENDP

SHRINK     PROC
           push    bp
           mov     bp,sp
           mov     si,[bp+4]          ; address of input buffer
           add     si,9               ; point to filetype
           cmp     BYTE PTR [si]," " ; no filetype if space
           je      no_type            ; not much to do
           mov     di,[bp+4]          ; address of input buffer
           add     di,8               ; point to for-sure end of filename
move_back:
           cmp     BYTE PTR [di]," " ; as long as there are spaces
           jne     end_found          ; the filename has not been found
           mov     BYTE PTR [di],"." ; add period separator
           dec     di                 ; bump back by one
           jmp     move_back          ; do again
end_found:
           inc     di                 ; bump off last char
           inc     di                 ; bump past period
           mov     CX,3               ; move filetype count -> 3
to_here:
           movsb                      ; move [si] -> [di]
           loop    to_here
```

Listing 15-5. Continued

```
            mov     BYTE PTR [di],"$" ; add a terminating $ for display
            pop     bp
            ret     2
no_type:
            dec     si
            mov     BYTE PTR [si],"$"
            pop     bp
            ret     2
SHRINK      ENDP
CODE        ends
STACK       segment stack
            assume  ss:STACK
            dw      64 dup (?)
STACK       ends
            end     START
```

SUMMARY

When you are able to follow the logic and structure of this program (and get it running), you should be able to venture out to use other functions of MS-DOS. Remember that it is easier to modify and expand a program that works than it is to struggle with a broken and unorganized program.

The BEB program illustrates several of the easier concepts that we have covered in the text. We've seen how MS-DOS functions can make your programming tasks and problem-solving easier by providing several standard functions through a fairly simple interface. As a standard method of accessing these features on a computer, your programs can work on several brands of computers even though they may be electronically different.

I hope that the discussions and illustrations in this guide have shed some light on the use of MS-DOS by a programmer. I have to admit that I have learned some new ways of doing things.

Appendix A

ASCII Symbols

ASCII Value	Character	ASCII Value	Character
000	(null)	026	→
001	☖	027	←
002	☗	028	(cursor right)
003	♥	029	(cursor left)
004	♦	030	(cursor up)
005	♣	031	(cursor down)
006	♠	032	(space)
007	(beep)	033	!
008	☗	034	''
009	(tab)	035	#
010	(line feed)	036	$
011	(home)	037	%
012	(form feed)	038	&
013	(carriage return)	039	'
014	♫	040	(
015	☼	041	)
016	►	042	*
017	◄	043	+
018	↕	044	,
019	!!	045	—
020	¶	046	.
021	§	047	/
022	▬	048	0
023	↨	049	1
024	↑	050	2
025	↓	051	3

ASCII Value	Character	ASCII Value	Character
052	4	087	W
053	5	088	X
054	6	089	Y
055	7	090	Z
056	8	091	[
057	9	092	\
058	:	093	]
059	;	094	∧
060	<	095	—
061	=	096	`
062	>	097	a
063	?	098	b
064	@	099	c
065	A	100	d
066	B	101	e
067	C	102	f
068	D	103	g
069	E	104	h
070	F	105	i
071	G	106	j
072	H	107	k
073	I	108	l
074	J	109	m
075	K	110	n
076	L	111	o
077	M	112	p
078	N	113	q
079	O	114	r
080	P	115	s
081	Q	116	t
082	R	117	u
083	S	118	v
084	T	119	w
085	U	120	x
086	V	121	y

ASCII Value	Character	ASCII Value	Character
122	z	157	¥
123	{	158	Pt
124	¦	159	ƒ
125	}	160	á
126	~	161	í
127	⌂	162	ó
128	Ç	163	ú
129	ü	164	ñ
130	é	165	Ñ
131	â	166	ª
132	ä	167	º
133	à	168	¿
134	å	169	⌐
135	ç	170	¬
136	ê	171	½
137	ë	172	¼
138	è	173	¡
139	ï	174	«
140	î	175	»
141	ì	176	░
142	Ä	177	▒
143	Å	178	▓
144	É	179	│
145	æ	180	┤
146	Æ	181	╡
147	ô	182	╢
148	ö	183	╖
149	ò	184	╕
150	û	185	╣
151	ù	186	║
152	ÿ	187	╗
153	Ö	188	╝
154	Ü	189	╜
155	¢	190	╛
156	£	191	┐

ASCII Value	Character	ASCII Value	Character
192	└	224	α
193	┴	225	β
194	┬	226	Γ
195	├	227	π
196	─	228	Σ
197	┼	229	σ
198	╞	230	μ
199	╟	231	τ
200	╚	232	Φ
201	╔	233	θ
202	╩	234	Ω
203	╦	235	δ
204	╠	236	∞
205	═	237	$\emptyset$
206	╬	238	ϵ
207	╧	239	$\cap$
208	╨	240	$\equiv$
209	╤	241	$\pm$
210	╥	242	$\geq$
211	╙	243	$\leq$
212	╘	244	⌠
213	╒	245	⌡
214	╓	246	$\div$
215	╫	247	$\approx$
216	╪	248	°
217	┘	249	•
218	┌	250	·
219	█	251	$\sqrt{}$
220	▄	252	ⁿ
221	▌	253	²
222	▐	254	∎
223	▀	255	(blank 'FF')

Index

About the Author

Dennis Jump is the president of The Great SoftWestern Company, Inc. and the author of The Auto-Board System.

Dennis received his B.S. in Mathematics/Computer Science option from Cal-Poly in San Luis Obispo, California and a M.S. in Information and Computer Science from Georgia Tech in Atlanta. He has been a member of the faculty at Texas Woman's University in Denton.

Dennis has a background in compiler design and software tool development. While at Sperry Univac, he implemented major sections of a Pascal/Graphics compiler and runtime system. He also wrote the "front end" of a FORTRAN-77 compiler for a Navy contract. Later, with Texas Instruments, he was involved in the design and implementation of a source-level Pascal debugger, three laser-printer-oriented text formatters, a database manager for trouble reports, and, most important, the design of the "front end" and optimizer phases of Texas Instruments, Ada copiler (USAF design competition).

Dennis lives in Denton, Texas, with his wife, Gwynn, and two daughters, Shelly and Hilary.